Also by Parag Khanna

The Second World:
Empires and Influence in
the New Global Order

HOW *to* RUN *the* WORLD

Random House | New York

HOW *to* RUN *the* WORLD

Charting a Course to the
Next Renaissance

Parag Khanna

Published in the United States by Random House,
an imprint of The Random House Publishing Group,
a division of Random House, Inc., New York.

RANDOM HOUSE and colophon are registered trademarks
of Random House, Inc.

ISBN 978-1-4000-6827-2
eBook ISBN 978-0-6796-0428-0

Printed in the United States of America on acid-free paper

www.atrandom.com

2 4 6 8 9 7 5 3 1

FIRST EDITION

Book design by Laurie Jewell

For Manjula and Sushil Khanna,
aka Mom and Dad

Contents

Part One

THE NEW WORLD ORDER . . . REALLY

Chapter One

Mega-diplomacy

Breakdown and failure reveal the true nature of things.

—Karl Jaspers

*Two millennia of experience and mountains of
knowledge have not made us much more capable of
managing our affairs than stone-age people.*

—Mahathir bin Mohamed,
former prime minister of Malaysia

*There is one way to run the world: with diplomacy. Yet for many
people, "diplomacy" is a historical term more than anything useful. That needs to change. Until we evolve a new diplomatic design,
we will fail to confront and prevent the constant stream of crises—
from financial turmoil to failed states—that engulf us. We are running
out of time.*

*Twenty-first-century diplomacy is coming to resemble that of the
Middle Ages: Rising powers, multinational corporations, powerful
families, humanitarians, religious radicals, universities, and mercenaries are all part of the diplomatic landscape. Technology and money,
not sovereignty, determine who has authority and calls the shots. This
can be a good thing if it means getting all hands on deck to manage*

challenges that no government or organization can tackle alone. Suc-
cess in this new world of mega-diplomacy hinges on bringing the key
players together—governments, businesses, and organizations—into
coalitions that can quickly move global resources to solve local prob-
lems. This is not your grandfather's diplomacy, but today's Genera-
tion Y intuitively gets it.

Diplomacy Is Dead! Long Live Diplomacy!

At least once every hundred years, the world goes to war—and then
tries to make lasting peace. During six intense months in Vienna in
1814, ministers of Europe's major powers—Britain's Lord Castle-
reagh, France's Talleyrand, Russia's czar Alexander I and Count Nes-
selrode, and Austria's Prince Metternich—were entrusted with
redrawing Europe's political map after the defeat of Napoleonic
France. Their conservative order, the "Concert of Europe," lasted es-
sentially until World War I. When the great powers gathered again for
six months in Paris in 1919, they were represented by France's
Georges Clemenceau, Britain's David Lloyd George, Italy's Vittorio
Orlando, and America's Woodrow Wilson. As the statesmen negotiated military disarmament, exchanges of territory, payment of repara-
tions, and the dismantling of colonies, it seemed the whole world was
in their hands—until it all fell apart again. After World War II, America's Franklin D. Roosevelt envisioned a global version of the Concert
of Europe, this time with "Four Policemen"—the United States, the
United Kingdom, the Soviet Union, and China—guaranteeing global
stability. However, despite the growing membership of the United
Nations, Cold War superpower summits reminded the world that
some countries were still more equal than others.

Luckily, the Cold War ended without nuclear catastrophe, but the
vacuum of the past two decades has yet to give birth to a new global
architecture that reflects the rapidly changing realities of power and
influence. The nineteenth-century world was run by a few key powers
overseeing their colonies, and the twentieth century by power blocks.

In the twenty-first century, however, manipulating world order from above won't be enough.

The past decade—from the 9/11 terrorist attacks to the global financial meltdown—has taught us the dangers of interdependence and that outsourcing leadership is a recipe for disaster. Some now fear a breakdown of our global order, but isn't it scarier to realize that the present order has already been broken for years? It's the kind of moment the philosopher Karl Popper had in mind when he argued that tearing down our existing order and constructing a new one from scratch might lead to a more workable system.

How bad is it? Well, today the powers that are expected to keep the peace sell the most weapons, the banks that are supposed to encourage saving promote living beyond one's means, and food arrives to hungry people after they've died. We are hurtling toward a perfect storm of energy consumption, population growth, and food and water scarcity that will spare no one, rich or poor. Our ever-growing list of crises includes financial instability, HIV/AIDS, terrorism, failed states, and more. Any one of these can magnify another, creating a downward spiral for individual nations and regions. Within the next twenty years we could see proxy skirmishes escalate into major war between America and China, more weak states crumbling, conflicts over submerged oil and gas resources at sea, drought-starved refugees streaming out of central Africa, and sinking Pacific islands.

Henry Kissinger said it best: "You do not design a new world order as an emergency measure. But you need an emergency to bring about a new world order." Finally, there is a global debate under way about how to redesign the way we run the world. It's about time—and hopefully not too late. Globalization has thrust us into a chaotic era with which our leading powers and institutions only pretend they can cope. Americans believe they can lead a "multi-partner" world, Europeans think they can tame the world through "civilian power," the Chinese try to buy the world off, most other states just want status without responsibility, and the United Nations is barely spoken of anymore. They all need to seriously rethink how the world is run. The notion of a "G-2" axis between the United States and China is the latest misguided incarnation of our quest for a simple global framework—it ignores the fact that the two powers can't agree on currency, climate, censorship, or many other issues, and that few if any countries want to be dictated to by either the United States or China.

There is no doubt that we need a global redesign to confront this perfect storm—one that doesn't just react to crises but proactively prevents them. What we have right now, though, is global policy gridlock: The West demands interventions and human rights, while the East prefers sovereignty and noninterference; the North is scared of terrorism and proliferation, while the South needs food security and fair trade. Stock prices are crucial for the capital rich; commodities prices for the resource rich. Americans are suspicious of Chinese state-owned companies, while the Chinese are suspicious of American regulators. We seem as far away as ever from a new consensus.

In 2004, the British historian Anthony Sampson published the widely acclaimed book *Who Runs This Place?* He was motivated by the simple question "Who is accountable to whom and for what?" Inside the book are Sampson's hand-sketched Venn diagrams depicting "The Establishment," interlocking circles of power whose fuzzy relationships seem to lack an obvious purpose of public good: the prime minister, accountants, pension funds, the monarchy, corporations, lobbyists, the rich, aristocracy, diplomats, intelligence, the treasury, Parliament, academia, churches, political parties, lawyers, the military, the insurance industry, television, editors, trade unions—and that's just for Great Britain.

Sampson was worried about British democracy; in international relations there is no such thing. What we have today is a worldwide perpetual no-holds-barred contest for power and legitimacy between regimes, companies, nongovernmental organizations (NGOs), religious groups, and super-empowered individuals all pursuing their own interests. From economic nationalists to resource-hungry companies to religious fundamentalists, everyone is out for themselves. Interest groups are not a marginal sideshow to some "real" politics; they *are* the politics. The best term for it: mosh pit.

Ironically, our ambition often prevents us from recognizing this reality. Because issues such as the climate and economy are "systemic" in nature, meaning they have worldwide scope and impact, we reach for grand, silver-bullet remedies such as "America must take charge" or "strengthen the United Nations." But just as there is no one nation that can rule the world, there is no one institution that can run it, either. Some experts offer strategies to "fix" the world, but their utopian schemes for new international bureaucracies are as boring in theory as they are unworkable in practice. There are also countless appeals to "save" the world through a variety of "grand bargains." But running the world isn't about one-off solutions.

"Diplomacy" is the one-word answer to how to run the world—and improving our global diplomatic design holds the key to running the world better.

Diplomacy is the world's second oldest profession—but it comes as naturally to human beings as the first. Among ancient Sumerian city-states, it was a means to channel the messages of deities among kings. But as we know from the fascinating Amarna letters (a set of cuneiform tablets inscribed in the second millennium B.C. in the Akkadian language), diplomacy was also a sophisticated code of conduct among merchants and ambassadors, who were often the same person: "Between kings there is brotherhood, alliance, peace and good words if there is an abundance of precious stones, silver and gold," went one Amarna adage. By the time of the Athenians, diplomacy was a robust system of trade and political dialogue, even featuring the first "Olympic truce." The Byzantines elevated diplomatic deception to a fine art, compensating for their material weakness by quarantining foreign officials in opulent chambers to cut them off from the reality of inner decay. Such tactics staved off the empire's collapse for four hundred years. The Venetians carried forward Byzantine practices in Europe, dispatching diplomat-spies abroad to send back coded messages that were instrumental in formulating strategies against its rival city-states Genoa and Milan, as well as the encroaching papacy. It was at the height of this turbulent period in the early sixteenth century that Machiavelli wrote *The Prince,* emphasizing a statecraft that blended the arts of diplomacy and war. Within a century, legendary French nobleman Cardinal Richelieu constructed the world's most extensive foreign ministry, while the Dutch and British East India companies acted as mammoth public-corporate agents of imperial expansion, forcibly creating a single international society of states, empires, and territories. The Ottoman Empire, China, Japan, and Russia were all brought into a global diplomatic web. British historian Arnold Toynbee marveled that the West's mastery of war, technology, and diplomacy had "unified the whole world in the literal sense of the whole habitable and traversable surface of the globe."[1] From Vienna in 1814 to Paris in 1919, diplomacy took on the aura of a clique of white men carving up the world—a secretive parlor game played by arrogant statesman with heavy accents.

Since that time, diplomats have been charged with negotiating how to run the world. Diplomacy remains an element of everything we do. Carl von Clausewitz declared that war is the continuation of politics by other means. Diplomacy, by contrast, is supposed to play the role of "words that prevent us from reaching for our swords," according to Bosnian scholar and diplomat Drazen Pehar. Yet war and diplomacy have often been two sides of the same coin, from the time of the Babylonians through Napoléon and Stalin. Diplomacy uses war as a threat, while war uses diplomacy to buy time. American diplomacy helped build a broad coalition (even including other Arab nations) for the first Iraq war in 1990 but failed to do the same in 2003. Diplomacy, then, is even part of anti-diplomacy.

It is more important now than ever. In an age when America can't impose its will on the world but instead must negotiate with everyone, when military might wins battles but not wars, and when the scope of global challenges goes far beyond what our current institutions can tackle, we should focus on diplomacy above all else.

We all know how technology has transformed the weapons of war from bows and arrows to robots and lasers, and from field armies to insurgent networks, but we often overlook how diplomacy has been changed as well. More than two centuries ago, Thomas Jefferson mused, "For two years we have not heard from our ambassador in

Spain; if we again do not hear from him this year, we should write him a letter." When Lord Palmerston received the first diplomatic cable at Whitehall in the mid-nineteenth century, he proclaimed, "This is the end of diplomacy!" In the 1970s, Canadian premier Pierre Trudeau remarked that he could replace his entire foreign ministry with a subscription to *The New York Times,* whose correspondents presumably provided better information than embassy cables. Today's communications technologies are doing to diplomacy what they have done to print media: demoralizing it and pushing it to the brink of extinction—while also reminding us just how important the media and diplomacy are.

Technology, capitalism, and moral agendas such as human rights have drastically multiplied the number of players in the diplomatic game. Diplomacy today takes place among anybody who's somebody. There are about two hundred countries in the world that have relations with one another, close to one hundred thousand multinational corporations that constantly negotiate with governments and one another, and at least fifty thousand transnational NGOs that consult on international laws and treaties and intervene in conflict zones to provide assistance to regimes and peoples in need. All these actors have acquired sufficient authority—whether through money, expertise, or status—to become influential. Cyberspace today is alive with virtual diplomacy: Sweden, Brazil, and other governments have opened virtual consulates in the universe of Second Life, where former U.S. undersecretary of state for public diplomacy James Glassman held debates with Egyptian bloggers. Senator John Kerry has even proposed the creation of an ambassador for cyberspace. Now that Google and the U.S. Department of Defense's research and development office DARPA (Defense Advanced Research Projects Agency) have pioneered handheld universal translation devices, everyone is a diplomat.

The who, what, when, where, why, and how of diplomacy have thus all been thrown into flux. That is a good thing. It allows us to step back and think about what kind of world it is we are trying to run. Since diplomacy is as old as history itself, history is a good place to start in understanding our new world.

The New Middle Ages

Sitting in one of the glassy towers of the United Nations on New York's East Side, the world seems very tidy. There are councils for security and human rights, commissions for social development and peace building, a division for women, a program for the environment, and an organization for global health. Name the issue, the United Nations has it covered. But how can an organization that caters to bordered states solve the problems of a borderless world? Are pandemics a health issue, a security issue, or both? Is terrorism a political issue, an economic one, or both? What about crop-killing insect infestations at higher altitudes caused by global warming—should the Food and Agriculture Organization or the UN Environment Program handle that? Surely population growth is a cause of ecosystem stress and poverty; do all three really require separate bureaus? How about the fact that there are suddenly as many environmental as political refugees? Whose problem are they? Technocrats sitting halfway around the world are often the worst placed to understand the links among these problems, and bureaucratic micro-splicing all but ensures that no issue gets enough resources to ever get solved. In fact, it's impossible to make sustained progress in any one area if the others are ignored: Disease can't be successfully tackled without considering overpopulation; inequality and state failure won't be overcome unless corruption is reigned in; and biodiversity can't be protected unless populations can afford sustainable consumption. Health, wealth, and education all track together—both upward and downward.

But most bureaucrats in international organizations are more fixated on setting targets and goals—and forming new and expensive agencies—than helping us find actual solutions. Lately they have asserted their relevance by declaring everything—food, climate, health, and poverty—a "security" issue, another fund-raising tactic that achieves nothing. Only inertia explains why some of these agencies are still around: They exist because they do, not because they do anything.

The United Nations is not a definitive superstructure hovering above the earth—it is at best a set of small pebbles attempting to hold the world in place, or prevent it from rolling off into an abyss. Like the Soviet Union, the international system today is collapsing not physically, but organizationally. According to the U.S. National Intelligence Council, by 2025 the very notion of a single "international community" will seem quaint and anachronistic. There will be no universal Leviathan, no global parliament of all mankind, no American hegemony. Instead we are in for a fractured, fragmented, ungovernable, multi-polar or non-polar world. All these adjectives hint at our emerging reality: a new Middle Ages.

It was a millennium ago—in the *pre*-Atlantic era—that the world was genuinely Western and Eastern *at the same time.* In the West, Europe was nominally ruled by the Holy Roman Empire while the vast and multiethnic Byzantine Empire centered in Constantinople faced perpetual tension with its neighbors. Yet Europe's darkest period was the era of Chinese and Indian glory. The Song, Yuan, and post-Mongol Ming dynasties represented the zenith of Chinese culture and exploration, and India under the Mughal Empire dominated southern and central Asia while its trade links flourished with East Africa. Furthermore, between the Umayyad and Abbasid caliphates, Islam reached its apogee, ruling lands from Andalusia to Persia and rivaling Christianity in prestige.

During the Middle Ages, Europeans, the Chinese, and the peoples in between all came into direct, sustained contact with one another in history's first world system. In the aftermath of the Crusades, explorers including the Arab Ibn Battuta and the Venetian Marco Polo traversed Eurasia's Silk Road and made civilizations more cognizant of one another's grandeur. The eager trade delegations of today, from Arab traders in China's Wuxi to Chinese businessmen across Africa, are reminiscent of the grand caravans and bazaars of thirteenth-century Champagne and Samarqand. Furthermore, the past decade's efforts on interfaith reconciliation have their roots in English philosopher Roger Bacon's thirteenth-century recognition of the importance of Islamic scholarship on Western thought and appeals to the pope to pursue global learning rather than crusades. Remember: Empires have soft borders, not hard ones. The more powers that rise, the more open the world becomes.

What does this mean for an America that no longer controls globalization? Rather than the usual comparisons to ancient Rome or nineteenth-century Prussia, a medieval analogy to the Byzantine Empire is more apt. Byzantium staved off decline throughout the entire Middle Ages until the fifteenth century, extending its influence through espionage, bribery, and alliances. Even when Constantinople wasn't able to impose its will on the chaotic medieval world, it remained relevant as a powerful military, economic, and cultural force.

After a decade of unnecessarily damaging American-led interventions, it's hard to see how the United States will regain either its post–World War II or post–Cold War stature. America's visibility may be global, but its influence actually boils down to very specific factors: Is the military active somewhere? Where are its companies investing? Which lobbies are shaping policy toward a country? Asking such questions—not rhetoric about the "indispensable nation"—is the right way to think about a diminished America in a complicated world.

Balancing East and West in the twenty-first century would be hard enough—but that isn't even half the picture. The post–Cold War era will be remembered for the rapid emergence of a postmodern Middle Ages—a world without any single power in control. The East will not replace the West, China will not replace America, the Pacific will not displace the Atlantic—all of these power centers and geographies will coexist in a *hyper-complex ecosystem*. In the Middle Ages, empires, cities, corporations, churches, tribal hordes, and mercenaries overlapped—all competing to rule territory, control resources, win trade and investment, and seduce hearts and minds. The same tableau is unfolding again. By empowering transnational terrorist networks, organized criminals, and drug traffickers, globalization has made some weak states even weaker, while multinational firms and NGOs have grown in power and stature. The number of meaningful communities is proliferating rapidly: Our maps of the world no longer reflect reality on the ground.

Power in such a complicated landscape is not fixed but fluid. Armies and nuclear arsenals don't matter in absolute terms but only in specific contexts such as deterrence, occupations, and interventions. Resource power and ideological power are as important as military and financial might. If the power you have is the wrong sort to get you what you want, then it is useless. The only correct answer, then, to the question of how much power someone has is "Over what?" Even under the nominal reign of Emperor Charlemagne in the late eighth century, bishops recruited their own vassals and knights, monasteries built up fortresses and ramparts, duchies and castellanies were run by military commanders, and barons had sovereignty over their manors. Today the similar fragmentation of societies from within is clear: from Miami to Bogotá to London to Bangalore, gated communities with private security are on the rise. Private military companies have sprouted in America, Russia, Germany, and South Africa not only to support U.S. operations in Iraq and Afghanistan, but to protect banks, ships, mines, and posh neighborhoods wherever people can afford them.

The other essential question in a neo-medieval world is "Who?" The state has been the form of polity that served the industrial age best, but now we are moving into a postindustrial age. Scholars pontificate about the centrality of "the state" as if it were one uniform thing. But the German philosopher Georg Wilhelm Friedrich Hegel was right when he said the state is a "work of art": No two are the same. There are states with strong nationhood (America and Brazil, for example), empires veiled as states (China), states acting as empires (Russia and Iran), empires made up of states (the European Union), natural-resource states (Qatar), market-states with more foreigners than citizens (the United Arab Emirates), quasi-states (Palestine and Kurdistan), and states that exist mostly in name (the Democratic Republic of the Congo). There is nothing natural about "the state"; some will survive while others will give way to new modes of organizing people through technology, resources, ideology, and money.

Undoubtedly, we witnessed a strong "return of the state" in the aftermath of the 2008 financial crisis, with leading governments pumping out $3 trillion of economic stimulus—about 5 percent of global gross domestic product (GDP). Some states are also flexing their muscles in creative ways: Chinese state-owned companies are buying up natural resources across Africa; Arab sovereign wealth funds determine which countries and companies to bail out and what assets they want in return; and Russian oil czars and Saudi Aramco dictate oil prices and pipeline routes. But even strong states act in multiple, distinct ways. Saudi Arabia has two foreign policies: that of the House of Saud and that of the radical Wahhabi clerics and Islamist charities. California (itself one of the world's ten largest economies) effectively has its own immigration, climate, and energy policies, while most Indian and Chinese provinces now have their own export promotion offices overseas. Ministers of the Canadian provinces of Ontario and Quebec, Germany's Rhineland, and Spain's Basque Country all travel the world to attract foreign investment to their own regions. They know better than to wait for a central government to act on their behalf.

Rather than think of the world as run by coherent states, we should instead realize that we have more *islands of governance* than we have effective governments—and just as in the Middle Ages, these islands are not states but *cities*. Today, just forty city-regions account for two-thirds of the world economy. Their power lies in money, knowledge, and stability. New York City's economy alone is larger than most of sub-Saharan Africa's. Port cities and entrepôts such as Dubai act like twenty-first-century Venice: They are "free zones" where products are efficiently re-exported without the hassles of government red tape. Such mega-cities as Rio, Istanbul, Cairo, Mumbai, Nairobi, and Manila are the leading urban centers of their countries and regions, yet each teems with hundreds of thousands of new urban squatters each year. The migrant underclass lives not in chaos and "shadow economies" but often in functional, self-organizing ecosystems, the typical physical stratification of medieval cities. Whether rich or poor, cities, more than nations, are the building blocks of global activity today. Our world is more a network of villages than it is one global village.

Alliances of these agile cities, like the medieval Hanseatic League of the Baltic Sea, are forming. They will use their sovereign wealth funds to acquire the latest technology from the West, buy up tracts of agricultural land in Africa to grow their food, and protect their investments through private armies and intelligence services. Hamburg and Dubai have forged a partnership to boost shipping links and life sciences research, while Abu Dhabi and Singapore have developed into a new commercial axis as well. No one is waiting for permission from Washington to make deals with whomever one wants.

Not only should we think more in terms of cities than states, but we must also distinguish between the *state* and the *government*. At a time when global commerce trumps fiscal and monetary levers, where trade barriers barely allow nations to protect jobs and industries, and where networked activists can destabilize regimes, many governments have become at most *filters* between domestic priorities and international demands. They are more regulatory than provisory: The best ones collect taxes widely and fairly, run efficient courts, protect property rights, defend national borders, police equitably, maintain economic stability, and provide some social safety net. How many governments can you name that do this? In many parts of the world it is increasingly civic groups, religious charities, and corporations that provide these basic goods. Very few citizens still say "It's the government's job" and expect the job to get done.

In such a fragmented world, who can we count on to deliver the goods? In the fourteenth century and for hundreds of years thereafter, Florence's Medici family was the archetypical hybrid of public and private power, producing three popes, building opulent palaces, commissioning art to shape values, and intermarrying with royal families across Europe. Today we see the Medici-like blurring of boundaries in spades: Gazprom oligarchs control the Kremlin; the billionaires Berlusconi in Italy and Thaksin in Thailand have also been heads of state; Persian Gulf royalty oversee semi-official ministries and investment funds simultaneously. Detroit's new mass-transit rail system is being funded largely by the CEO of Penske Corporation and the owner of the Red Wings ice hockey team. Today the main businesses of France, Turkey, Korea, Jordan, and other countries remain in the hands of big families and a clutch of businessmen who populate such guilds and clubs as the Young Presidents' Organization. Furthermore, family businesses and small enterprises are asserting themselves as the backbone of the world's real economy. As investment banking shrinks, private banking and wealth management firms are growing. Then there are the mega-billionaires-cum-philanthropists such as Bill Gates,

Richard Branson, and Ratan Tata who combat deadly disease, sponsor African schools, and govern steel factory cities, respectively. They represent the interests of their companies and projects far more than their home nations as such, and millions of lives depend on their good works. They increasingly run their own borderless worlds.

From clans to corporations, all of the players active in diplomacy a millennium ago are back. The word "diplomacy" stems from the Greek *diploun,* meaning "to fold," and refers to the folded diplomas authorizing entry into foreign territories that emissaries carried inside sealed metal plates. Today, the right business card will do. This isn't new. In the Middle Ages, diverse merchant communities were a driving force of diplomacy, managing to translate languages, exchange currencies, and trade a cornucopia of goods across Eurasia. In America's case, until the late nineteenth century its diplomacy was so sparse that National City Bank and Standard Oil both operated and deployed their own diplomatic corps extensively throughout Latin America and Asia. Worried by the dearth of American ambassadors in these regions, they helped finance the founding of Georgetown's Edmund A. Walsh School of Foreign Service, effectively America's first diplomatic academy, where "international business diplomacy" is a coveted major today. It's only a matter of time before an uber-corporation issues its own passport with pre-negotiatied visa-free access to countries large and small.

Even for large countries—Canada and India, for example—their growing business presence *is* their diplomatic presence: the substance of diplomacy without the ceremonial form. Corporations now have grand strategies just like countries. Weapons dealers and oil companies are just the most obvious examples of how these economic emissaries trove the planet in search of labor, fuel, food, and consumers. Of the one hundred largest economic entities in the world, half are companies. At the 2010 World Expo in Shanghai, corporations had their own pavilions alongside countries. With its network of thousands of reporters worldwide pumping data into proprietary terminals, Bloomberg is not only a media company that operationally dwarfs *The New York Times* and *Financial Times* put together, it is also effectively the world's largest private intelligence service with super-filters that allow clients to cull from thousands of sources. All over the world, private equity funds are taking stakes in farmland, gold, and other resources in exchange for building basic services and serving as friendly intermediaries with Western governments. The writ of the state has become at best hybrid sovereignty over supply chains, special economic zones, and reconstruction projects. Governments can attempt to monitor or regulate corporations, but they cannot control them.

At the same time, "corporate citizenship," once an oxymoron, is now a cliché. Today the willingness to build an airport or develop a medicine comes as much or more from companies who view these as necessary for their markets and consumers as from governments. One of the world's largest banks, HSBC—known for its multicultural "visual values" ads in airport Jetway ramps—has twenty thousand offices in eighty-three countries, three hundred thousand employees, and 150 million customers. In a world where people care as much about their cash balance as their citizenship, such banks are vital lifelines of dependable service. Businesses find it increasingly difficult to escape public responsibilities with the Milton Friedman–esque claim that "the business of business is business." They are right that unprofitability is not sustainable, so they increasingly pursue the path of profitable sustainability. The UK Companies Act requires that firms report on their social and environmental impact. Market incentives and government regulation can go hand in hand, but make no mistake: The former is indispensable.

Technology and finance have torn apart the relationship between borders and identity. In ancient Anatolia, Mesopotamian merchants embedded themselves in foreign societies to build cultural and commercial ties. Today, trade diasporas are again a key driver of economic and political links: Witness the emerging "Sinosphere" enlarged by fifty million overseas Chinese around the Pacific Rim and extending as far as Angola and Peru. China has begun to offer compelling incentives to these overseas Chinese to invest more and more in the mainland, soon potentially including even dual citizenship. The more than twenty million Indians concentrated in the Persian Gulf, East Africa, the United Kingdom, and Silicon Valley also form a "Desi" diaspora of growing ethno-political and economic weight. More than one hundred countries have external voting rights for diasporas, and eleven countries reserve seats for them in parliaments. In 2009, Lebanese political parties flew in expats from as far away as Canada to vote in parliamentary elections. Diasporas and cross-border economic dependencies can create unpredictable political and social rifts. What will the politics of Arab monarchies look like if the Indian government starts demanding a political voice for its millions of guest workers who outnumber the local populations by five to one?

In a neo-medieval world, multiple identities are possible according to your nation, profession, religion, ethnicity, or even your online avatar. The talent arbitrage of companies has become the citizenship arbitrage of countries as statelets such as Qatar try to acquire the best and brightest athletes and engineers from oversees, just as America offers fast-track citizenship to Latinos who fight in Iraq. Dubai even hires South African and Australian expats to carry out its commercial diplomacy. One of them recently asked, "Why can't they make a global passport for people who belong everywhere, who aren't representing just one country?"

Loyalties are strengthening beyond money, power, and kinship toward faith. Islam is spreading today as quickly as it did in the seventh and eighth centuries, its appeal equally political and social in such places as Egypt and Lebanon, where the Muslim Brotherhood and Hezbollah are both political parties and welfare providers. Christianity, too, is rerooting itself in Africa, Latin America, and even China, while in the United States millions of Americans join evangelical mega-churches and profess faith in messianic prophecies.

Once again we live in an age of superstitions that call to mind the Middle Ages, when the church banned paganism and magical practices it deemed either anti-religious or even too religious. The infamous "Toledo letter" predicted a world-ending planetary alignment in 1186, prompting the archbishop of Canterbury to declare a three-day fast. (It seems to have worked.) Today the rapid spread of AIDS, avian flu, and other pandemics perpetually raises the specter of another Black Death. If you live in a tall building, you fear terrorists crashing a plane into it; if you live near the shore (as 50 percent of the world's population does), you fear getting wiped out in increasingly frequent tsunamis or hurricanes. Today's Nostradamus figures are bestselling authors such as Eckhart Tolle and Paulo Coelho, who preach salvation through spirituality and raise self-help to a cosmic level with undertones of a "radical crisis" requiring that mankind "evolve or die."*

Fear of the future is growing as welfare states are dismantled and retirement accounts empty. Some predict that coming out of the financial crisis, members of religious traditions with high birthrates such as Jews, Muslims, and Catholics stand the best chance of economic stabilization because of their religions' focus on trust-based kinships and self-financing communities—the foundations of local stability in the Middle Ages.

We are never more than a hair's length away from the symptoms of medievalism: Economic chaos, social unrest, depraved morals, wild expenditures, debauchery, and religious hysteria all lie just under the surface of our many veneers of sophistication. After Saddam Hussein was removed from power in Iraq in 2003, it was only a short time before barbaric sectarianism was stoked and unleashed. During the 2008 credit crisis, hoarding gold became a sound financial strategy, while in Italy, the Naples mafia sprang into old-school action, providing large cash loans to needy businessmen—and showing up at their doorstep with pistols on payment day. In the United States, banks sold uncollected subprime debts to vulture agencies that harassed the overburdened poor like bounty hunters. In Russia, an estimated 10 to 20 percent of the economy quickly reverted to the barter system, while the country's politics remained focused on private feuds among modern-day robber barons. Around the world, cyber crime, boiler room frauds, fake check scams, and sellers of counterfeited batteries and toothpaste all flourished. Rape, pillage, and massacre are still indistinguishable weapons in African conflicts, where greed and grievance justify warlord control over minerals and slaves against nominally sovereign governments. Arab and African nations

---

*Comedian Stephen Colbert joked that the 2008 U.S. presidential debates reminded him of a "world in which cause and effect were divorced, when we could respond to events completely randomly—like the thirteenth century."

are always just a food price spike away from peasant revolt like the one that overran London in 1381.

NGOs and multinational corporations are a huge part of the response to the new medievalism: a new colonialism. Medieval churches, not kings, were responsible for the sick and helpless, and obliged universities and trade guilds to set aside charity money. Today, super-NGOs including Oxfam, Mercy Corps, and the International Rescue Committee run hospitals, schools, and refugee camps. For years in some places they have been the only barrier between humanity and chaos. In the poorest two dozen countries of sub-Saharan Africa, Médecins Sans Frontières (Doctors Without Borders) treats millions of AIDS-infected youth while feeding malnourished children and rehabilitating refugees. Together, strong powers and strong private actors run hopeless postcolonial nations in all but name. The now perpetual tension between building public legitimacy and the need to expeditiously deliver security, food, electricity, health, and education—which corporations and NGOs often do better than governments—has given rise to a new kind of hybrid sovereign state in which the actual government is not necessarily the most influential actor in its own territory.

As a result, the notion that governments do "high policy" while NGOs just "fill gaps" is outdated and insulting. NGOs are the tugboats of progressive diplomacy, steering supertanker governments and international organizations in the right direction on human rights and climate change. It was civil society groups that promoted direct micro-loans to the poor and pushed to ban antipersonnel land mines, and scientists and academics who made climate change prominent. Oxfam tells the UK Department for International Development what to do more often than the reverse, and the Bill & Melinda Gates Foundation sets the public health agenda more than the World Health Organization, for which Gates provides up to one-third of the budget. Through their guerrilla diplomacy campaigns, NGOs have become the chief advocates for reforming bloated and wasteful international organizations such as the World Bank, and they are a major force behind corporate responsibility activity as well. As one German diplomat put it, "Civil society does its own work, but its other role is to monitor and be a pain in the ass if things aren't working right." Even after the financial crisis, NGOs have delved deeper into the global citizenry to raise funds, and they continue to thrive, delivering welfare faster, cheaper, and better than many governments.

Today, comparisons to the interwar period of 1919–39 are tempting. Then it was Japan rising in Asia, today it's China; then it was the great influenza, today AIDS; then it was the Great Depression, today the Great Recession; then the League of Nations failed, today the United Nations is in crisis. Yet the Middle Ages parallel is superior in that it emphasizes the complexity of a world populated by many diverse types of actors. It is a mistake to think of the Middle Ages only as history's darkest era. It was also a time of great East–West commercial expansion and the rediscovery of classical wisdom. The new Middle Ages also need not be a permanent purgatory of uncertainty— in many ways it perversely gives some hope that our present situation may resolve itself in a Renaissance rather than a world war. But the Middle Ages only fully gave way to the Renaissance with the rise of the European nation-state in the sixteenth century. Establishing a new architecture for our current neo-medieval world could take decades.

The New Rules of the Game

There are few terms more fashionable in diplomacy today than "New Deal." Upon Barack Obama's election as U.S. president in 2008, European Commission president José Manuel Barosso called for a "New Deal for a new world." Other leaders seek a "New Deal" to balance global trade with sustainable development. Still we are waiting. Those who seek a grand global "New Deal" should remember that President Franklin D. Roosevelt delivered America's "New Deal" through what he called "bold, persistent experimentation." Where is that experimentation today?

Running the world is about much more than making laws and rules. That is the easy part. The hard part is implementing, evaluating, fixing, and spreading best practices. Crises such as the Indonesian tsunami, Darfur genocide, and the financial meltdown persistently re-

mind us of the gaps in our control over events and their consequences. There are plenty of resources in the world to solve our problems; what we really lack is the *capacity* to efficiently bring them to
bear. Fortunately, the solution is not to rip up our existing world
order and start from scratch. We just need to load new operating software onto our emerging global network.

That software is called *mega*-diplomacy. It is the key that unlocks
and unleashes the resources of governments, corporations, and
NGOs—none of which can run the world alone. Globalization has
splintered the world into an infinite milieu of actors, but technology
allows them to quickly and strategically recombine. Rather than a stiff
waltz of rituals and protocol among states alone, mega-diplomacy is a
jazzy dance among coalitions of ministries, companies, churches,
foundations, universities, activists, and other willful, enterprising individuals who cooperate to achieve specific goals. Twenty-first-century
challenges will be solved through such coalitions of willing government, corporate, and civic actors who not only sign their names but
also put manpower and resources on the table. Mega-diplomacy is the
triumph of *mini*-lateral action over multi-lateral stasis.

There will be no reform of global policies without a reform of
global political structure. Historically it takes either a major crisis or
a technological revolution to initiate such change—today we have
both. Whether combating terrorism, AIDS, or climate change, mega-
diplomacy has bounded ahead of traditional interstate diplomacy.
Whereas the old diplomacy was about affirming the *separateness* of
each nation through sovereign representation, mega-diplomacy is
about creating *unity* across communities to manage our collective
space. The great sociologist Émile Durkheim believed that society has
an essence beyond the sum of individual actions; within this social
milieu, an increasingly complex division of labor creates a dynamic
sense of solidarity. Scholars and politicians search for boundaries
among the state, market, and society, but in reality these have blurred
into irrelevance. It is hard to imagine anything getting done today
without the action-oriented networks that are becoming the corner-
stone of twenty-first-century diplomacy. It used to be possible to
count how many active public-private partnerships there were; today

the number is effectively infinite. Short-term politics cannot deliver the high start-up costs of global solutions, but smart diplomatic coalitions can.

Mega-diplomacy is the best hope to confront a world of high-stakes, neo-medieval chaos. Everyone seems to have micro solutions to macro problems. Mega-diplomacy brings those micro solutions to the macro level as a *systemic process*. The world needs very few if any new global organizations. What it needs is far more fresh combinations of existing actors who *coordinate* better with one another. This is not about money, but efficiency. The infrastructure of mega-diplomacy is the roads, or connections, among relevant agents, and the superstructure is the signs or guideposts that steer their coordination. Mega-diplomacy's success or failure comes down to following three principles:

- *Inclusiveness:* Getting all hands on deck through multi-stakeholder involvement of governments, companies, and NGOs.
- *Decentralization:* Spreading capabilities widely, and as close to problems as possible, promoting empowerment and resilience.
- *Mutual accountability:* Building communities of trust among participants, creating obligations to one another and the mission.

There is no better example of public-private collaboration than the Internet, which was invented by the U.S. military and is now governed by a single small nonprofit, the Internet Corporation for Assigned Names and Numbers (ICANN), which registers domain names and IP addresses. Though it has corporate funding from such companies as Cisco and Deutsche Telekom, its twenty-one-member board holds its elections online. The Internet is wider, deeper, and safer than ever because it is a distributed network. Cloud computing—not big buildings and bloated bureaucracies—is the future of global governance.

Mega-diplomacy forces us to cast aside ideologies. In the new marketplace of actors and solutions, collective wisdom is captured through diversity, making the whole smarter than the sum of its parts. As leading political scientist Robert Keohane puts it, "If only the world knew what the people in the world know!" Diplomacy needs more of Guy Kawasaki, the serial Silicon Valley entrepreneur who distrusts elitism in favor of passion and trial and error. As Jeffrey Immelt, CEO of General Electric, likes to say, "Fast failure is good." We should experiment, learn, share lessons, and move on. Harmonization and synchronicity, not control and direction, are the new virtues of management. There is not one authority or solution, but many; rules emerge not from the top down, but from the bottom up; there is no either-or between state and market, but both-and.

Diplomacy is not about perfection, but accommodation. Diplomacy can't stop every arms dealer, sex trafficker, forest logger, or rogue trader (and will not persuade Great Britain or its former colonies to drive on the right side of the road), but it can embody principles that will help us manage a messy but interconnected world. Mega-diplomacy can't be practiced the way bureaucrats tussle over org charts, focusing on who has the most power on paper. Instead, it should be thought of the way the best designers and mechanics work together to build cars—focusing on how to get energy flowing most efficiently through the vehicle—or like architecture, where form follows function. In flat organizations in which people can see what others are doing, everybody faces performance pressure and no one can hide behind bureaucratic silos.

In a world of constantly shifting coalitions, where does the buck stop? Who is ultimately responsible? Aristotle was skeptical of democracy; he wanted rule *for* the people but not necessarily *by* the people. For him, a regime's virtue lay in its ability to maximize the collective ends of citizen security and welfare. Similarly today, it matters far less *who* conducts an intervention than that it produces positive results. The diplomacy of action—"diplomacy of the deed"—is the new currency of legitimacy. Actors who want to be perceived as legitimate must *prove* they can do the job best.

Contrary to popular perceptions, this is where some parts of the UN system are strongest. Specialized agencies such as the World Food Program (WFP), the Office of the United Nations High Commissioner for Refugees (UNHCR), and the United Nations Children's Fund (UNICEF) not only save lives where great powers don't bother, but in the process change the way the world deals with such issues as food security and public health—both of which have a major impact on political stability. Since they are not top-heavy or centralized, their work happens where the problems are, and they enthusiastically partner with business and NGOs to get the job done. These bodies deserve the Nobel Prizes they have collected. As for the rest, the permissive consensus that allowed the UN Security Council, the World Bank, and other bodies to crawl along doing business as usual is over. They find themselves in a bizarre paradox: They are meant to promote efficiency, but it is most efficient to circumvent them.

Inertia is giving way to impatience. Vague notions of global democracy are not the solution to our problems; more accountable diplomacy is. Government bureaucrats may claim that "sovereign states are the only vehicles for legitimacy and accountability," but this orthodox lack of imagination has no place in a world needing fresh solutions. We will not have a meaningful global democracy of nations and peoples anytime soon, but we can have more accountable diplomacy today. Globalization doesn't have a global constitution, but dot-gov, dot-com, and dot-org diplomats can still monitor and hold one another accountable. Informal mechanisms can be more effective than laws that are neither obeyed nor enforced. Think eBay, where peers set value and clients and suppliers monitor one another for honesty and efficiency.

Accountability comes most fundamentally from the strategic use of shame. With so much technological sophistication in the world, it seems that only our own inner personal development is lagging—and shame accelerates our learning curve. Shame has recorded a number of victories: It was integral to ending the practice of slavery in the late nineteenth century, convinced Dow Chemical to stop producing napalm during the Vietnam War, compelled McDonald's and other fast-food chains to declare the calorie content of their foods, got Nike and Levi's to improve labor standards in their factories, forced cigarette makers to publicize the deadliness of their products, embarrassed a number of European leaders so that they canceled their visits to the

Beijing Olympics over the Chinese crackdown on Tibetans, pressured Persian Gulf states to switch from boy jockeys to robots in camel races, and convinced some Wall Street firms to curb outlandish executive compensation.

Today we rely on the media for transparency: to shame the impudent, deliver accountability, and make us feel informed and empowered. But the media has a limited bandwidth and a dangerous power to exaggerate both good news and bad. Television can generate moral disgust and act as a virtual conscience, but civil wars and famines don't go away when the press crews pack up after a few days. Haiti is nowhere near "back to normal" after its early 2010 earthquake. Indeed, such traumas make the news only when it's already too late. Also, the media is no longer—if it ever was—a neutral source of information. Privately owned cable channels, newspapers, and websites dominate the media landscape, and many of them now depend on private philanthropy to provide deeper reportage. Even public television networks such as America's PBS rely heavily on private support. Still, the more informed the global public, the more transparency we will have. But remember, on issues from climate change to rallies on the streets of Tehran, the media only highlights people's power; it doesn't supply it. You must do that.

The bumper sticker to capture the spirit of the new diplomacy is "Govern globally, act locally."

We have fallen into the habit of treating the most significant issues of our time—terrorism, climate change, the economy—as if they are global first and local second. But, in fact, the opposite is true. Movements that many consider global—jihadism, anti-corporatism, environmentalism—are far more rooted in local injustices. There is no "global poverty," but rather varieties of Latin American, African, Arab, and Asian poverty, each with its own blend of drivers, including overpopulation, geography, and corruption. We have an interlinked global economy and a fragile global ecosystem—but making them both more resilient will happen through local or regional measures. Such global ideals as democracy and human rights mean almost nothing until they are accepted and embedded by local actors within local contexts.

The word "global" can inspire, but global action requires the most elusive of forces: political will. How much political will do we have in global reserve? When the genocide in Darfur was unfolding in 2003–4, U.S. secretary of state Colin Powell and UN secretary-general Kofi Annan refused to speak the term "genocide," as it would legally require the international community to act. Instead they just called it a "catastrophe," leaving the Sudanese regime to continue sponsoring its genocidal pogroms. The year 2010 was supposed to be big for political will, with the United Nations measuring progress toward its development targets. Kofi Annan recently claimed that achieving these goals is still feasible, but the "political will remains largely absent." Brazilian president Luiz Inácio Lula da Silva also implored, "The world has enough resources to satisfy the needs of a population twice as big as the present one. But it lacks the political will to overcome this inequality." Upon receiving the Nobel Peace Prize in 2008, former Finnish prime minister Martti Ahtisaari called for peace in the Middle East: "It's only a matter of will." The sad fact is that few nations demonstrate political will, and fewer still agree on what changes to make. For most leaders, political will lasts at best until the next election.

Because there is no more deafeningly empty phrase than "political will," the desire for global consensus should never take precedence over local action: *human will*. Political will makes the perfect the enemy of the good, while human will is a bottom-up force. Rather than allowing "justice" to be defined by a distant bureaucracy, human will means taking matters into your own hands. Confidence in top-down approaches is declining, but faith in bottom-up solutions is growing. There will be inconsistencies in the forms of human will— but that's the point. One-size-fits-all solutions frequently fail, while the "right" approach to countering terrorism, achieving fiscal stability, or reducing poverty is different across continents and cultures. The devil is in the details: If you're not on the ground, chances are you don't know the details.

In basketball there is no more efficient and dazzling act of team-work than an alley-oop: passing the ball right into the hands of a leaping player already within inches of the net. This is the best metaphor for the most important principle for redesigning global order: *Political will must support human will.* If global resources are not supporting local solutions, then what are they doing? After decades of "analysis paralysis," there is nothing left to do but to do.

Cosmopolitan—or cause-mopolitan—"citizens of the world" aspire toward a global consciousness, a superego for humanity. How do we do it? British scientific journalist Matt Ridley put it best: "For St. Augustine the source of social order lay in the teachings of Christ. For Hobbes it lay in the sovereign. For Rousseau it lay in solitude. For Lenin it lay in the party. They were all wrong. The roots of social order are in our heads, where we possess the instinctive capacities for creating not a perfectly harmonious and virtuous society, but a better one than we have at present. We must build our institutions in such a way that they draw out those instincts."[2] Pushing resources from the global to the local level is the surest step to getting there.

Generation Y Geopolitics

When thirty-four-year-old Andry Rajoelina seized power in Madagascar after a military coup in early 2009, he had food on his mind. Most of the large Indian Ocean island's population lives at the poverty line, a fact that didn't stop his predecessor, Marc Ravalomanana, from cutting a deal with South Korean corporation Daewoo to lease more than one million hectares of farmland to grow food crops for itself. Within days of the coup, Rajoelina axed the deal. A former disc jockey whose work ethic earned him the nickname "TGV" after the high-speed French train, Rajoeline remains widely popular with the country's majority under-eighteen population who don't care that he is well below the constitutionally required age of forty to serve as president. Nothing says "To hell with the old order" like an underage coup d'état.

People under thirty, who are now most of the world's population, never experienced life before globalization. 9/11 is their defining moment—and interdependence is their lesson from it. Thanks to technology, generational identity—more than geography—shapes their worldview. Years before Henry Kissinger began his diplomatic career, he wrote, "Each generation is permitted only one effort of abstraction; it can attempt only one interpretation and a single experiment, for it is its own subject." Machiavelli argued that change has no constituency. Today it does. For Generation Y, *im*patience is a virtue. This millennial generation, who voted overwhelmingly Democrat in the 2008 U.S. election, is getting in the driver's seat faster than ever, and its ability to quickly mobilize using smartphones and Facebook makes autocrats as nervous as sanctions do. It intuitively supports greater trade, faster communication, more migration, and multiple identities, and it subscribes to postmaterial values such as equality and ecology.

Idealism has become practical again. Twenty years ago, only 18 percent of American college graduates said they wanted to "go out and change the world." Today that number is 40 percent. Whereas the postwar generation found public service noble, and baby boomers were convinced by Reagan that government is the source of problems, Generation Y's leaders will likely have five or six jobs across public, private, and nonprofit sectors over the course of their careers, and thus be pragmatic rather than ideological about the role of the state. They see problems functionally, not nationally, and see diplomacy not as vertical and hierarchical, but rather as a distributed network: All are connected, and there is no center. They take for granted that working for corporations such as Google, or NGOs such as Oxfam and the Gates Foundation, means participating in political agendas that operate without official approval, yet the work is as diplomatic as that of a foreign ministry. They are the ones who will reshape governments, corporations, and other pillars of the establishment from the inside out. Generation Y will own mega-diplomacy.

But can this global generation create a fair world? Unfortunately, Generation Y is divided as well. From Darfur's refugee camps to Pakistan's madrassas, many youth have learned to take a hard line against the existing order: revolution, not reform. Somalia's militant al-Qaeda affiliate calls itself al-Shabaab—meaning "youth." Are we in for generations of cosmic struggle? The answer depends on who runs this place. *You do.* Everyone has a role in running the world.

Chapter Two

The New Diplomats

*Diplomacy will always have ambassadors and ministers;
the question is whether it will have diplomats.*

—JULES CAMBON (1925)

*Changes are now under way which make it
extremely difficult to predict the future of diplomacy
or prescribe its conduct.*

—GEORGE KENNAN (2005)

If you think you are far removed from the back rooms and smoky
chambers of diplomacy, think again. Globalization and the end
of the Cold War have empowered ambitious entrepreneurs, academics, activists, and celebrities to deploy their own strategies on the
world stage. Many of them are today's most visible avatars of
mega-diplomacy. Excluding them guarantees diplomacy's failure.
They change the way issues make it onto the global agenda, how
and what policies are formulated, and how they are implemented.
They put their money where their mouths are, and use prestige and
shame to provoke the complacent establishment. Without these
new diplomats we still wouldn't have a land mine ban, debt relief,
or an International Criminal Court. Most of all, the new diplomats

*inspire millions of people around the world to join their causes.
You can be like them.*

*Who are these mega-diplomats who cross in and out of the public
and private worlds? What makes some more successful than others?
America is home to the greatest number of the new diplomats, yet its
foreign policy will continue to stumble until it learns to leverage them
into a seamless diplomatic-industrial complex. The new diplomats already have a big edge over the U.S. State Department and traditional
international organizations when it comes to fusing public and private power into a whole greater than the sum of its parts. Rather than
just the White House and Whitehall, the World Economic Forum and
the Clinton Global Initiative are the new go-to venues for new diplomats as well as the most promising examples of mega-diplomacy in
action. Their fastest-growing following is among students and young
people, meaning they represent just the beginning when it comes to
redesigning how the world is run.*

From Model United Nations to Model Medievalism

On a small college campus in Virginia, far from the limelight of the
White House or the United Nations, a diplomatic experiment is under
way. Each summer, the fledgling organization Americans for Informed
Democracy (AID) gathers several hundred high school students for a
unique simulation. Rather than at the Model United Nations, with
which many young internationalists are familiar and where all that
matters is if your country is big or small, these students don't just role-
play presidents. Instead, each delegate is just as likely to represent the
OPEC oil cartel, Gazprom, Amnesty International, Greenpeace, Bono,
Bill Gates, the *New York Times* columnist Nicholas Kristof, the head
of the World Trade Organization (WTO), Al Gore, or the CEO of Citigroup.

The exercise is realistic not only for the players *at* the table, but the
issues *on* the table. They negotiate sovereign debt, gas pipelines, and
agricultural subsidies. In the 2008 simulation, these next-gen diplomats negotiated an oil price cut for China through Russian energy

giant Rosneft in exchange for China's curbing its rapid construction of heavily polluting coal-fired power plants. Russia would then levy an export tax that it would use to enhance Eurasian oil and gas pipelines and power grids. China's payback of the fuel subsidy would be directed toward investments in alternative energy technologies. UN veterans should be jealous.

Students at the AID simulation are learning a far more accurate picture of the twenty-first-century landscape of power and influence than many diplomatic trainees today. Their role-playing exercise wasn't the "real" world, and yet it was: Energy security and climate change are two sides of the same coin, not parallel conversations in bureaucratic silos. Seth Green, one of AID's founders, realized early on that young change makers are inspired by alternatives to the UN system: "By playing not just Gordon Brown but also Bill Gates, students take on roles that allow them to navigate a much more complex world." The bottom line, says Kate Willard, another AID leader, is that "there are far more players working on far more levels of global policy than any single organization can reflect." Thanks to AID, these students are prepared for the open yet sometimes opaque world of neo-medieval diplomacy in which individuals can play multiple roles and juggle multiple issues at the same time.

There is no better example of this than Zalmay Khalilzad. After the U.S. invasion of Afghanistan in 2001 and the ouster of the Taliban, Khalilzad—an Afghan American working for the RAND Corporation—was appointed special envoy and then ambassador to the country. Armed with knowledge of Dari and Pashto and billions of U.S. dollars, and eventually backed by tens of thousands of American troops, he set about nation building and playing warlord politics. For three years he was constantly whispering in Afghan president Hamid Karzai's ear, and allegedly also in the ears of his opponents, earning him the label "viceroy." Later on as U.S. ambassador in Baghdad, "Zal" (as he is known to insiders) broke with protocol and negotiated directly with Sunni insurgents in Iraq to get them to participate in elections. In his next stint as U.S. ambassador to the United Nations, he again called his own shots, secretly advising Asif Ali Zardari, widower of Benazir Bhutto in Pakistan, on his election strategy. Even as a private citizen, he turned up in Kurdistan during the region's elections—to do what, no one seemed quite sure. Such boldness, while admirable, points to the fraying of modern diplomacy: Ambassadors can be more than just messengers of others' policy. Indeed, many still wonder whether Khalilzad represents American interests or his own—or sometimes the former but always the latter. Could his next step be to run for the Afghan presidency? Perhaps Khalilzad plays multiple agendas simultaneously simply because he can. As he himself put it, "Who is the ambassador in the age of BlackBerry?"

During the Cold War, diplomacy was intentionally ambiguous as the superpowers sought to fake each other out and call each other's bluffs. But ever since, diplomacy has become unintentionally ambiguous as technology and power allow anyone to penetrate borders and pursue their own agendas. The early 1990s was a thriving period for such shadow elites crossing public, private, and international networks. Privatization con artists flourished, such as Viktor Kozeny, a Czech émigré who fleeced thousands of his native citizens of their stock vouchers promising 1,000 percent returns, only to hide the money in offshore tax havens. Around the same time, the United States Agency for International Development (USAID) effectively outsourced its Russia policy to the Harvard Institute of International Development, which brokered loans as if it were a U.S. government agency.

From Bruce Jackson, the Lockheed Martin vice president who as head of the U.S. Committee to Expand NATO seemed to make official security guarantees to countries such as Georgia (which learned the hard way in the summer of 2008 that it has no protection from Russian intrusions), to Ahmed Chalabi, the head of the Iraqi National Congress who teamed with U.S. neoconservative Richard Perle to make the case for a falsely premised Iraq war in 2003, the line between diplomacy and lobbying has blurred to the point where foreign governments now use lobbyists as much as their own embassies to influence American policy toward Turkey, India, Taiwan, and many other places, especially targeting congressmen whose districts may benefit from business deals with their nations. Diplomacy has become "Diplomacy, Inc."[1]

Good diplomacy is making connections any way one can. To be

relevant, twenty-first-century diplomats need to be adventurous and multilingual. As a Swiss ambassador in Washington once put it, "My job isn't well-defined, but that's better than writing cables to Berne after every conversation. Instead, I build relationships that can be useful whenever we might need them." Today there are "digital" diplomats who are plugged in and "analog" ones who hide behind pointless paperwork.

Scurrying around the corridors of the WTO in Geneva is Falou Samb, a member of Senegal's lean mission to the powerful body's headquarters. Samb is tasked not only with promoting Senegal's access to markets as a small exporter, but also with lobbying for greater technical assistance for all West African nations. There are few tougher jobs than being an African diplomat, yet they best represent what diplomacy is becoming. Using just Gmail accounts and cell phones, young Africans serving in Europe and Asia today go door-to-door at ministries and corporate offices lobbying for the easing of trade restrictions and for greater investment. Their countries' survival depends on their persuasiveness and thorough understanding of how to set up a corporate visit, arrange project financing through an export-import bank, ensure sound legal contracts, and provide security for a factory once it's set up. This is the diplomat as he was in ancient times: a do-it-all factotum.

Whether you want to run the world or save it, the only question to ask is "What kind of diplomat do you want to be?" In the cubicles of Manhattan today there are thousands of management consultants, investment bankers, and lawyers who embody an odd mix of dejection and passion. Unfulfilled by the monotony of Wall Street capitalism, they use their spare time to make business plans for start-up companies on the other side of the world, set up clean technology funds, and travel abroad to learn foreign cultures. Armed with a smartphone and some savings, each is crafting his or her own project to attack a problem somewhere and make his or her mark. How to use music to promote women's rights? How to get cheap water pumps to the most arid parts of Africa? They are the answer to Khalilzad's question: Everyone who has a BlackBerry—or iPhone or Nexus One—can be their own ambassador.

The Seven Habits of Highly Effective Diplomats

Some of the most famous diplomatic treatises put the weight of the world on the shoulders of negotiators. In 1716, King Louis XIV's faithful minister François de Callières penned *On the Manner of Negotiating with Princes* to provide guidance in selecting and deploying the rare breed of skilled special envoys. A diplomat was expected to be quick, resourceful, agreeable, courageous, patient, and knowledgeable. But, of course, "he should also entertain handsomely. A good cook is often an excellent conciliator." Almost three centuries later, the book caught on again when it was republished with a fresh introduction by business guru Charles Handy. As ambassadors and executives blend ever more into a single leadership caste, Handy sensed that management, diplomacy, and negotiation were becoming synonymous.

So what does it take to be a good diplomat in the neo-medieval twenty-first century? Cardinal Richelieu famously stated that "secrecy is the first essential in affairs of the state," but does diplomacy still work best in secret, even though secrecy is now considered a sign of nefarious intentions? What about other traditional virtues, including finesse, wit, patience, and self-control? Today these seem more like excuses and delay tactics. Indeed, what if the opposite traits are more effective: bluntness, impatience, stubbornness? These were certainly part of U.S. ambassador Richard Holbrooke's repertoire during his Balkan forays, when he was known as "The Bulldozer," but he successfully brought Serbs to the table for the 1995 Dayton Accords. At the same time, as special envoy to Afghanistan and Pakistan, Holbrooke didn't set deadlines or preach American interests. He did more listening than talking, meeting with locals in tribal regions, including the Taliban. Real diplomats don't use vague concepts such as "smart," "soft," or "network power." They calculate which mixture of ends and means will get the job done.

Stephen Covey, the world's bestselling leadership expert, unwittingly provided sage advice for today's diplomats in his book *The Seven Habits of Highly Effective People*. If each of his seven virtues were imported into the diplomatic circuit, the world might become a better-run place.

1. *Be Proactive.* Diplomats are often dispassionate messengers, reading démarches like stale B-movie scripts. But what if their promotions were actually linked to performance, as in the business world? If diplomats weren't allowed the cushy job in London until they did something good for Liberia, we'd see a lot less talk and a lot more action.

2. *Begin with the End in Mind.* The most recent WTO negotiations, known as the Doha Development Round, carried on for seven years—then collapsed in 2008. Rather than focus on specific goals, the agenda was saddled (by the United States) with additional items like an overburdened mule. Meanwhile, many poor countries still don't have the capacity to implement the earlier Uruguay Round's aims. Credibility depends on results, even if they are small wins rather than grand breakthroughs.

3. *Put First Things First.* Inside the U.S. State Department, hoarding assignments and portfolios gets you more face time and status, with success a secondary consideration. Rather than delegating authority, Condoleezza Rice spent years doing North Korea on Monday, Israel-Palestine on Tuesday, NATO on Wednesday, Iraq on Thursday, and Pakistan on Friday. Leaders have to trust regional-expert diplomats to navigate and manage specific situations on their own; otherwise they will just spin in circles.

4. *Think Win-Win.* If you win one round and lose the next, has either side won? Some Americans who observe China's resource-driven deal making in Africa and Latin America fear it will undermine democracy. But why not intensify anti-corruption efforts and budgetary assistance so that high growth rates can translate into greater welfare? The West's new rivalry with China for influence could still be good for everyone.

5. *Seek First to Understand, Then to Be Understood.* The United States has learned the hard way that what others want for themselves trumps what it wants for them—always. From Iraqis fighting American occupation to Congo's miners protesting Chinese contractors, everyone now has the power to resist if their needs aren't appreciated. So-called public diplomacy has been given second-tier status, but it holds the key to learning what Muslim societies want *prior* to launching ill-informed and kitsch TV and radio stations.

6. *Synergize.* Diplomats are often generalists, and only the most experienced know a lot about a lot. Unfortunately, interagency processes quickly devolve into one dominating the others. But experts in development, combat, and governance must think and work in teams to make a whole policy greater than the sum of its parts. Bureaucrats need to focus less on turf wars and more on combining skills.

7. *Sharpen the Saw.* If diplomats ought to be pros in one area, it's networking. But with whom? In fact, they spend too much time among their own kind, reinforcing stale information rather than learning from experts in business, academia, and NGOs. One digital diplomat is worth three analog ones.

Anyone who wants to be part of running the world—setting its rules, shaping its policies, and implementing its decisions—would do well to obey these principles. America and its diplomats have as much to learn as anyone.

America's "Diplomacy in Action"

Diplomacy is a force multiplier: It is the style that changes the substance. The United States under George W. Bush presented an irony of diplomacy: a powerful state whose tin-eared diplomacy actually diminished its leverage in the world. By contrast, within his first one hundred days as president, Barack Obama reached out to the leaders of countries previously labeled adversaries, such as Venezuela, Cuba, Russia, Iran, Myanmar, and Syria—bursting the myth that isolation, either of America or its rivals, serves the "national interest." But while Obama attempted to replace Machiavelli's duality between fear and love with "tough love," he has yet to prove that diplomacy is more than the lesser cousin of force. To do that requires putting much more muscle into the U.S. State Department's new motto, "Diplomacy in Action."

American diplomats today aren't nearly empowered enough for the job. Instead of being nimble and resourceful, they often regurgitate such platitudes as "It's a top priority"—and in the same breath follow them with deflating deflections like "We don't know when it will happen." The State Department's archaic org chart separates economics, security, public diplomacy, and other areas from regional offices and has a catchall bureau for "Global Affairs" that covers everything from climate to disease to human rights and democracy. To span these stovepipes, posts for envoys, special representatives, and senior advisers are created for everything from the war on drugs to the war on terror—"enough czars to make Vladimir Putin jealous," one commentator noted. Meanwhile, more and more ambassadors are political appointees chosen from the ranks of campaign donors who "serve at the pleasure of the president," rather than career diplomats who can build continuity in relations. Between superenvoys grabbing the glory, an inner circle of the White House and National Security Council staffers making all the key decisions, and friends of the president occupying about half of all ambassadorships, it's no surprise that so many American diplomats exist in a state of semi-depression.

Even worse, the embassies most diplomats work in often confine rather than empower. U.S. foreign service officers used to venture afield to survey land, build inroads with local populations, and learn vernacular languages. But since 9/11, diplomats have been barricaded inside fortified embassies—more and more of which are being moved from the center of capital cities out to remote suburbs behind barbed-wire fences. In Baghdad, nine hundred diplomats are hunkered behind sandbags in the world's largest embassy. As Edward Peck, himself a former ambassador to Iraq, put it, "I don't know how you can conduct diplomacy in that way." The American embassy in Islamabad, Pakistan, has been similarly built up, with little clarity as to what it will actually do.

It doesn't have to be this way. Diplomats used to be granted immunity on the promise of not intervening in the domestic affairs of host countries. Today successful diplomacy requires exactly that. Few foreigners care anymore what American officials think—it matters far more what they deliver. Embassies must be outposts for economic, intelligence, military, development, and other experts to bring about positive change in societies, helping them provide services their governments might not. In Pakistan, for example, this means agriculture teams, education programmers, and culturally astute negotiators regularly ferrying in and out of troubled parts of the Pashtun tribal regions and working seamlessly with NGOs—both American and Pakistani—to deliver tangible benefits to villages that are more accustomed to military campaigns and corruption. In such places, diplomats shouldn't lecture locals on natural resource management or child labor but actually roll up their sleeves and help them improve their standards. It's not surprising that so many diplomats have admitted that Peace Corps volunteers are the best ambassadors America has ever had.

For the United States to even conceivably regain a global leadership role, it needs to think along three dimensions in all its foreign activities: which agencies to bring together (the "whole of government" approach), which nations to cooperate and coordinate with (the "multi-partner" approach), and how to leverage private sector and NGO resources and talent (the "public-private" approach). Combining public and private resources can generate a sophisticated *diplomatic-industrial complex*. America already has a military-industrial complex: the "iron triangle" of industry, politicians, and the military assailed by President Dwight D. Eisenhower in his 1961 farewell address. Now it must do the same for diplomacy. From oil companies to chambers of commerce to environmental activists,

America's corporations, civic organizations, universities, churches, youth groups, and charities already have their *own* foreign policies—and Americans are expressing their diplomatic voice through these channels more than any other.

No other country has such a deep pool of resources *outside* of its government to beneficially shape the world. The greatness of America lies in the talent, depth, wealth, and generosity of its citizenry. Its corporations have been the most innovative and respected in history. Its universities have educated much of the world's elite, and have now located campuses in the heart of the Middle East, potentially introducing free thinking and ideas more potently than any other force. The United States sent $192 billion to the developing world in 2006, most of it in foreign investment, portfolio capital, foundation grants, and philanthropic giving. No other large country (with a population of one hundred million or more) comes even close. In 2010, President Obama brought together big American companies with Arab entrepreneurs to partner up on job-creating investments across the Middle East, while the U.S. Overseas Private Investment Company boosted loans and insurance to Arab start-ups. Obama also hosted a "Citizen Diplomacy" summit to build connections among schools, companies, and communities in the United States and abroad "one handshake at a time." This is the way to use mega-diplomacy to "drain the swamp."

In the globalization age, states will prove themselves *stronger* if they can harness private forces rather than try to suppress or control them. The more open a society, the more ambassadors it has. America needs all the diplomats it can get, especially since the number of foreign service officers (approximately five thousand) is less than that of the crew of a single aircraft carrier.

Celebrity Diplomats: Does Life Imitate Art?

Some diplomats are also big celebrities. In France, Foreign Minister Bernard Kouchner—the 1960s Parisian radical and founder of Médecins Sans Frontières—is perennially the country's most popular politician. In 1992, as minister of health, he marched up the Somali shore with sacks of rice donated by French schoolchildren. He brow-beat Serbs as UN high representative in Kosovo in the late 1990s, and in 2008 he demanded that the international community intervene militarily if necessary to deliver essential supplies to the stranded Burmese victims of Cyclone Nargis. If a man of his stature were married with the resources of America, we might see more UN resolutions result in actual action.

Ever since the first American "celebrity-diplomat" Benjamin Franklin worked his charms in the court of French king Louis XVI, the terms have become increasingly de-hyphenated—but the concepts are merging once again. Celebrities possess one of the core ingredients of diplomatic success: *prestige.* They have a healthy skepticism of the rigidly defined acronyms traditional diplomats swear by, favoring instead an emotive appeal that transcends bureaucratic barriers. They represent not only themselves, but also the potential of millions of fans young and old whom they inspire, whether through songs or tweets. Hollywood raised as much money for Haiti's reconstruction as any government, and Madonna has helped put Malawi on the map by adopting children from there. Madonna cites her resilience and tirelessness as the reasons why she remains at the top of her game. Regular diplomats should learn from her staying power.

For every current celebrity diplomat there is a predecessor. Audrey Hepburn's success as a UNICEF ambassador inspired the birth of an entire industry of celebrity diplomacy featuring Princess Diana and Angelina Jolie, who has humanized the plight of refugees. Bill and Melinda Gates took their initial cue from Ted Turner, the CNN founder who pledged $1 billion to start the UN Foundation and support UNICEF and the UN Population Fund, and began partnerships with companies such as Vodafone to fight measles and AIDS. The UN Foundation has spent more than $1 billion and partnered with over one hundred NGOs to deliver ten billion doses of polio vaccine to two billion children. Now such partnerships are the norm, with Barcelona's soccer club contributing $2 million to UNICEF projects and wearing its logo on its jerseys.

Turner was also something of an anti-diplomat, worrying less about numbers and protocol than about getting things done. Bono's perhaps unconscious role model is Richard Gere, who as chairman of the International Campaign for Tibet worked with everyone from Senator Jesse Helms to the Beastie Boys to confront China's smothering of Tibetan human rights both in reality and in UN debates. Bono launched the One Campaign through which he practices shuttle diplomacy between London and Washington to build trust with world leaders while nagging them about targets for increasing development assistance; he famously brought Helms to tears once on the issue of debt relief. He also never misses a chance to shame corporate executives, telling the Global Business Council for HIV/AIDS in 2004: "I'd like to talk about getting on the right side of history. If you thought this dinner was off the record, it's not. History is taking notes right now. Frankly, history couldn't care less what you or I say tonight. History only cares what we do when we leave, in the weeks, months, years even, that follow."[2] Corporate funding to combat AIDS has grown year after year. Bono's sometimes partner in crime, British ex-rocker Bob Geldof, is known for a less subtle approach. At Live Aid in 1985, he simply screamed into the microphone, "Give us the fucking money!" As far as the people of destitute villages are concerned, it doesn't matter if the person bringing freshwater, food, or vouchers is bug-eyed Bono or a stiff man in a suit—it's what he delivers that matters.

Even absent an "Actors Without Borders" organization, the celebrity-diplomat model has rapidly spread from West to East. Yao Ming is not only China's most famous export, but he has also promoted many charities across his home country as well. In India, Nobel Prize winner Rajendra Pachauri's Lighting a Billion Lives solar power initiative received little attention until Bollywood starlet Priyanka Chopra got involved: Millions of dollars were raised instantly for solar electricity projects in one thousand villages. Global celebrities can do nothing more important than inspire their own kind in every country they can reach. The most important heroes are local ones.

It's cynical to claim that celebrities divert attention from those truly responsible for atrocities or poverty when they attempt to shine the spotlight on precisely those who are in charge—and it's naïve to think those who are responsible on paper will act responsibly in practice. Author and activist Naomi Klein dismisses the "Bono-ization" of protest because it is less dangerous and less powerful than street protests. But the trouble with this logic is that the rich have never stormed their governments on behalf of the poor. That some intellectuals and politicians feel insecure about the prominence of celebrities pressuring them while educating the masses is deeply disturbing. They should instead be encouraging anyone with resources and influence to chip in, since they know how little they are doing themselves. Stale and emotionless political debates have yet to mobilize more money from governments to tackle poverty, so why not let celebrities—who excel at insinuating themselves into people's emotions—have a chance? Some actors are perhaps just doing what they do best—but even if that's the case, we can still hope that life will imitate art.

Stateless Statesmen and Super-NGOs

Nobody tells George Soros what to do. The billionaire currency trader, fund manager, and philanthropist is one of the few individuals who seem to be a pole of power in their own right. Due to his destructive capacity, a Chinese military report once ranked him just behind Osama bin Laden—after all, he is also known as the man who "broke the Bank of England" in 1992 and is accused by former Malaysian prime minister Mahathir bin Mohamed of torpedoing Asian economies through his market speculations in 1997. Today financial markets react not just to G-8 declarations, but also to Soros's response to those declarations. In economics, Soros boasts that he is rich only "because I know when I'm wrong." He appreciates the principle of reflexivity, by which other market participants' decisions are crucial to determining prices and trends. In other words, he is powerful but also knows he is not the only person in charge.

Soros's view of politics is much more linear. In his parallel life as a postmodern diplomat, Soros vehemently believes in an inexorable path toward the "open society," the phrase coined by his London School of Economics mentor Karl Popper. Unlike shadow elites with multiple business cards, Soros is entirely overt about what he represents. In the 1970s he began funding anti-apartheid students at the University of Cape Town, then turned his full attention to his native Hungary and Eastern Europe, from which he had fled Nazi occupation. As the Iron Curtain fell, building a new education infrastructure was the only way to reverse decades of Soviet-Communist brainwashing. Soros therefore endowed the Central European University in Budapest and funded upgrades and reforms in dozens of other universities across the region and in Russia, focusing especially on ensuring access to the Internet. Between the Open Society Institute (OSI) and the Soros Foundation, he has given away close to $10 billion.

Some Russians view Soros as an agent of Western policy, but he is much more a "stateless statesman": He sets his own global strategy. He funded UN operations to "save Sarajevo from Serbian fascism" in the early 1990s and financed legions of NGOs involved in the "Rose Revolution" in Georgia in 2003 and the "Orange Revolution" in Ukraine in 2004. That same year, he spent $25 million trying to oust George W. Bush from the U.S. presidency. Believing that "global attention is the only lifeline available to the oppressed,"[3] Soros opened offices focused in Haiti and Zimbabwe, as well as in Myanmar, which OSI-funded backpacking medics infiltrate to provide assistance to persecuted minorities in the country's highlands. Rather than deal with the "spend or lose" funding that plagues such government agencies as USAID, OSI can recycle unspent funds, quickly regranting the money to where it's needed most. Soros's approach is the real "transformational diplomacy" America and Western powers seek: changing societies from the inside out.

Super-NGOs like Soros's OSI are sometimes referred to as "diplomats with opinions," shaping some of today's most important questions, including whether to open dialogue with oppressive regimes, or whether investments in oil and gas should be encouraged or violently protested. They are among the shrewdest practitioners of mega-diplomacy. Oxfam uses its $500 million budget to supply radios to UN peacekeepers in Rwanda (who didn't have any), buy shares of pharmaceutical giants such as GlaxoSmithKline to influence their vaccine policy, and publish key reports on how the WTO can manage climate-damage funds to subsidize clean technology for poor countries.

Critics of the rising power of NGOs insinuatingly ask whom they actually speak for. The answer is that their legitimacy derives from their authority of expertise, impartiality, representativeness, and transparency of operations. In many ways they act far more accountably than governments: The more exposed they are, the more they are held to account by donors, charities, customers, and their own competition. Their funding is certainly more efficient than official sources: Almost all of it goes to frontline operations and partners, making it less susceptible to government leakage and meddling, while training local civil society in the process.

Other super-NGOs, including CARE, Save the Children, and Mercy Corps, have also established themselves as truly independent global players. Their ability to leverage technology and capital enables them to bypass governments altogether. They no longer refer to their contributors as donors but as investors. The largest humanitarian NGOs (whose annual giving exceeds $20 billion) have teamed with Microsoft in an "NGO Connection" platform to assist them in compiling and sharing best practices. This kind of interoperability planning is what we typically expect from members of the NATO alliance—now anyone can do it.

Flash Diplomacy: The World Economic Forum

On a typically sunny day in the Persian Gulf emirate of Dubai, more than one thousand men and women gathered for anything but a day at the beach. All top figures in their fields, they were convened by the World Economic Forum (WEF) for a "Summit on the Global Agenda," lending their minds to what the BBC's Nik Gowing dubbed a "fundamental reboot" of global problem solving. But rather than formulating extravagant proposals, they huddled in "Global Agenda Councils" to perform mental brain dumps, sharing the latest thinking on alternative energy, food security, Mideast peace, financial risk, social entrepreneurship, biodiversity, trade liberalization, and dozens of other issues. No oversized groupthink here: Each expert group appointed ambassadors to fan out like intellectual hunter-gatherers, identifying linkage points: How can more efficient construction and transportation cut emissions while also creating jobs? How can skill-building centers be used to mitigate interfaith tensions? Even in the wake of the worst economic crisis since the Great Depression, win-win solutions are still possible.

From the outside, the WEF is just another nonprofit foundation in Geneva with a staff of about 250 people. Yet it has engendered a revolution in where and how diplomacy gets done: Its summits are sophisticated flash mobs. On location from Africa to China, and each January in the secluded Swiss mountain resort of Davos, hundreds of top business, political, economic, academic, and civic leaders congregate to network, argue, lobby, and collaborate. Scholars don't need appointments to see presidents, who it turns out would rather hear ideas from their authors than filtered through assistants and ministers. CEOs get the latest trends and analysis without waiting for cumbersome reports and come away with a growing sense of social obligation beyond the bottom line. At WEF gatherings, everyone at the table is at the top of their game, so there is no question as to who is in charge and on whose shoulders responsibility falls.

North and South, public and private, West and East: All the new power centers are present within the WEF's activities, making it the world's only organization truly devoted to mega-diplomacy. Whereas the United Nations and World Bank speak of "reform" as a code for strengthening themselves, the WEF creates the space for thinking about a genuine *redesign* of how we run the world—always partnering governments, businesses, and organizations. Indeed, while official diplomacy has been slow to recognize the importance of NGOs, their participation has grown so rapidly at WEF summits that the waves of anti-globalization protests that racked international gatherings over the past decade have ceased to bother the organization. The WEF brought the protesters inside the tent and set them on par with government leaders and CEOs. Another advantage the WEF has over its state-centric peers is that it has rapidly adjusted to the world's shifting balance of power. To show respect for emerging powers, you have to take the show to them. Summits in China and the Middle East have maintained the WEF's relevance as U.S. power wanes. Capturing the shift in influence under way in Africa, the cochairs of the forum's 2009 Africa Summit in Cape Town included the chairmen of the Dubai Group and the Industrial and Commercial Bank of China.

Over the past forty years, the WEF has grown into the archetype of the new diplomacy: informal, efficient, and involving all relevant types of actors on equal footing. At WEF summits, collaborations among companies, NGOs, and government agencies are both incidental and facilitated. Organizations with obvious complementarities waste no time in launching joint projects. One of the most common refrains one hears is "We should have met ages ago!" Importantly, WEF meetings are not places where the only people you meet are those you already know. Instead, bloggers, social entrepreneurs, and a host of "change makers" under the age of twenty build networks with one another and otherwise far-off leaders. Many great ideas and projects are born through connections made at these summits. The WEF will never get any credit—but who cares?

The WEF itself has evolved into a hybrid structure not seen before: corporate funding, nonprofit status, current and former government officials on its board, and summits accorded the status of official diplomatic events. Its staff has come on secondment from member companies and governments such as Singapore, and it has seconded staff to UN agencies and think tanks. The WEF also embodies our postmodern age because it allows people to maintain the multiple identities they carry today. Bill Gates has appeared at Davos as Microsoft CEO and as head of the Gates Foundation at the same time, gradually speaking much more about malaria than software. Indeed, it was at Davos that Gates first had the idea to found his pioneering foundation. George Soros comes as a billionaire fund manager giving signals about currency markets but also as a democracy activist. Richard Branson attends as Virgin chairman but also as an environmental crusader dangling massive rewards in front of tech start-ups willing to tackle climate change. And Bono shows up as the head of his African development outfit the One Campaign—playing rock star only at night.

There need not be tension among the roles the rich and powerful play, and the WEF gives them the space to evolve their priorities.

Advocates of some form of global democracy evoke the ancient Greek *agora*, a marketplace free of coercion. The term that best captures the WEF, however, is the Latin *consilium*, meaning a consultative assembly. Many detractors complain that the WEF masks secretive corporate activity and conspiratorial deal making with corrupt governments. But no CEO needs to go to Davos for this—they can do that year-round in London, New York, Geneva, Moscow, or Riyadh. What the WEF reveals about corporate activity is that transparency *within* industries—that is, among companies—is as important as government regulation: They want to monitor one another on a level playing field. Furthermore, the WEF gets industry giants to undertake projects together; for example, construction companies lend resources to disaster relief projects in Latin America, mining companies run health clinics in Africa, and information technology companies set up e-learning academies in the Middle East. Companies now go to Davos and other WEF summits to learn precisely how to become better corporate citizens, and increasingly do so under WEF auspices.

WEF meetings and the increasingly numerous initiatives the forum sponsors are vehicles for leaders to find out what they can do together and what each can do better than another, and then devise a division of labor to get a job done. Presidents and ministers leave the UN General Assembly or its regional group meetings having recited pro forma speeches and defended their turf. Executives, ministers, and NGO heads all leave WEF meetings with stacks of business cards of potential partners and ideas for mega-diplomacy projects to undertake together. The WEF gives all these diverse leaders homework, making them smarter year after year.

The Broker: The Clinton Global Initiative

Each September, New Yorkers are subjected to a midtown traffic nightmare as the world's political leaders come to town for the UN

General Assembly. Impatient pedestrians on Park Avenue stand behind blue barricades for up to an hour waiting for the blitz of armed motorcades to go by, ferrying presidents, kings, and despots from JFK International Airport to the Waldorf Astoria Hotel to UN headquarters. In the past five years, the congestion has gotten only worse because of a parallel event at the Sheraton Hotel near Times Square. Many New Yorkers may not know it, but they are witnessing a crosstown diplomatic duel over how to run the world.

In 2008, diplomats asked to recall the overriding theme or priority for that year's UN General Assembly were dumbstruck. Yet there was no such confusion a few blocks west at the Sheraton, where what many have dubbed "Clintonpalooza" was taking place. Bill Clinton of course schedules the annual Clinton Global Initiative (CGI) to coincide with the United Nations in order to lure about sixty heads of state (as well as hundreds of business leaders and NGO representatives from ninety countries) to validate his mission—but by so overshadowing them with the array of successes CGI achieves, it also seems they are really brought there to be shown the light. At his 2009 gathering, which ran under the motto "Actions speak louder than words," he mused that "ninety percent of politics is about what you are going to do and how much you are going to spend." While spending and action are out of synch in politics, Clinton wants money to actually do something. "We know what to do," he says. "It's only a question of organizing ourselves to do what needs to be done."

Like the World Economic Forum, CGI needs no public funding to sustain itself, yet it produces the same aura of great consequence. Underwritten by wealthy entrepreneurs and the Children's Investment Fund Foundation, CGI gets regular support from about a dozen major corporations, foundations, and governments. Rather than stiff speeches, CGI panels feature notables such as Partners in Health founder Paul Farmer and Nobel Prize winners Muhammad Yunus and Wangari Maathai sharing examples of how they impact thousands of lives every day. All CGI sessions end with concrete action items, not just recommendations. Plenary sessions take place at CGI only to praise major commitments, with recognition taking the form of a handshake or bear hug from Clinton himself. Such public gratitude shows why Clinton would have made the best UN secretary-general had he considered the post: His personal authority to name and shame would be vital to changing bad behavior. But now that he has found his groove, it makes more sense that he pioneer a new model than wrestle with fatally outmoded bureaucracies.

The simplicity of Clinton's premise is elegant: Connect the world's top billion with the bottom billion in as many ways as possible. Bridging the first and third worlds is not about socialist redistribution schemes and whopping aid programs, however. Rather, it's about expanding the corporate world's focus on high-value branding and products toward low-cost but wide-scale opportunities. If ever there was a place to see how far we have come from the anti-globalization movement of just a decade ago, and how far corporate funding can go to change the way so many various places are run, CGI is it.

CGI also works because it brings politicians, business, and civil society leaders together on the same plane to devise a division of labor in their activities. No CEO or head of state is entitled to attend CGI—he or she has to earn it. The only way in the door is to first stop at the Commitments Office and put forth a workable and funded plan to support local development, environment, health, or education initiatives. The Clinton Hunter Development Initiative, for example, is a suite of efforts to promote Rwandan fair-trade coffee while also making coffee production more eco-efficient through smarter planting of shade trees. In 2008 alone, companies with extensive Africa operations pledged $300 million for small enterprise support and another $100 million to expand mobile banking services. NGOs that used to lobby governments for funding now go to CGI instead to join forces with companies. For the past three years it has also run a "CGI University," inspiring thousands of students at colleges worldwide to make their own commitments to sustainable projects.

It's easy to dismiss Clinton's efforts as a vanity project, but then why do more and more companies want to make their corporate citizenship commitments via CGI? The most important factor underscoring the CGI's sustainability is that it is backed by a foundation with year-round activity—the annual capstone event serves mostly to generate public awareness. Indeed, the William J. Clinton Foundation boasts accomplishments perhaps greater than the CGI statistics, particularly in the arena of access to low-cost HIV vaccines. Rather than engage in endless policy debates over intellectual property rights at the WTO, the foundation identifies bottlenecks in vaccine distribution and supplies funding to incentivize companies to increase volumes and lower costs. Clinton has brought down drug costs much faster than would otherwise have been the case—saving countless lives in the process.

The Clinton Initiative seems like a quixotic forum to the old guard who feel that diplomacy is their turf—as if the diplomats who sign climate treaties are more important than those who actually innovate emissions reductions, as if those who allocate development aid are more important than those who liberate people from it, and as if those who debate political and military interventions are more important than those who act based on their conscience. Clinton ends that debate. We are all part of the dam preventing the flood. We *are* the new global architecture.

Chapter Three

The (Fill-in-the-Blank) Consensus

At the April 2009 summit of the Group of Twenty (G-20) countries in London, President Obama mused during a press conference about how the United States and Great Britain put together the post–World War II economic order: "If it's just Roosevelt and Churchill having a brandy, that's an easier negotiation . . . but that's not what it's like anymore." If the world economy were a company, it's no longer clear who the chairman of the board would be. Today every country wants a seat at the high table; otherwise, they'll shop around for another forum that gives them more respect and voice. A former Mexican diplomat in London put it best: "If you're not at the table, you'll be on the menu." Economic diplomacy is now a dizzying game of musical tables—with the fate of globalization hanging in the balance.

The first global economy took shape during the Middle Ages, but it was one in which different regions had their own anchors and rules. Similarly, today there is no more free-market "Washington Consensus" to which the world's economies subscribe. Instead, each is searching for ways to manage globalization to its benefit. Yet all seem to agree with the mantra that the world coming out of the financial crisis must be different from the world going in. For that to happen, however, the public and private sectors need a new kind of partner-

*ship: one fast enough to manage risks and progressive enough to ben-
efit the masses. Countries that get public-private synergy right will oc-
cupy the commanding heights of a global economy that has become
as much Eastern as Western. If you want to know who sets the rules
for the new global economy, follow the money.*

"Twenty HUBS and No HQ"

Utter the word "Sherpa" and one name—Tenzing Norgay—usually
comes to mind. Certainly not Michael Jay, who with his lanky frame,
wiry spectacles, and balding head looks more like an accountant than
the record holder in Mount Everest expeditions. But after a long career in and out of the British government, Jay was tapped by then
prime minister Tony Blair to help him navigate the rapidly shifting
landscape of club diplomacy. His title was the coolest one can attain
in the diplomatic world: "Sherpa." As Robert Hormats, a veteran
America Sherpa recently returned to the Obama administration, recalls, Sherpas think of themselves as "munchkins," like the old but
diminutive *Wizard of Oz* characters. So many young diplomats today
want to become Sherpas—but first they have to do an apprenticeship
as "yaks." For Jay and his counterparts, being a Sherpa is the peak of
professional achievement in diplomacy: "It's a tough job, but huge
fun!"

Since the 1970s oil shocks, the Sherpa job has attracted some of
the best troubleshooters from the world's leading governments. For
thirty-five years, their main job was to coordinate financial stability
policies among the Group of Seven (G-7), which until recently was
the exclusive club of the world's leading industrial economies.*

But in late 2008, their task was nothing less than saving the world
from a looming depression. Unfortunately, by this point the G-7 had
degenerated into group therapy for Western leaders. When the global
economic agenda is set by Italy and not China, you know your club

---

*With the inclusion of the European Union and eventually Russia, G-7 has actually
been more a G-9; it is also referred to as the G-8.

is in the wrong century. Sherpas nonetheless sprang into action, this time activating the dormant G-20 network: twenty countries that collectively represent 80 percent of the world's population, 80 percent of its economy, and 80 percent of its emissions.* In lightning speed, Sherpas coordinated treasuries and central banks across the G-20 to craft the mother of all global bailout packages. Shifting from the G-7 to the G-20 was no problem for Sherpas: It was as easy as adding friends on Facebook.

Indeed, what Sherpas do is what World Bank president Robert Zoellick calls "Facebook diplomacy": They are a cabal of policy experts constantly in touch by phone and e-mail. When they do meet in person, it's for working lunches, not six-course meals. Sherpas don't show up at meetings with prefabricated statements; they exchange ideas and negotiate on the fly. Members of this trusted behind-the-scenes network keep negotiations going no matter who's in power and help their bosses prepare for the most delicate diplomatic face-offs. As one former European Sherpa said, "Leaders get along best after they've yelled at each other behind closed doors. That builds empathy and trust."

But is the G-20 the new "steering committee for the world"? It certainly surmounts the inherent inflexibility of the United Nations. It has no secretariat, and chairmanship rotates each year, sometimes pairing one old and one new member to ensure a balanced agenda. In this sense, the G-20 embodies the latest in thinking about decentralized management: It has "twenty hubs and no HQ."[1]

Yet the G-20 is already in danger of becoming a victim of its own success. The 2009 Pittsburgh summit resembled a new diplomatic Woodstock with hordes of media, lobbyists, and protestors swarming in to give free advice, point fingers, and trash the city's downtown. Also, just because the G-20 is legitimate, it doesn't mean that Indonesia, Mexico, and South Africa are states strong or competent

---

*The G-20 actually first convened in 1999 after the Asian financial crisis, but it did not gain momentum until 2008. The G-20 members are Argentina, Australia, Brazil, Canada, China, the European Union, France, Germany, India, Indonesia, Italy, Japan, Mexico, Russia, Saudi Arabia, South Africa, South Korea, Turkey, the United Kingdom, and the United States.

enough to be considered world leaders. Indeed, the G-20 has proven not to be a global regulatory mechanism but at best a semi-global one, including both those with the resources and will to regulate and those who just enjoy the spotlight. It can coordinate financial regulation to prevent a repeat of this crisis, but what about preventing the next one?

Still, the G-20 model ensures that diverse perspectives are aired quickly and policies are coordinated efficiently. The G-20 itself should stick to what it knows best—fiscal and monetary policy—but there should be more networks of Sherpas—lots more—across North and South, East and West, coordinating activity on climate change and failed states. Perhaps the G-20 will ultimately fail since, after all, so much of the world's geopolitical tension is among G-20 members themselves, not least America and China. Or maybe a new and more exclusive G-8 will form, kicking marginal members, such as Argentina and Italy, out of the larger group. Still, as we experiment with the G-20 and push leading nations to focus on coordination rather than communiqués, the global diplomatic system will evolve—and so will we.

Who Has the Money Makes the Rules

At the World Economic Forum's 2009 Davos meeting, Chinese premier Wen Jiabao succinctly articulated what became the dominant narrative of the global financial crisis, claiming it had its roots in an "unsustainable model of development characterized by prolonged low savings and high consumption" and the "blind pursuit of profits." What part of that do Washington and Wall Street not understand as they continue to demand higher consumption from Asians? Privatization and price liberalization—tenets of the Washington Consensus— have been steadily controlled by Asian governments ever since their late 1990s financial crisis. Indeed, the "global imbalances" that we constantly hear about are as much ideological as fiscal and monetary. The United States wants Asians to reverse an innate savings culture and more than a decade of insuring themselves against economic volatility by suddenly becoming voracious consumers. But Asians have heard enough hypocrisy from the high priests of Western finance. As America has gone from the lender of last resort to the world's leading debtor, they won't listen to its leaders' denunciation of high savings rates and their suspicion of sovereign wealth funds—which they quietly begged for bailouts when corporate America tanked.

Importantly, at the same Davos meeting, both American and Chinese leaders confessed they are looking to continental Europe for inspiration on how to manage a balance between economic growth and social security. For decades, Europe has been building world-class infrastructure and generous welfare systems, and reducing inequality while merging into the world's largest trading block. In the words of one prominent academic observing the discussions, "When the world's biggest economy and the world's biggest emerging economy look for lessons in the same place at the same time, you know something is up. We are seeing a paradigm shift toward a more European state."

America represents a late-twentieth-century role model for managing political-economic modernity, but the future will reveal an increasing number of variants and formulas. The more universal the acceptance of capitalism becomes, the more its many shades of gray are revealed, most notably between what was once American laissez-faire capitalism and the surging Asian state capitalism. Within that spectrum, only two real criteria separate winners from losers among models of entrepreneurial capitalism: those that enforce contracts and attract innovation and those that don't.

In other words, we are in an up-for-grabs era of economic management, one in which mixed models compete to pull their countries ahead and, in doing so, set examples that others will follow. The response to the financial crisis has looked more Chinese and European than American. The Beijing government controls its currency value to keep exports cheap, maintains strong oversight of the financial sector to avoid external control and overexposure to toxic assets, restricts procurement policies to benefit national suppliers, guides research and development to benefit national innovation, and selectively curbs imports of goods to maintain high domestic employment. In this way, semi-open economies from Brazil to India fared best in the financial crisis. Eventually, America wound up pursuing much the same course. Even George Soros has remarked that he is impressed by the China model, or what some are already calling the "Beijing Consensus." There is something to be said for a system that peacefully transitions more than one billion people from revolutionary communism to Confucian capitalism.

Westerners have complacently forgotten one of the eternal axioms of world affairs: Who has the money makes the rules. Today the head of the People's Bank of China, who sits atop $2 trillion and more of foreign exchange reserves, is a far more significant player in global finance than any head of the International Monetary Fund (IMF). Eight of the ten largest currency reserve holders are Asian countries. Their capital, companies, and contracts are already reshaping the way economies are run and business gets done worldwide. Americans who cynically ask what a world led by Asia would look like should get out of their chairs and go there. Good luck finding the border between state and market.

Since China favors state capitalism to unbridled laissez-faire, that is how it will be. In the thirteenth century, the Chinese state already played a strong but invisible hand in partnership with its merchants. Today, as Shanghai joins Hong Kong—what some call "Shangkong"— as a world financial hub, corporate rules are bending the Chinese way. Among China's more than one hundred thousand state-owned enterprises are the Industrial and Commercial Bank of China and the China Construction Bank, the two largest banks in the world by market capitalization. China's method of listing state-owned companies on stock exchanges and strictly regulating currency value and capital outflow are not only fair game today but are being widely emulated.

The integration of the China model within a greater Asian coprosperity sphere holds the greatest potential to force a rethinking of the basic geographic and economic building blocks of global order. Asia now follows Europe's lead in building an integrated regional market in which the majority of trade is within its borders rather than outside it. Led by China and Japan, Asians have rapidly increased their currency swap lines and pool of reserves in the Asian Monetary

Fund, while also doubling their contributions to the Asian Development Bank. With the three pillars of regional self-reliance in place—a free-trade zone, a development bank, and a monetary fund—eastern Asia can make its own rules. More than half the world's population falls within this increasingly self-reliant system. An Asian economic zone with global hubs including Shanghai, Hong Kong, Taipei, Tokyo, Seoul, Singapore, and Sydney doesn't need its talented and experienced managers to stay awake to listen to what bankers in New York want. Indeed, what London most has going for it today besides its legacy as a global financial capital is its time zone: Its bankers can conveniently talk to Tokyo and San Francisco in the same day.

China is undoubtedly Asia's biggest global spender, pressing ahead with explicit loan-for-resource agreements valued at $10 billion to $30 billion with oil and mineral giants Russia, Kazakhstan, and Brazil. China can afford to bail out its own banks, invest massively in domestic stimulus, reinforce regional institutions, and increase its global influence through international buying binges—all at the same time. The China Investment Corporation spent as much per month in late 2009 as it did in all of 2008—but now it focuses on American mortgages and real estate rather than treasuries. When Treasury Secretary Timothy Geithner went to China and told an audience that their holdings of U.S. bonds were safe, they laughed. The United States wants a "Buy American" policy, and China is buying America.

Soon America will be borrowing just to pay the interest on its debt, hardly in tune with its officials' frequent touting of their responsibility in managing the world's main reserve currency. China is leading the charge toward the next monetary order with calls for a stable neutral currency dominated by no one nation. Some believe the IMF should manage this most delicate transition—and even become something of a Global Central Bank. During the past decade's commodities boom, the IMF's role was reduced to that of a lifeguard watching an empty pool, but in the aftermath of the 2008 financial crisis, its funds were tripled by G-20 countries. Still, rearranging chairs and shares at the IMF's headquarters can't change the fact that no central body is running the global monetary show. Instead, the

IMF is evidence of how going local is the only way to stay relevant. Rather than commanding from afar, the IMF has learned to take its services to the root of problems. It has begun to lend to any country with low inflation, current account deficits, and public debt, and it has opened new technical assistance centers in Central America and central Asia, and two in Africa. If it doesn't back up the priorities of Asians and Africans, they will get the money they need from powerful new friends such as China, India, and Brazil. Indeed, even as G-20 countries have reinforced the IMF's liquidity, they are also buying allies through well-timed loans and increasingly trading in their own currencies. They will still make their own rules.

Public *and* Private

French president Nicolas Sarkozy has made a habit of claiming that the global financial crisis was not a crisis *in* globalization, but a crisis *of* globalization. That is nonsense. In the long run, globalization is additive: It survives pandemics, financial crises, and world wars. Even though the world economy shrank in 2008 for the first time since 1945, in the intervening half century world exports in merchandise increased from $58 billion to almost $14 trillion, and global foreign direct investment (FDI) rose from less than $100 billion to more than $1.8 trillion.[2] And yet globalization's reach has always been underestimated: After 9/11, many feared it would reverse, yet instead the world experienced an economic boom with trade volume jumping a further 70 percent. The stability of global currency markets today reminds us how important integration can be. Countries, companies, and consumers have chosen: Globalization is not optional. For America, Hollywood, high-tech, and higher education are all earning as much abroad as at home.

Of course, globalization means mutual vulnerability as much as it brings mutual gain. The nearly simultaneous food, fuel, and financial crises of 2008 spread *faster* and more *globally* than any before. Leaders are now asking themselves: How much globalization is too much?

Yet even as each country struggles to protect itself from the whims of unfettered globalization, all still seek a place in a global economy that will continue to widen and deepen.

But this is not the time to pretend that a grand "new consensus" is in the offing. The symptoms of instability haven't been removed; they've just been shifted. To save the balance sheets of companies, countries have harmed their credit ratings. The global economy is very much still in uncharted territory: The state has an uncertain role, a precarious imbalance exists between savers and consumers, global trade reform is a stalled process, and the role of international financial institutions is unclear. Even as economies recover, they face huge public deficits that can be redressed only through default, inflation, higher taxes, or tighter spending—all politically volatile options. From banking regulations to reserve currencies, building the next global architecture won't happen through grand design but rather, in the words of financial journalist Moisés Naím, by "focusing on the plumbing and wiring."

Human nature is hard to regulate. Not just greed but other equally human traits such as creativity were in play to bring about the massive privatized gains and socialized losses that Western economies experienced in the financial crisis. Regulators can limit capital leverage ratios and break up banks, but regulations without monitoring and enforcement will be toothless.

Even strong G-20 states such as the United States and China have not suddenly brought the market under control—it is still a mutually exploitative relationship. The global economy is a highly complex system, one that can only be managed if the public and private sectors see each other as partners, not competitors. Gordon Brown's proposal for a "B-20" group of business leaders to help the G-20 design financial sector reform is just one example of the new public-private diplomacy shaping the global economy moving forward. Indeed, the U.S. Treasury hasn't so much bailed out banks as created a Public-Private Investment Program (PPIP) and invited major asset management firms to step in and help clean up and restructure toxic balance sheets. And to keep short-term loans flowing to corporate America, the Fed turned to PIMCO, a private bond-trading firm, to revive credit markets.

By and large, the companies that earn our dollars are still in many ways more accountable than the governments that get our votes (and dollars). As Gordon Brown argued in London, "The key is for the practices of most of the private sector to be followed by all of the private sector." Even when it comes to complex derivatives, the solution is fairly simple: require banks offering high-risk products to buy appropriate amounts of insurance for them as well. Instead of squashing the ambitions of hedge funds and pension funds, more of them can be encouraged to think beyond profit the way Warren Buffett does. There is plenty of lending left to be done without fake derivatives: Main Street is still waiting.

Capitalism can again become more social without being socialized. Medieval guilds were professional associations that trained their members from apprenticeship to master craftsmen. After the Industrial Revolution in the United States and the United Kingdom, it became a privilege for charted companies to build railroads in the service of the nation. The American Bar Association is today's equivalent of a guild, with membership requirements, ethical standards, and internal policing and accountability. Rather than overbearing regulation that backfires, companies and their industry associations can wear a public hat as well as a private one so that investment bankers, derivatives traders, and other financial, consulting, and accounting professionals undertake more internal controls over their behavior. This means stronger associations of independent regulators such as the Financial Industry Regulatory Authority—maybe even with government funding. Catching ethical lapses has to happen at the source before it's too late. Making laws to catch up with ethics is a half solution—constant monitoring is much better.

Can any country—even the United States—afford interminable public-private hostility when its overall competitiveness is at risk from rising powers? Rather than speaking of boundaries between public and private, with both sides accusing the other of short-term thinking, we should assume the need for a hybrid middle ground.

Companies have always been part of "governance": Governments alter their investment laws and other policies to become more attractive to business. Even though governments can temporarily bail out their economies, much of what the economy does—create jobs and innovate—cannot be done by governments. All emergent sectors of the twenty-first-century manufacturing and services economy—clean technology, health care, education—require sensible public *and* private synergy to spur job creation and growth. Business and government can't forever point to each other's leaks. If the boat sinks, everyone is a victim.

Part Two

SAVING US FROM OURSELVES

Chapter Four

Peace Without War

*Diplomacy without power is like an
orchestra without a score.*
—Frederick the Great

*Diplomacy is the art of saying "Nice doggie"
until you can find a rock.*
—Will Rogers

D uring the Cold War, nuclear bipolarity and third world proxy
wars were two pillars of a truly global security order. The uni-
polar world resulting from the Soviet collapse hardly felt like a stable
substitute as civil wars erupted and states fragmented from the
Balkans to Africa to the Caucasus. Twenty years on, there is no such
thing as "global security." Grand international bodies such as the UN
Security Council, and even powerful alliances like NATO, are frail
and fraying. How can power be subordinated to norms when no one
agrees on those norms? Does the lack of a single global leader or master plan mean the world is collapsing onto itself?

Paradoxically, the more we allow political autonomy to spread,
the more peaceful the world can be. Much as in the Middle Ages, the
world is organizing itself into discrete regional systems with their

own sets of rules. This should be encouraged. Restoring any sense of global stability begins with regional stability. And within each region, the greatest single step that can be taken to advance mutual security is to redraw the most unstable boundaries. Medieval borders were fluid as thousands of political and economic entities navigated an increasingly open world. Today that will be possible only if we remap parts of Africa, the Middle East, and southern Asia, where colonial borders have been nothing but trouble, and allow new regional organizations to take responsibility for them. Freelance diplomats have emerged from the bottom up to rectify history's many cartographic mistakes and injustices one by one—while companies build the cross-border roads, railways, and pipelines that can eventually make those borders irrelevant.

A World of Complexes

When Russian tanks rolled into the tiny republic of Georgia in the summer of 2008, multilateral diplomacy was an afterthought. Just a decade prior, diplomats from fifty-four countries had gathered at a grand ceremony in Istanbul to sign the new security charter of the Organization for Security and Cooperation in Europe (OSCE). Between the NATO-Russia Council, the UN Security Council, and the OSCE, the United States, Europe, and Russia had abundant opportunities to talk about moving from suspicious spheres of influence to shared spaces. But when national pride is at stake, charters are cheap. To slow Russia's armored advance toward Georgia's capital, Tbilisi, French president Nicolas Sarkozy jumped in to mediate behind the scenes with his newly installed counterpart Dmitry Medvedev of Russia. Meanwhile, President Bush scowled during the opening ceremony of the Beijing Olympics with Russia's prime minister, Vladimir Putin, sitting smugly right behind him.

Several years on from the Russia-Georgia conflict, the names "Georgia" and "Kosovo" are shorthand for very different interpretations of how to manage flare-ups in dusty corners of the world. For America and Europe, NATO's 1999 bombardment of Serbia was a legitimate if legally unsound action to protect the ethnic-Albanian Kosovars. For Russia, it became a preview of the arbitrary American imperialism that later came to be embodied in the George W. Bush administration. For the West, "Georgia" today represents *Russia's* cantankerous neo-imperialism, while for Russia it stands for Western meddling in places it doesn't understand and backing immature and pugnacious leaders such as Georgia's Mikhail Saakhashvili. Teenagers around the world are not all reading the same textbooks.

Global security no longer has a dominant narrative to which everyone subscribes. At the high tables of diplomacy, the diplomats are mostly talking past one another. Local and regional concerns dominate, global norms matter little, and actions are justified on the fly. As American dominance fades region by region, upstart powers fill the gap. Today's major emerging powers—Russia, China, Saudi Arabia, India, Brazil—are more focused on establishing primacy in their own neighborhoods than contributing to an ethereal global stability. At the same time, terms such as "alliance" and "partnership" are thrown around by countries that cooperate at best opportunistically: the United States and India, for example, or Russia and China, or the United States and Saudi Arabia. The difference between dalliance and alliance is just one letter.

The gap between global ideas and action couldn't be wider. Former government officials and ambitious academics propose grand ideas, including a "Trans-Eurasian Security System," a "GlobalSecurity Alliance," and a set of "Global Authorities." Yet no such scheme has ever made the leap from the op-ed page to reality. How would any of these deal with the collapse of North Korea or a Saudi-Iranian proxy war in Iraq?

The UN Security Council's structure hasn't changed in several decades despite the fundamental shifts in the world's power balance. As a result, what the P-5 (the five permanent members, who have veto power) view as a club of special responsibility is viewed by the rest of the world as a club of abusers of privilege. The P-5 are the world's five largest arms dealers, while three of them (the United States, Great Britain, and France) ignored the council in NATO's 1999 attack on Serbia. Though the Security Council is supposed to be the only institution that can compel the international community to do something, it is increasingly illegitimate because its decisions are made on the basis of great power clientelism—such as China's defense of Sudan, Russia's of Iran, and America's of Israel—and ineffective because it serves as a collective mask for individual failures, such as the lack of American and European leadership in intervening in Darfur. It presides over international law but hardly stands in the center of any nation's moral compass.

Instead, each major regional center of gravity—for example, China, India, Brazil, Russia, and Nigeria—wants to be sheriff of its own neighborhood rather than follow the lead of any global policeman. Whether the Security Council backs a country's decision legally or militarily is a secondary concern at best.

Each region of the world has thus become a *complex unto itself,* with its own rules and codes. The world is already structured as much by *regions* as by nations. For most countries—and most people—geography is still destiny. Their security depends much more on relations with their neighbors than with far-off nations. While global friction between great powers appears manageable, regional tensions are rife between China and India, or Saudi Arabia and Iran. There are no global solutions to better neighborly relations, only regional ones. From South America to sub-Saharan Africa to eastern Asia, regional trust building has been the main reason countries have chosen to dismantle or abandon nuclear weapons programs. Brazil has anointed itself leader of the Union of South American Nations (UNASUR), the Association of Southeast Asian Nations (ASEAN) is deepening its charter and building its own peacekeeping force in Southeast Asia, the European Union (EU) has undertaken close to a dozen stabilization operations of its own from the Balkans to Congo to Lebanon, and the African Union (AU) is authorizing its own missions as well. Furthermore, Asian-African, Asian-Arab, and Latin-African summits increasingly grab the economic headlines.

Rather than fight this tide of devolution in the name of some grand but toothless global architecture, we should encourage regional responsibility as much as possible. Indeed, regional security organizations should be stronger than global ones—if there is a fire next door, would you rather have the fire station close by or far away? A decade after America began to hand over leadership of Balkan security to Europe, each micro-state of southeastern Europe has some form of agreement with the European Union. Europe should, and finally will, guarantee their stability.

Where regional security organizations are strong, there is order; where they are weak, there is chaos. Not surprisingly, today the world's two most unstable regions are the two most lacking in inclusive regional institutions: the Middle East and south-central Asia.

Over the past several centuries, Arab security has rarely been defined by Arabs, but rather by Britain, France, Ottoman Turkey, the United States, and more recently Israel and Iran. The Gulf Cooperation Council does not include Egypt, Jordan, Syria, or Iraq, and certainly has no regular security dialogue with Israel and Iran. And yet these Middle Eastern countries need above all else a common diplomatic mechanism through which to deepen economic cooperation and debate nuclear proliferation and energy, Iraq's rehabilitation and reconstruction, and the contours of a new Palestinian state.

When the Iran-Iraq War ended in 1988, the final paragraph of the UN resolution called for a Persian Gulf security conference that never happened. Instead, America tried dual containment and two invasions of Iraq. Meanwhile, Iran has acted as both arsonist and fireman. Yet the Arab world finally has competent diplomatic players such as Qatar—home to both U.S. Central Command and controversial satellite broadcaster Al-Jazeera—who are potentially ideal hosts for a permanent Middle Eastern security organization that would build mutual transparency. An Asian diplomat stationed in Doha calls Qatar "a geographical exclamation mark perched on the Persian Gulf, a maverick minnow maneuvering around the region's geopolitical and sectarian fault-lines between Sunni giant Saudi Arabia and Shi'a colossus Iran." In other words, Qatar is in the eye of the storm and wants to stay there. To broker any long-term nuclear détente between Israel and Iran, or negotiate the presence of Arab League peacekeepers to restore Palestinian unity, an all-inclusive Gulf security conference will be essential. But in the Mideast, there is no "resolution" to conflicts, only evolution. That is precisely why the region needs its own institution to mediate disputes rather than constant outside intervention.

Similarly, south-central Asia is caught in a geopolitical no-man's-land among the Middle East, India, China, and the Turkic former Soviet republics. Here, too, a standing mechanism is needed to curb Taliban sanctuaries and drug trafficking across the Afghanistan-Pakistan frontier, to promote cross-border pipelines, roads, power grids, and trade—and to remind NATO that victory needs to be defined in Afghan, not American, terms. The lack of a robust regional body has meant that the United States has had to bring together Afghan and Pakistani parliamentarians, cabinets, foreign ministers, intelligence chiefs, and even agricultural experts to get cooperation going on a variety of levels. If the United States and Mexico require joint military and police patrols to monitor drug and weapons trafficking across their long mutual border, then Afghanistan and Pakistan certainly do as well. Taliban mastermind Mullah Omar has called for Muslim peacekeepers to replace NATO in Afghanistan. Eventually, neighbors must mind their own fences.

The world desperately needs stronger regional security organizations to take their places alongside the EU, ASEAN, the AU, and other major groups as the lead arbiters of stability in their regions. Indeed these regional groups—not France and Britain—should even hold permanent seats in the UN Security Council. Together they can deliberate on the legality of interventions and loan troops and money to support one another, as the United States and European Union have done in donating more than $2 billion in aid and equipment to the African Union. Stronger regions helping weaker ones manage their own problems: This is the design for global security from the bottom up, not the top down.

Building better regional systems and a better global system are two sides of the same coin. Neither NATO's presence in Afghanistan nor the creation of the U.S. African Command by the U.S. Defense Department can substitute for the long-term necessity of regional solutions for regional problems. The common lesson of all of America's recent military adventures is that the only viable long-term strategy is to help others help themselves. This is more than strategy: It is states-manship.

Can an Oxymoron Stop a War?

Carne Ross is as frenetic as a chain-smoker but has no time to smoke. He's too busy—certainly more than he ever was as a senior British diplomat inside the closed box of foreign embassies and UN Security Council negotiations. That was a world of orderly illusions—a world Ross wants to turn on its head. State-to-state diplomacy suffers from the democratic deficit in spades: unrepresentative elites create plans out of sight from the noisy masses below. Instead of working with the "real" diplomats, who are sheltered on the "inside" by high walls and barbed wire, Ross now practices diplomacy from the *outside*, a position of grave disadvantage.

Ross's organization, Independent Diplomat, is an intentional oxymoron—how can a diplomat not represent *someone else*? This is actually a perennial myth of diplomacy: that one is merely a messenger dispatched by a higher authority. But ever since the Renaissance, when ambassadors began to spend more time with one another than with their own national ministers, there have been diplomats who feel a higher calling in their duty to peace than to their prince. For Ross, being party to the contrived buildup to the Iraq war in 2002–3 presented such a conflict. He resigned and immediately launched Independent Diplomat—"a diplomatic service for those who need it most"—meaning stateless or unrecognized clients such as Kosovo, Western Sahara, and Somaliland, but also quite a few "normal" states that lack the diplomatic heft of great powers. Stripped of arbitrary cartographic simplifications, diplomacy fumbles. This is the gray area where Ross thrives—exposing but also exploiting the realities of improvised diplomacy.

Most new states are born of secessionism: seeking to rectify injustice by breaking free of their territorial master. Some secessionist movements and exile groups seek redress at the United Nations, believing that international law provides a sufficient moral foundation for their cases to be judged on their merits. They are still waiting. The United Nations is the repository of the guilty conscience of colonial powers who have mostly wiped their hands clean of messy withdrawals, such as Spain's from Western Sahara, or Great Britain's from Somaliland. These voiceless entities are a reminder that even "global" institutions aren't yet universal. One of Independent Diplomat's major advocacy platforms is therefore the "Universal Right of Address," a proposal that *all* parties to a dispute be allowed to speak directly before the UN Security Council. Currently, 80 percent of disputes on the council's agenda involve such stateless actors. Normally the United Nations sends a special representative to gather material and report back to the council, but why not cut out the middleman?

Independent Diplomat works hand in hand with its clients, becoming a part of their core teams. It provides legal and political guidance as well as the all-important press relations for a world in which perception is reality. Ross spends countless hours shuttling among fractious exiles, a staple irony of world politics. Whether anti-theocracy Iranians, aggrieved Uzbeks, or Miami's Cubans, exile groups' hatred for their home regimes is matched only by their own infighting. Independent Diplomat works with the democratically elected Burmese exile government to organize itself and generate an action plan for dialogue with the ruling junta on transitioning to democracy and protecting human rights, agricultural policy, and fair exploitation of the country's large gas reserves. Since the organization brings together opposition groups under one umbrella, the military will eventually have to negotiate with a more formidable civilian force.

Ross and his team demonstrate that the best diplomats, like Sherpas, know a lot about a lot. They have, for example, provided detailed assistance for Croatia to retool its government for EU membership, accelerating a process that will surely bring the country hundreds of millions of dollars of foreign investment. They've coached the nascent quasi-state of Somaliland to move away from counting on former colonial master Great Britain to support its independence and instead focus on lobbying the African Union. They recently crafted a new strategy for the desert guerrilla Polisario movement of Western Sahara, pushing it beyond harping about self-determination to emphasizing the human rights obligations of Morocco. And one of their newest projects involves working with the sinking island nations of the Marshall Islands and the Maldives to boost their capacity at major climate change negotiations where Independent Diplomat staff members sit alongside their clients—nonprofit *next to* government—and face off against the heavy-hitting delegations of the United States and other major carbon-emitting nations.

For would-be mediators, Independent Diplomat represents a new style of negotiation: crowd sourcing. Rather than wait for information to trickle through official filters, its staff constantly receives live, on-the-ground updates and recruits academic and commercial legal pro bono experts to help with specific cases. It is also a new type of consultancy. To most of its clients, the organization charges minimal fees; it receives grants from foundations such as George Soros's Open Society Institute. Yet still hundreds of seasoned diplomats from powerful nations apply unsolicited to work for Independent Diplomat, seeing it as a place to fight for the underdog.

The entrepreneurial role model for Independent Diplomat and similar outfits is the International Crisis Group (ICG), the NGO best known for having its finger on the pulse of conflict dynamics in every corner of the globe. It has been called on as a back-channel mediator in hotspots from Colombia to Indonesia to Liberia. ICG's main funding boost originally came from governments that didn't have embassies in far-flung places but needed access to the same quality of information as established powers. It has since become so well regarded that even China consults it to evaluate the country's risk exposure in conflict-prone areas from Sudan to central Asia.

It's easy to get overexcited about people-to-people diplomacy. Between all the "good offices," "special envoys," "quartets," "troikas," "contact groups," and "Track II" dialogues, there appears to be more mediation of the world's ongoing disputes than ever. Yet in so many conflicts, international law seems to be taken into consideration only after the militaries have had their way. Delegates at the UN General Assembly unite behind resolutions, while in their home countries people unite behind armies—against which UN resolutions seem equally useless. The United States, Israel, and Ethiopia have been known to sidestep the laws of war in their invasions of Afghanistan/Iraq, Gaza, and Somalia, respectively. Gaza is so densely populated that Israel's 2008 incursion to rout Hamas inevitably killed several hundred civilians, including many children. When Sri Lankan president Mahinda Rajapaksa (who with his thick mustache resembles a Bollywood villain) felt victory was near in the country's civil war against the Tamil Tigers, preventing a humanitarian nightmare was a distant second priority to "defeating a terrorist force" and "uniting the nation under the shade of the national flag." He probably knew that the world would prefer to have one less civil war on its to-do list than gripe with him later on about how he did it.

The United States has dispatched special operations forces to help the Sri Lankan government crush the Tamil Tigers, to help Colombia corner the FARC, and to help the Philippines defeat the Abu Sayaf insurgency on the island of Mindanao. In all three cases, American support for military allies has trumped international mediation efforts. When the New York Philharmonic performed in Pyongyang in March 2008, it inspired even hard-nosed former defense secretary William Perry to claim that a "breakthrough" may be at hand. But Kim Jong Il didn't show up for the concert, and in North Korea, it's been his way or no way.

Still, the only way to overturn generations of hostility and hate is to reach deeply across a new generation and instill a different psychology. Seeds of Peace, an American nonprofit that runs camps in Maine for Israeli and Palestinian youth, now has its first generation of alumni entering positions of influence in their respective governments. They keep in touch during times of crisis, and many alumni have become teachers in local peace centers that attempt to change perceptions of those on the other side of the fences and walls. Jimmy Carter has become a major backer of the Geneva process led by Israeli and Palestinian civil society groups—insisting that government officials attend only as observers. A nonviolent Palestinian group in the town of Budrus has gained back territorial concessions from Israel and built goodwill with Israelis in the process. Like celebrity diplomats, this new vanguard of civic mediators and reconciliation movements shouldn't be dismissed simply because they haven't yet been able to undo the mess colonizers and corrupt governments have made. A peace made without the people is a piece of paper.

Making Borders Irrelevant

In the mid-twentieth century, Sigmund Freud and Albert Einstein engaged in a long exchange of letters on the question "Why War?" They debated whether war originates in the human mind or if it is inherent in social existence, but agreed that war has been a permanent feature of human activity because communities naturally struggle to assert their identities and control territory. Intergenerational, cross-border political disputes fuel the world's exploding military-industrial complex—even in countries that can't afford their militaries and have little industry. Today, any enemy, near or far, real or imagined, justifies stockpiling more nuclear weapons, warplanes, ballistic missiles, tanks, and surface-to-air rockets. More often than not, conflicts are over borders—either within or between countries. As the late Columbia University sociologist Charles Tilly wrote, "War made the state and the state made war." These existential questions—who gets to *have* a country and who gets to *be* a country—are still as alive as ever. Our disorderly matrix of borders is still the biggest threat to peace.

Worldwide, so much energy is dissipated in perpetual *cartographic stress*. When tensions flared between Indonesia and Malaysia over the disputed islands of Sipadan and Ligitan in 2005, masses were mobilized and cyberspace was ablaze with hateful rhetoric from both sides. India and China have two outstanding disputes in mountainous areas that are of strategic value only if one side is shooting down at the other. Even peaceful diplomatic haggling—the two sides have exchanged maps for decades while waiting for the upper hand—demonstrates latent animosities unbecoming of powers that wish to be seen as great and benevolent. The World Court at The Hague has border dispute cases piling up, and overlapping maritime claims are now being registered according to the UN Convention on the Law of the Sea. But who will arbitrate these hundreds of potential flashpoints?

There is no better time to remap the world and move beyond the arbitrary postcolonial borders that have become the hand-me-down suits of international relations that never quite fit. This was President Woodrow Wilson's vision after World War I: to promote ethnic self-determination but also to embed nations as equals into economic and other institutional bonds such as the League of Nations. It may seem paradoxical that the antidote to the problem of weak states is to create more states. But if we don't proactively remap certain territories now, they will just continue to tear themselves apart. Only by more clearly defining the political lines on the map can we move beyond them. Why insist on imposing modernity when we should strive for postmodernity? Sometimes the former is the surest path to the latter. Only when states are comfortable within their borders can they confidently transcend them. Speedy and fair breakups can lead to better friendships.

When the ancient Greeks quarreled with one another and their neighboring Persians, they would often engage in the practice of *dike,* making truces on the spot and demarcating borders anew for the sake of avoiding fruitless battles. Ironically, this is what empires were good for. During several centuries of peaceful reign, the Ottoman Empire offered nominal autonomy to hundreds of ethno-religious enclaves but also protected them from one another. So, too, does the European Union, which requires the settlement of disputes by diplomacy rather than force. EU and NATO pressure compels Greece and Turkey (which almost went to war twice, in 1987 and 1995, over uninhabited islands in the Aegean Sea) to resolve Cyprus peacefully. Even Great Britain and Spain still sometimes deploy warships to intimidate each other over the British Mediterranean exclave of Gibraltar, but war within the EU commonwealth is effectively unthinkable.

The major reason Europe is finally at peace, though, is that almost all nations have their own states. They merged economically *after* they separated politically. Just look at the Czech Republic and Slovakia, which emerged from a partitioned Czechoslovakia in 1993 and are both now members of the European Union. Extending this logic to the Balkans is still necessary today. The savagery of the Balkans in the 1990s might have been even worse without the breakup of Yugoslavia. While Slovenia is already an EU member today, Bosnia is still governed by a fragile, forced coalition among Bosnians, Serbs, and Croats with untold resources wasted in the suspended animation of bickering and corruption. In Mostar, the restoration of the famous sixteenth-century bridge cannot hide the fact that the ethnic Croatian section of the city prefers the Croatian kuna to Bosnia's national currency. Meanwhile, the borders of the Republika Srpska still snake around Bosnia like a noose, with Serb-backed nationalist leaders insisting on autonomy from power-sharing structures with Muslim Bosnians in Sarajevo. Maybe both Serb territory *and* its disruptive proxies should be ejected from Bosnia instead. This isn't tantamount to giving in to the Serbs. Instead, it turns suspicion into settlement. Most important, it removes a major obstacle to *both* Bosnia and Serbia's eventual EU membership—without which neither state has a meaningful future.

States' borders are like amoebas: lacking a fixed shape, pulling in new directions, engulfing neighbors, and splitting randomly. In the Middle Ages, princely rulers forged alliances and crushed former vassals and mercenaries to centralize power. Governments today constantly struggle to build, maintain, and renew national unity, both physically and psychologically. Colombia, fractured for decades through a narcotics-fueled civil war, even ceded territory to the FARC guerrilla army in the 1990s before the government of Álvaro Uribe used the army and police—as well as construction engineers and road builders—to make the mountainous Andean nation whole again.

Then there are the largely abandoned zones where identity is being redefined at the ground level. Slowly and almost imperceptibly, even the world's most imposing cartographic presence, Russia, might be fragmenting. No empire has suffered greater losses in the past two decades—both territorially and demographically. Today, many of its cities remain unconnected to one another, with some roads literally ending where provincial boundaries do. Russia today has less usable highway mileage than it did in 2000. Without a sense of belonging to Moscow, Turkic identities are being resurrected as nomadic peoples and increasingly identify with their lineage tracing to Genghis Khan. Meanwhile, in the North Caucasus, Islam has deepened its roots in and around Chechnya despite the brutal war of a decade ago. Rather than broaden and deepen their governance, the Kremlin and Duma have granted two giant utility companies, Gazprom and Transneft, the right to raise private armed security forces to protect their gas pipelines across Siberia, while largely abandoning much of the massive Far East to the whims of resource-hungry Chinese firms and shuttle traders. On a map, Russia is still the world's largest country, but on the ground it is an archipelago of diffuse ethno-political experiments. Russia isn't "too big to fail."

Our present cartography does not have to be destiny. The map of the world is in perpetual flux—its many lines, either straight or curved, rarely represent orderly calmness. Often the opposite is true. Some countries such as Lebanon and Afghanistan are too ethnically entangled to be separable, so they exist in a state of perpetual negotiation with warlords or ethnic minority groups to maintain tenuous, always costly, and ultimately dubious stability. Yet still we look at Kurds, Pashtuns, and Baluchis—peoples who live across multiple national borders—as if they are bizarre historical anomalies, as if the borders they straddle are somehow morally superior to their far deeper cultural and geographic identities. This arrogance stems from a loyalty to sovereign territorial integrity over self-determination. But today no amount of counterinsurgency or promises of equality will cheat people away from their national aspirations.

Mediation can save time and lives, but partition can as well. Indeed, sometimes divorce is the most sensible option. Not every society can remain a multiethnic, democratic state. Nigeria, Sudan, and Iraq are just some of the former British colonial states fused out of ethnically, culturally, and religiously incommensurate communities that have found no peace with one another. Not all partitions necessarily end up in the genocidal violence that attended the independence of India and Pakistan in 1947. This is not to say that all examples of ethnic tension should result in splintering states into ethnically pure nations. In fact, it is the state failure resulting from predatory corruption that most often unleashes interethnic feuds. But once on this path, patching up grievances is an arduous and uncertain task and often not the most efficient option. Power-sharing agreements and more inclusive constitutions work in some places and not in others.

Realpolitik, of course, plays a crucial role in determining the fate of peoples. The United States, Europe, and even India have long abandoned the Tibetan cause in the face of China's growing clout, and if North Korea collapses, China might dominate its future, too, given that it provides 90 percent of the country's oil, 80 percent of its consumer goods, and 45 percent of its food—even if there is peaceful reunification with South Korea. Similarly, the West won't bother Russia about Chechnya so long as oil continues to flow undisturbed through the Baku-Ceyhan pipeline (which, indeed, Russia scrupulously avoided damaging during its 2008 invasion of Georgia). Now Russia has reappropriated for itself the Georgian enclave of South Ossetia, dispatching Federal Security Service agents cloaked as border guards and distributing Russian passports with little opposition from NATO. Such bargains are an inevitable part of great power relations, but they rarely help us find deep, long-term solutions to resolving the mismatch of territory and demographics that plagues so many parts of the world. There are at least thirty countries in the world in the midst or on the brink of civil war. Each dispute has its own solution.

Inertia is not a legitimate reason to prolong cartographically imposed suffering. Both interstate and intrastate rivalries require us to remain perpetually open to the option of remapping territory. This means first and foremost sorting out—and supporting—stable and self-governing entities wherever they may be. Many nations are not yet lucky enough to achieve statehood, but from the Eskimos of Canada to the Jews of eastern Russia, varieties of self-governing communities are becoming more and more the norm of world politics. Granting them some autonomy can grease the path to peaceful coexistence, while reflex nationalism is almost always a recipe for war. The Northern Ireland and Basque Country conflicts were tamed only after promises of more devolution from London and Madrid, and the restive Muslim-majority Pattani province of southern Thailand will only settle if Bangkok makes the same decision.

Talking about "making borders irrelevant" won't make it happen, but accelerating clear border demarcation and building cross-border infrastructure can. European governments and companies have built a dense network of roads and railways spanning almost thirty countries, promoting a single borderless economic space. In much of the rest of the world, these are the lines on the map that still need to be drawn—and each one can make borders increasingly irrelevant. For example, the Baku-Tbilisi-Kars railway in the Caucasus, supported by commercial banks around the region, will bring badly needed economic interaction to the fractious area. Similarly, the Trans-Asian Railway Network Agreement is perhaps the most important breakthrough in diplomacy across the former Soviet Union, a part of the world not known for warm cross-border relations. If this "Iron Silk Road" of publicly and privately financed pipelines and rail lines across landlocked central Asia is completed in the coming decade, it will triple the region's GDP while assuring that the region isn't bypassed in favor of the maritime Silk Road linking the Persian Gulf to the Far East. The places that most need to start emulating the European model today are Europe's former colonial spheres of Africa, the Middle East, and South Asia.

Facts on the Ground: Africa

We know to always be suspicious of straight lines on a map—and Africa is the continent left with more of them than any other. Many African states take their boundaries from the 1884 Congress of Berlin, which divided Africa among European powers along lines of latitude and longitude rather than by rivers or ethnic territories. Decades of interstate and civil wars have not undone these disfiguring colonial scars. According to the Fund for Peace, fifteen of the world's twenty worst failed states are in Africa.

Now is the time to ask what an Africa for Africans would look like. There may be little that Africans can do about droughts and climate change, but many do agree they would like to redraw the continent's borders—except when it comes to their own. This must

change. We can start with the biggest, most volatile, and most mean-
ingless cartographic fictions of Sudan and Congo. Both Sudan and
Congo need to be broken into more sensible and governable pieces if
Africa is to collectively make sense—even to itself.

A colonial construction almost twice the size of Alaska, Sudan is
the continent's largest country, a forced biracial crucible of Arabs and
black Africans. It has known more war than peace. With Arabs and
blacks, Muslims and Christians, nominally inside one set of borders,
the country actually suffers from three civil wars at once. In Darfur,
Arab *janjaweed* militias backed by the Khartoum government have
been engaged in what some call "slow-motion genocide." But like the
genocide in Rwanda, there is nothing slow about three hundred thousand people being massacred between 2003 and 2005 alone. In the
south, the Khartoum government is far more interested in controlling
lucrative oil fields than fairly governing the Christian and animist
population, which is more loyal to the Sudan People's Liberation
Army (SPLA). Neither judgments from The Hague nor a referendum
in 2011 will bring stability so long as Khartoum can still send proxy
militias to destabilize the SPLA regime in Juba and siphon off oil
profits. In the east, rebel groups are equally suspicious of inequitable
central control over the region's resources, making the region a perennial powder keg as well. By what logic do we cling to the arbitrarily
defined Sudan when it seems impossible that any government in
Khartoum will ever have the authority or legitimacy to rule over the
whole country again?

Then there is the Democratic Republic of the Congo, Africa's next
largest country and an equally obsolete colonial legacy. Plundered by
Belgium's King Leopold II for its rubber, and by the leopard-skin-clad
Mobutu Sese Seko for cobalt (essential for American fighter jets),
Congo has more speaking for its nonexistence than its existence
today. Its sixty-seven million people include more than two hundred
ethnic groups who share little in the way of a national language or a
sense of unity. The government has little reach beyond the capital,
Kinshasa, controls only an undisciplined army and police force, and
depends on patronage payments from mining operations to stay
afloat. The country's 1998–2003 civil war, in which four million peo-

ple were killed, has been called "Africa's first world war"—and one largely ignored in the West. With its child soldiers, empty schools, and exploding AIDS rates (a result of the use of rape as a weapon), the war has devastated the nation's human potential. Two scholars of Africa point to a simple, brutal fact: "The Democratic Republic of Congo does not exist. All of the peacekeeping missions, special envoys, interagency processes, and diplomatic initiatives predicated on the Congo myth—the notion that one sovereign power is present in this vast country—are doomed to fail."[1]

Many Africans genuinely want stronger regional bodies to help them deal with border conflicts, rebels, weapons, and refugees—and the African Union has the political respectability to oversee the gradual remapping of Sudan, Congo, and other parts of Africa as well. It can convene the relevant governments and provincial leaders to settle the future of Congo's California-sized Kivu province, which Rwandan forces regularly infiltrate to chase Hutu rebels, as well as that of the mine-rich "copper belt" province of Katanga, which is tied more to Zambia than to Congo. The AU can also openly shepherd the independence of Darfur and southern Sudan without waiting for referenda that are already being preemptively undermined by the Khartoum government. China has certainly wasted no time in beginning construction of an oil pipeline from southern Sudan across Kenya to the Indian Ocean, which may prove to be the key factor in liberating southern Sudan from Khartoum.

The AU won't look anything like the EU until fundamental territorial questions are resolved. There are many other frail corners of Africa needing such an approach. Somalia, held from total socioeconomic collapse only by the bandage of humanitarian efforts, has separatist regions such as Somaliland and Puntland, both more functional than the country itself, while the Muslim Somalis of the Ogaden region of Ethiopia suffer brutal military crackdowns at the hands of the Ethiopian military. With states so weak and illegitimate, the only pragmatic approach is to abandon efforts to shore up the current states dwarfed by their own geography and work with de facto powers on the ground toward a more pluralistic but coherent set of quasi-states.

Whatever the number of African states, increasing physical connectivity across the continent's hundreds of internal borders is its greatest hope. There are two kinds of countries in Africa—landlocked and not landlocked—the former always having to negotiate with the latter. Medieval European merchants took advantage of the Danube and other major rivers reaching deep into the continent's interior, providing economic lifelines even to landlocked communities. But Africa has fewer and less navigable rivers, so needs other forms of lifelines even more.

The only way to provide economic lifelines is through shared governance and by building infrastructure. The New Partnership for Africa's Development is focusing on channeling foreign direct investment into cross-border transportation, agriculture, electricity, and manufacturing, while the Pan-Africa Infrastructure Development Fund finances dams, highways, and airports in western and sub-Saharan Africa. Recently, the East African nations of Kenya, Tanzania, and Uganda have teamed up to appeal for foreign investment through a common board. Virgin Nigeria and Kenya's Flamingo Airlines are starting to build regional airline networks. Bringing in professional partners and demanding private-sector partners is perhaps the only way to noticeably improve the efficiency of these infrastructure projects while decreasing corruption. Furthermore, just about every sub-Saharan African border should be turned into a transboundary conservation park jointly managed by sustainable tourism agencies and tax authorities. Their collective motto should be "make safari, not war." Africa will achieve a broad renaissance only if its many micro-economies fuse into just a few.

Facts on the Ground: The Middle East

The artificial confines of the state have always been uncomfortable for Arabs, who once presided over mighty caliphates that fostered prosperous relations among the great cities of Cairo, Baghdad, and others. The post-Ottoman Arab world has suffered particular cartographic trauma ever since the Sykes-Picot agreement of 1916, in which the British and French divided up Arabic-speaking nations. European powers backed monarchies and dictatorships across the Persian Gulf and Levant and midwifed the creation of Israel in 1948. America then took over Europe's role, pushing a two-track policy of protecting Israel and the flow of oil. Egypt became an anchor of Arab-Israeli peace efforts, but the lack of progress since the 1979 Egyptian-Israeli peace agreement sank Egypt's credibility. The Arab world does not need a dominant hub to regain its unity. It needs a remapping of Palestine, stability in Iraq, and a rehabilitation of the Ottoman infrastructure that once made the region a proud global passageway.

When territorial disputes are left unresolved, children grow up in the shadow of barricades and barbed-wire fences and are raised on venomous myths about their neighbors. Many of Egypt's youth now want to reverse the 1979 deal they were never involved in, and they call for suspending ties and cutting off gas exports to Israel. Syrian and Israeli youth bicker on Facebook over the status of the Golan Heights. Which generation will actually put an end to escalating cycles of resentment and violence? One diplomatic axiom holds that the "triumph is in the timing." But when will the timing be right? In democratic Israel, leaders avoid moving too quickly toward peace for fear of being labeled sellouts. It won't contemplate allowing any formula on the right of return until all Palestinian survivors of 1948 have died. In autocratic Arab countries, anti-Israeli and anti-American sentiments are crucial to political legitimacy. If we're waiting on Arab democracy for this to change, then the Arab-Israeli conflict may indeed go on forever.

From Henry Kissinger's "shuttle diplomacy" to this past decade's "road map," no conflict has been awarded more Nobel Peace Prizes for the lack of peace, nor has the word "durable" been used more often to describe a "settlement" that is anything but settled. The 2001 Taba talks were the closest to a comprehensive settlement, but the elections of U.S. president George W. Bush and Ariel Sharon in Israel put that process on ice. Western policy since then has been an incoherent mess. The "Quartet" group was meant to marry the "power of the U.S., money of the EU, and legitimacy of the UN," but for most of the past decade has barely managed to conceal its internal differences. The United States backs Israel and provides assistance to Palestinians, but not as much as the European Union, which has a trade accord with Israel despite numerous European corporate boycotts. Russia has crucial demographic and economic stakes in Israel and thus pursues its own course while courting Hamas leaders to snub the United States. The theatrics of diplomacy create the illusion of progress through measures meant to generate momentum like in a stock market rally: In the waning days of the Bush administration, a UN Security Council resolution simply re-re-re-re-re-affirming the importance of the Mideast peace process was considered a breakthrough. But when the gap between what diplomats say and what nations or groups do becomes too vast, diplomacy loses all credibility; it becomes nothing more than an exercise in professional self-preservation.

After about a half-dozen Arab-Israeli wars, multiple intifadas, innumerable suicide bombings in cafés and buses, the construction of a massive barrier-wall encasing much of the West Bank, assassinations of Hamas leaders, kidnappings of Israeli soldiers, and the invasion of Gaza, support for an independent Palestinian state has grown worldwide and even within Israel itself. If the new yardstick is the creation of a formally independent and internationally recognized Palestinian state, then words and deeds on all sides should be judged by whether they promote or hinder it.

There is nothing wrong with the sentiment of the 1970s "land for peace" proposals. They are simple, sensible, and measurable—and they hold the only way out of the deadlock over who will recognize whom. Israel would withdraw all but a few settlements from the West Bank, allow some right of return for refugees that is arbitrated by a joint council, and give Palestinians full access to East Jerusalem and the right to hang a flag there even as Ramallah remains Palestine's administrative center. All this would be backed by a simultaneous mutual recognition among Arab states, Israel, and a Palestinian state. Israeli prime minister Benjamin Netanyahu has called for this new state to be demilitarized, a demand Arabs reject—but one that points to the likelihood that an independent Palestinian state could seek the sovereign assistance of Egypt and Jordan to guarantee the security of

Gaza and the West Bank and develop professional security forces to replace the armed Hamas leadership. Saudi Arabia and other Arab states and foreign investors might then more confidently invest in Palestinian infrastructure, particularly an "arc" of road and rail links connecting the West Bank and Gaza, where a commercial port could boost Palestinian trade. Independence without infrastructure is futile.

Clarifying territorial boundaries is not the path to higher walls, but to better neighbors. The deeper internationalization of the region—even the gradual restoration of an Ottoman-like, borderless coexistence—proceeds *after* each has achieved respected sovereignty, not before. The opening of the Shebaa Farms and Golan Heights as regional tourist centers and vineyards, for example, would reassure no one until the fundamental security dilemma is overcome. The road to Jerusalem runs through Jerusalem—and it needs to have signs in Hebrew *and* Arabic.

The deeper regionalism that can genuinely settle the Middle East also requires a resolution to Kurdistan. The post–World War I Versailles Treaty recognized the rights of the Kurds to statehood, but today the Kurds recount a saying for the centuries of empty promises of self-rule they have endured: "My one hand is empty and in the other there is nothing."

Sometimes one country has to die for another to be born. A century after Versailles, with neither Saddam's brutality nor the American military holding Iraq together anymore, Iraq's low-level intra-Arab civil war is giving the Kurds their chance to fulfill the promise of post-Ottoman statehood. The country is slowly moving from perpetually unstable Lebanon-ization to more permanently divided Balkanization. The Kurdistan variant of "land for peace" is being called "oil for soil": Kurdistan could defer its total claim over the oil-rich and Kurdish populated Kirkuk in exchange for security guarantees and the right to substantial profits. Another option is to cede Kirkuk to Kurdistan—but since Kurdistan is landlocked, it would have to share revenues fairly with Baghdad, lest the rump Iraqi government spike taxes on Kurdistan for exporting through its territory (which Kurdistan's other neighbors, including Syria and Turkey, could do as well). Through such territorial compromises, the Mideast may graduate from mutually assured destruction to mutual assurances—and use its armies to guard pipelines instead of borders.

Arabs want to restore the glory they enjoyed during the European Middle Ages, and they actually have the wealth to do so. But even more pointless territorial disputes stand in the way of regional integration. Iran and the United Arab Emirates continue to dispute three tiny Persian Gulf islands, while Saudi Arabia has disputed borders with all its Gulf neighbors. Despite being overwhelmingly larger than all of them, it has nonetheless taken land from them and raised customs duties at the borders, hampering the very useful movement toward a Gulf currency union. It should instead focus on financing the proposed high-speed rail link connecting all the Gulf Arab states from Kuwait through Saudi Arabia all the way to Oman. Even grander plans to restore the fabled Hejaz railway from Istanbul via Damascus to Medina—which also had a branch to Haifa on the Mediterranean Sea—won't get traction until territorial spats are solved. Colonialism is no longer an excuse: They have only themselves to blame.

Facts on the Ground: South-Central Asia

The largest military occupation in the world is neither in Iraq nor in Afghanistan but in Kashmir, where more than twice the maximum number of troops serving in both Iraq and Afghanistan combined (over six hundred thousand) is deployed in what so many poets and travelers have ironically referred to as a Himalayan paradise. The 1947 Partition of India and creation of Pakistan was one of the bloodiest national births in history, with more than one million people killed during the Hindu-Muslim population exchange. Over the decades since, India has ignored UN resolutions calling for a plebiscite in Kashmir, while Pakistani-backed terrorist groups and three cross-border wars have justified India's intransigence. But today neither India nor Pakistan can afford the status quo in Kashmir given how damaging and costly it is to both sides—and most of all to Kashmiris. Since 1990 alone, more than fifty thousand people have been

killed in Kashmir violence, far greater than in the Israeli-Palestinian
conflict. One major weekly Indian magazine in Delhi recently proclaimed on its cover: "Do we need Kashmir?"

India and Pakistan have consistently pursued secret negotiations
over Kashmir, and in recent years even publicly claimed to be close to
an agreement that would more liberally open the Kashmir border on
both sides—as briefly happened after the devastating earthquake of
2005, when the border was opened to deliver relief to Pakistan's side,
known as Azad Kashmir. But the ouster of Pakistani president Pervez
Musharraf and the terrorist attacks in Mumbai in 2008 by the
Pakistan-based Islamist militant organization Lashkar-e-Taiba emp-
tied that reserve of goodwill. With Pakistan in turmoil, however,
India has the crucial window not to seize Kashmir, but rather to draw
down its troops, a move that would allow Pakistan to refocus its
military—two-thirds of which sits on India's border—on the country's Afghan border, where it is needed most. This is what India also
needs most: to shift its approach to Kashmir the way China has recently won over Taiwan—by buying its loyalty. Indian leaders cannot
countenance independence for Kashmir (which Kashmiris themselves
are uncertain about), but they can fulfill decades-old pledges for economic rehabilitation and genuine autonomous self-governance. This
would be even more feasible if both India and Pakistan would declare
the so-called Line of Control the official border *before* pursuing more
goodwill missions across it. Opening official borders in the long term
means more than unofficial ones in the short term.

The Pashtun territory straddling Afghanistan and Pakistan pre-
sents an even greater headache to south-central Asia's political geography. Straddled between the Indus River and Hindu Kush mountains,
the Pashtun region is not a barrier between the more "natural" states
of Afghanistan and Pakistan—the former created as a buffer and the
latter in haste—rather, it is the cultural bridge between Persian and
Indian civilizations. In the 1960s and '70s, Pakistan's urban class
would cruise on scenic drives for shopping and picnic lunches from
Pakistan's Peshawar to Jalalabad in Afghanistan. But the Soviet invasion, the rise of the anti-Soviet mujahideen, the Afghan refugee crisis,
and overpopulation have changed all that. In the past three decades,

Pakistan's population has nearly tripled to 170 million people. Peshawar today is a place from which even Pashtuns now flee for safety from the Taliban—and some even flee into Afghanistan rather than elsewhere in Pakistan. In 2009, President Zardari declared that his country was "in a fight for our very survival."

It says a lot that the institution that Pakistan (and the United States) relies on most to fight the Taliban is the antiquated, British-colonial-created Frontier Corps. Since 9/11, American policy has declared its priority to be Afghanistan, then Pakistan, and now hyphenates them. But the trouble with defining the "Af-Pak" situation according to existing borders is that it eludes the real problem. Pakistan has two arbitrary borders containing it—the Radcliffe Line as its Indian border and the Durand Line as its Afghan border. The latter divides the Pashtun people across both countries. While Afghanistan is majority Pashtun, there are twice as many Pashtuns in Pakistan as in Afghanistan. Pakistan's largest city and commercial hub of Karachi is also its largest Pashtun city. Even by 2009–10, there was still waffling about whether Afghanistan or Pakistan is America's "main focus"—but in Pashtunistan they bleed together indistinguishably.

The Pashtun way of life has perennially mocked this border, and the Taliban's exploitation of it has equally embarrassed Western policy. Both the anti-Soviet mujahideen and the Taliban were homegrown in the madrassas and refugee camps of Pakistan's tribal areas and pushed into Afghanistan. After 9/11, America's invasion pushed the Taliban—and al-Qaeda—back over the "border." Each drone attack in the Federally Administered Tribal Areas has dispersed both Taliban and al-Qaeda leadership deeper into Pakistan, particularly into the restive province of Baluchistan. To contain them would require a pincer move coordinated and timed from both sides; instead American policy has treated the area like a balloon: squeezing on one side simply to inflate on the other.

But Pakistan has enough problems already. Afghanistan is a broken country, but not breaking apart. Pakistan, meanwhile, has actual separatist movements. Decades of alternating civilian and military misrule have led to a situation of mutual hostility among Pakistan's Punjabis, Sindhis, Pashtuns, and Baluchis—and a parallel mutual hostility among the military, Islamist groups, and civilian elites. In the absence of any delivery of development or justice, the Taliban and various Islamist militant groups and charities became important social service providers, not just in the border areas but also in Karachi and even deep in the Punjabi heartland. The Pakistani military's renewed operations have created another refugee crisis, which is fertile ground for recruitment by Islamist militias. Pakistanis today often say that this is "not their war," but it has become a war over their country. Many of them now think of the "real" Pakistan as that of Sind and Punjab—provinces east of the Indus River—rather than Pukhtunkhwa and Baluchistan, which lay west of it.

If Pakistanis themselves have given up hope of taming the frontier, why do we still treat the countries of Afghanistan and Pakistan as if they are superior to the Pashtun people? And even if Pakistan's many factions—the army, Inter-Services Intelligence, political parties, judges, tribal *maliks,* and Islamist movements—come together in a new national consensus, what can they actually offer to the alienated and assaulted Pashtuns of the frontier? Solidifying the Durand Line is a historically and geologically futile mission, and foreign occupation—including that by the Pakistani state—is largely unwelcome: NATO and Pakistani forces are battling far more local Pashtun nationalist movements than any unified Taliban, and bribing them will only harden their sense of independence.

But Pashtunistan does not have to devolve into another Somalia. Rather than suppress Pashtun autonomy, Pakistan's and Afghanistan's state-building projects should do the exact opposite. Active support for the revival of Pashtun self-governance is the only local antidote to a resurgent and radical Taliban. Pashtun tribes have been negotiating with outsiders for centuries: Talking with them is, if anything, more important than talking with the corrupt capitals of Kabul and Islamabad. A Pashtunistan legislature representing districts on both sides of the Durand Line could be created, and the Taliban, like the Islamic Salvation Front in Algeria, could be compelled to accept politics over jihad. Like Kurdistan and Kashmir, Pashtunistan may not become a sovereign country, but clearer autonomy carries clearer responsibilities for self-policing. The Pashtuns are a more honorable people to trust with their own security than the governments who claim to speak in their name.

Pashtunistan and Baluchistan are, like Kurdistan, potentially vital transit corridors for new oil-slicked Silk Roads. Rather than no-man's-land no-go zones, they can be bridges for the proposed Turkmenistan-Afghanistan-Pakistan-India and Iran-Pakistan-India natural gas pipelines. Putting the resources of an energy-rich region in the service of its energy-starved people is the best way to ensure economic development and cross-border cooperation. Pipelines are the lines on the map that central Asia needs the most.

There are still dozens of nations in need of states—many should have them. An impatient generation that has known only political suppression and legal limbo doesn't want to live in statelessness forever. Suppressing the fundamental desires of people isn't a strong or bold strategy but rather a weak and timid one. Peace agreements require concessions on both sides, and territory is the most meaningful concession that can be made. Talk of "containing spillover" is hardly an ambitious conflict-resolution strategy. A shock-therapy approach of fixing fairer borders and empowering regional organizations to manage them will bring stability much more quickly.

It is true that diffusing the world away from a rigid map of sovereign states will create confusion and costs: What country are people citizens of? How will they survive economically? But the benefits include diminishing accusations of foreign meddling and scapegoating of minorities by lazy and corrupt leaders, and the potential for subregions of the world to build their own stable structures from the bottom up. With autonomy comes responsibility, both to control security and to manage new infrastructure that can turn jigsaw puzzle borders into more meaningful and connected wholes. The slow and sometimes jarring mutations in the cartographic landscape will continue in search of such equilibrium. Since there is little "victory" to celebrate in wars today, this would be a good cause to pursue.

Chapter Five

The New Colonialism:
Better Than the Last

S ome states were never meant to be—and really never were. Centuries of Western colonialism created the modern world as we
know it, but that map is unraveling as some states splinter, collapse,
or seem to fall off it altogether. Terrorist cells striking from zones of
chaos and mass migrations from countries with no economy or stability are a constant reminder that even if we peacefully remap
volatile regions, the postcolonial world—which includes most members of the United Nations—is in a state of high entropy, fragmenting
into a fluid, neo-medieval labyrinth. Globalization has filled this void
with a twenty-first-century colonialism of strong states, international
agencies, NGOs, and companies. Beneath the veneer of independence, these players are running a growing number of countries.
From Oxfam and the Gates Foundation to Booz Allen Hamilton and
DynCorp International, the new colonialists keep many states from
failing—but also prevent them from becoming truly sovereign.

Building a stable global society hinges on getting the new colonialism right. There need not be a false choice between building
things and building institutions: Dozens of nations—new and old—
need both. And they are better off becoming hybrid states today than

the traditional, antiquated type of state decades from now. There is more to taming hot spots than creating new org charts, however. For the places that seem beyond salvation, it will require intrusive public-private peacekeeping forces and even subversive plots and assassinations. Afghanistan is just the beginning—and also a warning that without smart mega-diplomacy among the new colonialists, failed states may forever stay that way.

Colonialism New and Old

As supreme commander of the Allied powers in Japan, General Douglas MacArthur iterated a clear to-do list for postwar rehabilitation: "First, destroy the military power. Punish war criminals. Build the structure of representative government. Modernize the constitution. Hold free elections. Enfranchise the women. Release the political prisoners. Liberate the farmers. Establish a free labor movement. Encourage a free economy. Abolish police oppression. Develop a free and responsible press. Liberalize education. Decentralize political power. Separate the church from state." Just add the World Bank language of creating an "enabling environment" for the private sector and NGO-speak about "consultation with civil society" and you'd have today's standard prescriptions for how to fix broken or despotic societies.

The trouble with historical analogies—with Japan and Germany widely rehearsed as appropriate prologues for the reconstruction of Iraq—is that they bear little resemblance to the circumstances of today's failed states and deposed regimes. The details of demobilizing armies, reforming police forces, creating ethnic reconciliation programs, and jump-starting power plants and hospitals are unique aspects of modern state building: There is no template for them. Instead, we are mostly state-building in places where there never really was a state.

There would be no state building to speak of were it not for the aggressive European colonialism that created the international system we take for granted today. For centuries, European colonizers fanned out across the planet for commercial gain and geopolitical advantage—along the way creating one world under their hierarchy. They forced insular societies such as China and Japan to accept their consulates, compelled the modernization of the Ottoman bureaucracy, and in the name of a *mission civilisatrice* created coherent administrative structures in India and Africa. Even as European imperialism was dismantled through decolonization, former tribes and clans became states and parliaments, and took seats in the United Nations.

But beneath this veneer of sovereign equality, statehood never really took shape after colonialism's retreat. Civil wars, coups, and cronyism prevented real states from emerging. Today's optimists claim that the number of interstate and civil wars has fallen, and thus so have the number of casualties in warfare. But this has more to do with the fact that so many so-called states don't really exist anymore. In 2005, 130 countries received food aid from a hodgepodge of missions, agencies, donors, and other charities. If a state can't even provide food for its citizens, how sovereign is it, anyway?

Today we have no shortage of alarmist terms such as "failed states," "arc of crisis," "danger zone from Palestine to Punjab," and "Eurasian Balkans" to describe these places where "fragility" is a euphemism for illegitimate or nonexistent authority. But these terms describe rather than explain. What almost all these weak states are experiencing is *postcolonial entropy:* decay of European-built infrastructure they haven't upgraded, demise of administrative discipline as civil services become bastions of corruption, and fraying of cohesive national identities as the euphoria of independence fades. Identity crises occur, as Durkheim explained, when a society abandons one set of values without agreeing on the next. For at least fifty countries in the world today, from Congo to Afghanistan, the term "state" is a misnomer. Their governments' effective power rarely reaches beyond their capitals. These countries can't cope with high population growth and disease, social exclusion and ethnic tension, low economic growth and high unemployment, elite cronyism and widespread corruption. They exist more in name and on maps than in reality.

We often wait to act until the specter of the label "failed state" is stamped on a country's image. But the signs of a state being *in failure* appear far in advance. In Pakistan, Musharraf's 1999 coup was viewed as an effort to clean up corruption, but in fact his reign provided only a veneer of stability over a state in a continuous process of failure. Musharraf was not the antidote to state failure in Pakistan; he accelerated it. In the process, Pakistan, like so many other failing states, has lost the technical, fiscal, and even moral authority to run itself.

Failed states create the worst kind of terrorism. By far the largest number of martial casualties results not from wars between countries, but rather from civil wars *within* dozens of failed states. In the 1980s and '90s, two-thirds of sub-Saharan Africa's forty-three countries suffered from civil war—and the toll in lives from displacement and disease was far greater than the deaths during fighting itself. In failing states the leading killers are not tanks or guided missiles but AK-47s, available for as little as ten dollars on some street corners in Mexico, Central America, the Andean region of South America, central and sub-Saharan Africa, southeastern Europe, the Caucasus, and southern and Southeast Asia. Violence is the new war; the killing comes from within.

Since most of these failing states were never actually successful states, why do we pretend that they can be restored to some ideal of statehood? Is statehood itself the problem? Why is central government the metric of effective governance? Western nations now define such failing places as greater threats to their security than the mass armies of Asia's rising powers, but they have little in the way of a strategy to deal with them. If self-determination and nation-states were the resolution to empires and colonialism, then what is the solution to the crumbling of so many nation-states?

As far back as the eighteenth century, Immanuel Kant argued that it was permissible for nations to force others to join the republican league of states and adhere to the standards of civilization. Since then the bar of civility has risen from merely the "capacity to govern" (League of Nations) to "peace-loving nations" (United Nations) to the Copenhagen criteria of democracy, human rights, and free markets (European Union). Yet today many countries still remain a long way from meeting even the League of Nations' most basic standard of a century ago. The only way most failed states will ever meet the standards of civilization is if we abandon the quest for sovereignty in favor of hybrid statehood.

Across the world's failing states, the weak need protection from militias and floods equally—delivering human security cannot wait for government "capacity building." The foot soldiers of humanitarianism constantly relocate from Haiti to Afghanistan to Indonesia to confront the worst disasters, for which there is no strategy, only improvisation. After the Indonesian tsunami of 2004, the first aid to arrive in the remote Banda Aceh province came on planes and vans operated by Dutch logistics multinational TNT. Unilever distributed energy-fortified biscuits manufactured and donated by Danone, and the World Food Program used offices donated by Citigroup. Ultimately, the U.S. government's donation was $657 million, while private American citizens and corporations gave more than $2 billion. And where was the Indonesian government in all of this? Much of the $4 billion it received from international donors remains unaccounted for.

Then there are refugee camps: islands of permanent emergency. In regions from Mauretania to Myanmar, public and private aid agencies constantly struggle to meet basic survival needs while fending off assaulting militias and preventing the theft of food and the siphoning of fuel. Chad's best health care is found in UN camps set up for a half-million refugees from Darfur and the Central African Republic. The International Rescue Committee provides drinking water for millions and health training for tens of thousands worldwide; 90 percent of its budget goes straight into its programs, making it perhaps the world's most efficient humanitarian force. In all these ways, the new colonialists have become woven into the fabric of governance in weak states, preventing them from failing even further.

There are clearly big differences between the old and new colonialism. As Tony Pipa, director of the NGO Leaders Forum, says, "Equating the two is like calling the Prius the new Hummer. They both get you from here to there, but the goals and values behind the design are completely different." Unlike the previous European colonialism, which purposely sought to perpetuate dependency, the new colonialists want states to practice "responsible sovereignty" by which they protect their people and prevent threats from spilling over their borders.[1] The new colonialism isn't intentionally exploitative, condescending, or coercive—only unintentionally so. The new colonialists are certainly more committed to local ownership than either U.S. military occupations or traditional UN missions.

At their best, the new colonialists don't displace or ignore local politics, but instead lend global resources to make local politics progressive. If Haiti is to be "built back better" after its devastating earthquake, it will have to shift from an ad hoc "Republic of NGOs" to a new system for linking global resources such as money and building designs to local businesses, civic groups, and government agencies. But so far what we have seen is a global outpouring of material and financial support that is not coordinated enough to necessarily set the country on a new course.

The biggest challenge, then, to the new colonialism is inefficiency: Everyone wants to be the coordinator, no one the coordinatee. Britain's Lord Paddy Ashdown, the European Union's former high commissioner in Bosnia and Herzegovina, summed it up best: "Before I started my mandate I had been told that managing Bosnia was like herding cats. What I hadn't appreciated was that this applied to the international community too." The United Nations, United States, and NGOs all have a vision of seamless bureaucratic harmony under their leadership—yet none can succeed alone.

The new colonialists therefore have a bigger job to do than compete with one another. From Haiti to Niger to Myanmar, the countries that need emergency help after disasters also need to be rebuilt better than before: better roads, better housing, and more competent government. The best help the new colonialists can therefore give to the refugees and hungry villagers of failed states is to team up and meddle in their domestic politics, undermine bad leaders, and empower local groups to manage their own affairs. Only then will the new colonialists leave in less time than the old colonialists did.

The Responsibility to Be Responsible

What do we respect more: people or states? During the past two decades the high idealism of humanitarian rhetoric has been buried in the pettiness of international bureaucracy. The reactions to Somalia, Bosnia, and Rwanda in the 1990s, and Congo and Darfur in recent years, were too little too late, and poorly resourced and executed. To this day the catchphrase of "humanitarian intervention" is still far more often talked about than done. Even the recently minted Responsibility to Protect (R2P) doctrine is stillborn. It was supposed to require the international community to intervene when governments fail to protect their own people, but instead it became a victim of every nation's claim to conduct its own "war on terror" without outside interference. Right doesn't yet have might.

A smarter strategy is to focus on removing the heads of state that are often the roots of the problems. Ousting bad leaders—yes, violently deposing them—without punishing good people is one of the most sensitive topics in diplomacy and foreign policy, but it holds the key to liberating many societies to run themselves better. One of the new colonialists' main tasks is therefore to take down the leaders who are medieval in the worst sense of the term.

We often forget that, from Yugoslavia to Sudan, the descent into civil war and genocide is often not about genuine grievances and mass movements, but rather the megalomania of one single leader. During the 1990s, the northern and southern no-fly zones imposed on Iraq left it in a geopolitical gray zone with Saddam Hussein still in charge of whatever his Baathist regime could reach. Sanctions between the two Gulf wars cost five hundred thousand Iraqi children their lives due to pneumonia and other preventable illnesses. Zimbabwe was once sub-Saharan Africa's second largest economy behind South Africa, but President Robert Mugabe's violent seizure of land from white farmers and paranoid politics plunged what was once "Africa's breadbasket" into desperation, with hyperinflation requiring $500 million notes to be issued (enough for eight loaves of bread). Innocent people living under sanctions are twice oppressed: by their rogue leaders and by the international community.

This past decade's revolutions in Ukraine, Serbia, and Georgia gave us false hope that all odious regimes can be changed through relatively peaceful means. Where people power fails, "lawfare" has become a go-to weapon for the Western diplomats. From Nuremberg to the International Criminal Court (ICC), universal jurisdiction has reached countries whose own laws don't yet see it that way. But do we really live in a world where courts chase after mass murderers and armies don't have to? ICC indictments have targeted rebel leaders such as Liberia's Charles Taylor and Joseph Kony of Uganda's Lord's Resistance Army, rogue ex-presidents such as Slobodan Milosevic of Yugoslavia, and even heads of state such as Sudan's Omar al-Bashir. Yet setting up criminal courts while a conflict is still ongoing is an odd substitute for hard action—especially since indictments only further entrench despots. Bashir now restricts his movements to Khartoum and friendly countries, and Kony is hiding out in the jungles of eastern Congo. Bashir told the ICC that it should "eat" the indictment, calling it an "instrument of neo-colonialist policy."

We shouldn't need tribunals to tell us who the bad guys are. Regimes from Sudan to Myanmar seem impervious to shame, moral appeals, and even ICC indictments. Even though Mugabe eventually entered into a nominal power-sharing agreement and made his rival prime minister (due largely to the election of Jacob Zuma in South Africa), and even if Bashir allows more aid and peacekeepers in Darfur, these revelations of decency always occur after unconscionable damage has been done. Would it not have been more sensible—both morally and politically—to give robust support to efforts to oust the likes of Saddam, Mugabe, and Bashir?

The United States officially banned assassinations of foreign leaders in the 1970s, but since 9/11 the CIA has undertaken an expansive covert program to assassinate al-Qaeda and Taliban leaders. But rogue presidents have killed far more people than the most ruthless terrorists. Our neo-medieval world doesn't have a common code of sovereign noninterference. Leaders can quite easily be sorted out between those who are civilized and those who are barbarian.

There are many ways to seriously harass an intransigent regime before escalation goes overboard. Kautilya, the fourth-century B.C. Indian strategist of the Mauryan empire who was part-Bismarck, part-Machiavelli, provided a four-step strategy for subduing villains: *saam* (dialogue of equality), *daam* (bribery), *dand* (punishment), and *bhed* (sowing dissent). Revoking recognition, freezing bank accounts, and imposing travel bans can curb the spending habits of rulers who enjoy lavish shopping in London and Dubai while their people starve. Flipping defecting officers and bribing junior ones are more aggressive ways to make it less fun for despots to enjoy their perch. Patrolling no-fly zones, jamming radio and TV signals, blockading weapons imports and lucrative exports, and building up rebel defenses are other ways outsiders can isolate thuggish regimes. Flooding countries such as North Korea or Myanmar with money, mobile phones, and targeted food aid could also destabilize foul regimes from within.

Rogue leaders today are more likely to hold some form of elections, but they also win 90 percent of them through vote rigging, imprisoning opposition, stuffing ballots, and intimidating voters. Outside do-gooders will therefore have to be more cunning and persistent than ever in providing tactical support to remove the despots who are a primary obstacle to political evolution. This is not an invitation for more attempted thrill-seeking coups by unscrupulous retired British officers as in Equatorial Guinea in 2004, but rather to build opposition that can break the cycles of coups and countercoups. In Africa this will take a long time. Most African rebel movements aren't led by true revolutionaries but rather opportunists with little vision beyond profiteering from chaos. The 2008 coup in Guinea, led by officers who assassinated the long-standing authoritarian leader Lansana Conté (who had himself taken power in a coup), was followed by the public humiliation of politicians who had stolen millions. They were forced to return the money—but to whom?

Which countries deserve a crippling blockade to isolate their rogue regimes and which leaders deserve to be assassinated? The question comes down to whether behavior change is sufficient or regime change is necessary. Some states, such as Sudan, could reasonably establish a power-sharing order (or peacefully split up) once a particular regime is removed from power, while in others, such as North Korea, removing the leadership could give rise to something even worse. Large-scale interventions such as in Iraq can backfire, turning supporters of liberation into insurgents. Most Iraqis are grateful for the United States' removal of Saddam, just not for America's subsequent occupation. The former was necessary; the latter was not. Few will mourn the wicked once they are gone, and the sooner they are gone, the better so that people can get on with their lives.

Ultimately, the removal of tyrants should come from and be owned by the country's own citizenry. As people get access to wealth and voice, they will increasingly be prepared to fight to defend it. But until popular uprisings can overcome police states and cults of personality, progressive interventionists will have to continue to be guileful, and even play God, in the name of saving people from their leaders.

Finding the Peace to Keep

A couple of years ago, a famous Hollywood actress turned activist—let's call her Mia Farrow—had a quiet meeting with the head of the private security firm Blackwater to find out if the overpaid military contractor would be able to stage a humanitarian intervention in Darfur on behalf of its own people. Blackwater answered that it could "clear and hold," no problem. Farrow didn't pursue the idea any further. Perhaps she wasn't sure which was more disturbing: that the West had in its power the ability to protect those who remained of Darfur's beleaguered population but wouldn't, or that it was the most notorious private military company that was willing to do the job. If you could send in the troops—whether they wore green or black—would you?

In many places, the lofty term "international community" means no more and no less than the number of UN peacekeepers present.

Soon after the United Nations' founding, peacekeeping was quickly invented on the fly to monitor cease-fires in the Mideast and Kashmir. By the early 1990s, the humble United Nations had become the "Rolls Royce of conflict management." It facilitated transitions in numerous Latin American, African, and Southeast Asian countries, conducting elections, demilitarizing armed forces, and steering economic reform. Soon there was talk of UN-led international trusteeships for East Timor, Kosovo, Palestine, Somalia, and Sierra Leone as well. UN troubleshooter Sergio Vieira de Mello ran East Timor from its independence vote from Indonesia in 1999 until its UN membership in 2002.

But by 2006, it was clear that the Australian-led UN intervention in East Timor still wasn't up to the task of reforming the country's security services or resurrecting the economy. And in other interventions—particularly in Congo, Liberia, Haiti, and Sudan—peacekeepers were deployed to places where there was no peace to keep. Today it seems the United Nations no longer knows what it is doing in peace operations, even though peacekeeping is the most expensive UN function by far. The number of UN military and police personnel on duty in twenty-plus operations worldwide now stands at more than 110,000. Each intervention is cobbled together with piecemeal funding and supplies (from the first world) and troops (from the third world) without sufficient training or a clear mandate for today's more dangerous stabilization missions. Once on the ground, UN operations have fallen into every postconflict trap, from failing to confront local warlords to following mandates that don't match local realities to designing constitutions without popular buy-in. Peacekeeping has become the continuation of politics by other means: Some operations have gone on for so many years that they may have become part of the problem themselves.

For peacekeeping to not further degenerate into never-ending, half-hearted occupations, the more than $8 billion spent on it each year would be better allocated to building local, multinational forces managed by regional organizations. Regional—not global—peacekeeping forces are the future of conflict management. The United States, NATO, and the European Union can all give more financial, military, and logistical support for the African Union to halt genocide, stabilize conflicts, and enforce peace agreements—all legitimate mandates that Africans should learn to pursue themselves. Countries such as Kenya, Uganda, Tanzania, Ethiopia, and Djibouti have added troops to a standby peacekeeping force, while Nigeria has set up a training center for AU forces, and South African police are training their Congolese counterparts in crowd control. Spain has become the largest funder of the Economic Community of West African States (ECOWAS) because the organization can foster on-the-ground cooperation for interventions (as it did in Liberia), combat illegal migration to Europe, and promote economic relations in the region. The United Nations could never do these things without ECOWAS—but one day ECOWAS may be able to do them without any outside help.

With UN blue helmets, American troops, and NATO armies stretched all across Africa, the Mideast, and Afghanistan, great powers may have finally realized that consistent regional anchors for peacekeeping operations are the key to both alleviating the burden on themselves and encouraging self-policing. Regional forces have far greater on-the-ground knowledge, legitimacy, and acceptance even though they don't pretend to be neutral like the United Nations does. In Bosnia, the United Nations was accused of not distinguishing between the perpetrators of genocide and its victims. In Somalia, Iraq, and Afghanistan, aid workers, UN staff, and peacekeepers have come under constant attack while supplying food to refugees. Militants, insurgents, and terrorists don't care about their proclaimed neutrality: If you're not with them, you're against them. Local forces are better able to navigate these rifts, which constantly catch UN forces off guard.

No matter who is in charge of peacekeeping, constant security risks remain an obvious reason why the new public and private colonialists need to learn to get along for the long haul. If NGOs have to pull out due to attacks—as has happened in Afghanistan, Iraq, Sudan, and Somalia—their humanitarian gains can go up in smoke. Some NGOs already partner with private military companies. Military outsourcing has been given a bad name by the tens of thousands of contractors involved in the U.S. occupation of Iraq. But "contractors gone wild" is not a universal phenomenon. DynCorp successfully demobilized the Liberian militia. NGOs and modern-day mercenaries may seem strange bedfellows—altruism and profit—but they do, in fact, need each other: Firms stabilize and NGOs deliver services. There is no longer anything "inherently governmental" about providing basic stability. Public-private security is the order of the day in the neo-medieval world.

Taking the Reins of "Chaos-istan"

No place better exhibits the strategic stakes yet also the perpetual improvisation of public and private actors clamoring to rebuild a failed state like Afghanistan. Just months after the 2001 invasion, Pakistani journalist Ahmed Rashid remarked that "Afghanistan has a wonderful opportunity to experiment with small government." What it got instead was quasi-government at the intersection of heavy-handed military occupation, insipid donor politics, corrupt national institutions, traditional warlord rivalries, and vainglorious NGOs. To fix Afghanistan will be hard enough; incoherent strategies and arbitrary timelines only make it harder.

The U.S.-led occupation has lacked vision, lurching from election campaign to campaign—both American and Afghan—and donor conference to donor conference, each event marked by clashing agendas rather than collective strategy. Why, for example, were democratic elections such an early priority, when the delivery of services remains to this day inadequate, making the very inclusiveness of the elections a challenge to their own legitimacy? While the West focused on shoring up Hamid Karzai, the rest of the country became what former finance minister Ashraf Ghani called a "narco-mafia state." Poppy eradication policies lacked complementary programs to offer alternative livelihoods, strengthening warlords who reemerged as governors and drug-trafficking commanders. Meanwhile, most Afghans have seen only "phantom aid" while international bureaucrats siphon off educated Afghans to work as drivers and translators, cause traffic jams, and all but invite suicide bombings with their hulking SUVs.

Human security remains hard to come by: Some $30 billion has been spent by donors and yet at least half the population suffers from perpetual food shortages.

There are now two "What are we doing in Afghanistan?" questions. The first is about *why* we're there in the first place. The second is about *how* we go about our activities there. Afghanistan's persistent failure has many parents. Since 2009, both military and civilian resources have received a big boost, yet the coordination between them has been pathetic. Almost a decade since the invasion, the collective international presence is still asking the most basic questions: What type of government should Afghanistan have? What resources should be provided and at what level of society? Who should lead reconstruction projects? In the midst of a surge of troops, funds, donors, and civilians, a far more effective division of labor is still needed. Afghanistan remains an American war rather than an Afghan war.

In Afghanistan as much as in any other failed state, the global should support the local. In counterinsurgency, terms such as "tactical level," "security halo," and "population-centric" are all utterly redundant—the local is *everything,* particularly against Pashtun tribesmen turned Taliban who are genetically expert at guerrilla warfare. But it took until 2008 for America to commit serious resources to an Afghan Public Protection Program, which trains local Afghan community forces across ethnic lines, and for international forces to work more systematically with local *shura* councils to build community defense mechanisms. Similarly, on the political level, foreign diplomats built up new political parties as if they could replace tribal *jirgas* as the main mode of arbitration—but at best the former could be a manifestation of the latter. Also, UN reports refer to such *jirgas* as "alternative dispute resolution mechanisms" as if they weren't *the* mechanisms of justice in Afghanistan, handling up to 90 percent of legal claims.

A better model than pouring billions into Kabul's or Islamabad's black holes has been the National Solidarity Program in Afghanistan, which has disbursed block grants to twenty-eight thousand villages that have a participatory and transparent process for determining how the money is spent. What Afghanistan needs is more competent provincial security and administration, not a bloated government in Kabul: It can have central government without *centralized* government. Otherwise outsiders are practicing too much old colonialism and too little new colonialism. The goal of helping others help themselves is no less worthy simply because working through local players exposes the weakest links in the chain. Those links need to be supported even as outsiders overcompensate.

The travails of Afghanistan's tribal population have never been in doubt: poor irrigation and seasonal flooding, lack of safe drinking water, poor health care, and shoddy roads. Unconnected spaces are often ungoverned places. A century ago, British colonialists attempted to tame the frontier through road building, turning unsettled areas into settled ones. Even in the twenty-first century, American generals invoke the old adage that "where the road ends, the insurgency begins." Stabilizing settled population centers and then building roads to connect them is thus perhaps the most crucial step in state building. Under the mantra of "clear, hold, and build," soldier-diplomats of the U.S. military have overseen some important successes, such as restoring the Kabul-to-Jalalabad road. But insurgents frequently target Western-built infrastructure, making the Kabul-Jalalabad road impassable—at least to Westerners. Yet when *locals* build them themselves, they gain the means to pursue their own livelihoods and a reason to fight for their future. As Afghans say, "If you sweat for it, you'll protect it."

In Afghanistan, which is cut off from global markets (except the opium market), all important economic activity is local as well. Eighty-five percent of Afghans depend on agriculture. Afghan farmers could earn as much from pomegranates as poppies, but they lack the roads and access to ports to efficiently transport their harvests to India and the Persian Gulf. With better irrigation they could grow rice in one season and fruit and nuts in another, and with small processing plants they could make fruit juices for sale. Rather than wasting millions on large-scale commercial agriculture as USAID did during the Bush administration, the U.S. military and agriculture experts from American universities are finally spreading across

Afghanistan to increase rural efficiency. Mint, pomegranate, soy, saffron, and raisins could all grow in the provinces where opium has been strongest. Rapid-response bodies such as the Office of Transition Initiatives—whose diplomats-for-hire get things done by putting money straight into local players' hands—should get fifty times their meager budgets to jump-start such local projects. Afghans can also be employed to make toilet paper, soap, and bicycles—anything China and India are becoming too expensive for. When a Canadian commander in the southern Helmand province was asked how he managed to pacify one district, he replied: "Carpet bomb the area with projects."

Achieving human security hinges on improving the coordination of fledgling regimes, NGOs, UN agencies, and foreign militaries. Lord Paddy Ashdown, the European Union's former high representative in Bosnia and Herzegovina, urged that foreign occupiers should always prepare for their own obsolescence rather than fortify their often unwelcome presence. But in Afghanistan, that horizon might be too distant to prepare for. Instead, the country is emerging as a semipermanent model of the hybrid public-private governance taking hold across the postcolonial world. It represents the new normal of globalization and failed states across Africa, central Asia, and Southeast Asia: Flights come in and out of Kabul ferrying Western consultants and Chinese businessmen, each pursuing his or her own agenda amid chaotic politics and an uncertain future. The American military even guards the Chinese-operated Aynak copper mine in Logar province, their cooperation contributing to resurrecting Afghanistan's place along the new Silk Road.

Neo-colonialists need to learn the lessons from their present foray in Afghanistan for potential future interventions in Sudan and Congo in Africa, but also for Yemen, Myanmar, and North Korea—all strategically located states with sensitive great power interests and all populous countries with starving people. As these states' regimes weaken and potentially collapse, geopolitical and humanitarian factors will collide in unpredictable ways. There is no choice as to whether or not to pursue the new colonialism—but there is a choice as to how to do it right.

Chapter Six

Terrorists, Pirates, Nukes

*I*f you're looking to traffic young girls, Haiti is the place to go. The
*latest in stolen electronics? Paraguay is where the action is. Pushing
cocaine? Colombia has what you need. Smuggling cigarettes? Albania
is a treasure trove. Selling heroin? Myanmar is a top source. States
don't have to be failing or in the midst of civil wars to be hubs for the
export of trouble—often that is their main export. Opium from
Afghanistan kills five times more citizens of NATO countries than the
number of NATO troops killed in Afghanistan itself. Today there is a
global black market for everything, from poached hides of exotic animals to high-end virility drugs to nuclear material. Real or fake, they
flow off assembly lines, get ferried across borders and waved through
customs by airport crews, and are sold to both willing and unsus-
pecting buyers worldwide.*

*Terrorism, piracy, warfare, and organized crime have blended to-
gether into one public-private underworld of state sponsors and nefarious shadowy groups. Market dynamics are impervious to moralizing
debates: So long as demand exists, there will be supply. Since governments no longer control the market for mass crime and violence, the
market for solutions is wide open as well. Only an equally robust
mega-diplomacy of intelligence cooperation, investment for job cre-*

ation, and prying open closed societies can effectively deal with insurgent jihadists, Somali pirates, and Iranian mullahs.

Terrorism as War

Before 9/11, terrorism experts used to say, "Terrorists want a lot of people watching, not a lot of people dead." Today's terrorists clearly want both. In theory, warfare is between armies while terrorism targets civilians. In practice, they have become all but indistinguishable: Civilians are by far the greatest casualties of both war and terrorism. The term "terrorism" remains as contested as ever: One man's terrorist is still another man's freedom fighter. More fundamentally, terrorism isn't going away because, if used cleverly, it is undeniable that terrorism works. The "war on terrorism" fared no better than the "war on drugs." Every couple of years the strongmen of Asian powers from Russia to Uzbekistan to China get together and raise their arms in the air declaring they will together "stamp out the scourge of terrorism." One of them is usually hit with a terrorist attack within a week or two.

Terrorism is a dirty business, but it is very much a business; the boundary with organized crime is blurry at best. The notorious Bank of Credit and Commerce International was perhaps the most successful drug-money-laundering, weapons-financing, and terrorist-sponsoring (from Abu Nidal to Osama bin Laden) corporation in history until it was shut down in 1991. Without the continued ubiquity of money launderers, al-Qaeda and other terrorist groups would be a far weaker force. Whether they want independent statehood or a global *ummah*, terrorists and guerrilla insurgents use similar strategies: fragmented expertise across multiple cells, coalescing when they need to conduct large operations, pooling and directing money and weapons to wherever they are needed. They are shadowy in their diffusion, but strong in their unity.

Borderless trade and communications technology, the forces that empower citizens and consumers, also empower the terrorism-warfare-criminality nexus of banks, gunrunners, charities, training camps, spies, gangs, and corrupt officials reaching every corner of the globe. The notion of "allies" fully united and committed to a global counterterrorism compact is antiquated. Saudi Arabia and Pakistan aren't unified in any such way. Some parts of their governments cooperate, while others are among the main feeders and financiers of terrorist groups. The U.S. State Department blocked families of 9/11 victims from suing Saudi Arabia, but not Saudi charities that directly and indirectly fund the Taliban and al-Qaeda. The transnational nature of the new terrorist-criminal enterprises has thus ripped apart the traditional confines of international negotiation. Nonstate groups such as the FARC in Colombia or the Taliban in Afghanistan have held territory without having statehood, but we treat them much the same. Even the truly stateless Osama bin Laden has made peace offers and called for negotiations, which European diplomats have seriously considered despite accusations of appeasement.

States sponsor terrorism through public-private networks—so thwarting terrorism requires the same approach. Cross-border problems need cross-border solutions, not UN resolutions. Chasing terrorists across the Afghanistan-Pakistan border, drug smugglers across the Colombian-Venezuelan border, and arms traffickers across the Moldovan-Ukrainian border all require cooperation among neighbors to catch and prosecute the miscreants. International terrorist groups by definition violate state sovereignty, so violating it further to catch them should hardly be illegal. In the aftermath of 9/11, UN resolution 1373 mandated greater international intelligence cooperation. From there, some officials suggested the creation of a global counterterrorism organization. But how would such a central body be even remotely nimble enough to deal with the diffuse threat of terrorism? What value could it add to the more than seventy regional and subregional counterterrorism efforts that already exist?

The hodgepodge of UN and other international agencies and committees that deal with transnational threats treat terrorism, organized crime, weapons proliferation, small arms, and drugs as if they each have a unique set of solutions. But they don't: Border security, export controls, legal reform, well-paid police, and well-trained judges and prosecutors are part of any effective strategy against these ills. A far greater premium should be placed on networking that allows intelligence and law enforcement agencies to share information on terrorist suspects and money-laundering charities and financial institutions. The Financial Action Task Force (FATF), which names and shames countries with weak money-laundering safeguards, and Interpol, which receives only $60 million per year from its member states, deserve much larger budgets. Without the FATF, the U.S. Treasury's outreach to more than forty major international banks such as Barclays to freeze and reduce dealings with Iran would have been much more difficult to coordinate.

Intelligence cooperation can catch terrorists before they blow up buses, trains, planes, police stations, and parliaments, but it doesn't address underlying grievances. American foreign policy has favored the "long war" over the more important local war. We no longer use the term "global war on terror," yet the reality of multinational jihadism remains a daily ordeal in the Mideast and southern and Southeast Asia. Despite its global connections, most terrorism is local. Al-Qaeda can strike worldwide, but its grievances are local, as are most of its targets. Some Islamist militias in Pakistan and radical Salafists in North Africa have clearly benefited from al-Qaeda links, but when we refer to groups as al-Qaeda "affiliates" or "copycats" we reify them into amorphous global movements, ignoring their tangible local agendas, which, if addressed, could take the wind out of their sails. The poor political performance of Islamist parties in Indonesia or Hezbollah in Lebanon is at least partially explained by this. As a 2008 RAND study of more than five hundred terrorist campaigns unequivocally demonstrates, integration into political processes and joint intelligence-police operations (rather than military operations) are the most successful mechanisms sapping terrorist support.[1] But if poor and fractured societies could do this by themselves, they wouldn't be criminal-narco-terrorist havens to begin with. Indeed, beefed-up security alone isn't a total solution to terrorism, simply because most countries can't afford it. More police cameras in the West and in authoritarian states simply drive terrorists to lawless safe havens such as Yemen or Pakistan. Military strikes kill the terrorists of today, but they also alienate local populations and breed the terrorists of tomorrow. Australia's goal in Indonesia, therefore, is not only to conduct joint 'operations and training with the army, but also to provide a steady flow of experts in police and justice reform to improve the quality of governance in restive areas.

Instead of a high-altitude "war of ideas," the way to win "hearts and minds" is through the wallet and the stomach. Tacky television programs boasting the virtuous lifestyle of Muslim Americans and appeals to brotherhood with a mythically vast global Islamic community do nothing for the prosaic problems of Muslim youth. The Obama administration has moved beyond conflating the global struggle against al-Qaeda with the larger challenge of rehabilitating the economy and governance of postcolonial Muslim societies, but has yet to penetrate deep enough to help them see a better future. The Arab world has the greatest share of its population in Generation Y, but this cohort is also a generation in waiting: waiting for jobs, education, marriage, and homes. All the reports about a "missing middle class" and "youth bulge" should focus on how to build more vocational centers, factories, and call centers in the Middle East.

This is the time for American companies—not its military—to be the tip of the spear. Foreign investment reinforces alliances: Now that the U.S. military has pulled out of Saudi Arabia, it's increasingly up to multinationals such as Alcoa, which recently announced a $10 billion investment in a new aluminum complex, to bring jobs in modern facilities and goodwill to the Saudi people. In the other direction, Saudi prince Alwaleed is the largest single private investor in the United States. Together Alcoa and Alwaleed are the new Army and Aramco.

America's universities can also "drain the swamp" better than any invasion. From the outskirts of Cairo to glitzy new quadrangles in Qatar, top-tier schools—including Georgetown, Cornell, Texas A&M, NYU, and Carnegie Mellon—are now the best face of American foreign policy in the Middle East, educating the next generation of Arab entrepreneurs and politicians in making business plans and managing ministries.

Business for Diplomatic Action, a private group of executives alarmed by America's diminished global brand, has also taken matters into its own hands. It has launched a CultureSpan program to promote dialogue between American businesspeople and foreign citizens, urged American firms to maintain robust overseas operations, and partnered with business schools and companies such as Boeing and Microsoft to fund dozens of Arab entrepreneurs to tour American firms and visit the United States. One Arab participant exclaimed, "We don't like America. . . . We *love* America!"

Terror on the High Seas

As if there were not enough ungoverned spaces on land, there are even more at sea. Even though globalization has brought us jet travel and e-commerce, 70 percent of all interregional trade, including two-thirds of the world's oil shipments, is still transported by sea. With the rise of Asian economies, most of the world's container and tanker traffic crisscrosses the Indian Ocean from the Mideast to the Pacific Rim, passing through the narrow choke points of the Bab el-Mandeb Strait connecting the Red Sea to the Gulf of Aden, the Strait of Hormuz connecting the Persian Gulf to the Gulf of Oman, or the Strait of Malacca, which connects the Indian Ocean to the South China Sea. Land and sea are not unconnected spaces—they give way to and shape each other. From Somalia to Aceh in Indonesia, whenever instability has risen on land, so, too, has piracy at sea.

Most of the world is covered by oceans that are mostly controlled by no one. The eighteenth century was not only a pivotal period of global capitalist expansion and colonialism, but also an age of piracy from the English Channel to the Straits of Malacca. The Barbary pirates of Tunis, Algiers, and Tripoli demanded $1 million from Thomas Jefferson (then one-tenth of the U.S. budget) to suspend attacks on American ships. While Europeans regularly paid such tribute, the United States eventually dispatched the precursor of today's Mediterranean fleet to crush the pirates and restore free commercial flows. But clearly, robbery on the high seas has not gone away. Across the centuries, the combination of depraved conditions on land and opportunism at sea has always led to piracy. Indeed, as coastal development continues along the sea lanes of Africa, the Middle East, and Southeast Asia, we are entering another era of global piracy.

The violence in Yemen and Somalia, the littoral states of the Gulf of Aden, knows no shoreline as pirates threaten the twenty thousand ships passing through the water between them every year. In early 2008, pirates seized a Ukrainian ship loaded with dozens of battle tanks. Later the same year, when Somali pirates hijacked the Saudi-owned supertanker *Sirius Star,* carrying two million barrels of oil worth $100 million, a ransom of $3 million was air-dropped in a giant brick of $100 bills at a designated beach. In 2010, a ransom of $7 million was paid for the release of the crew of a Greek super-tanker. Somali pirates don't care whether the ships they raid are owned or flagged European, Arab, or Asian—often they have no idea whom they're assaulting or what booty they might win. And since their country's banking system is virtually nonexistent, cash is king.

Somalia-based piracy is estimated to be a $100 million annual business, a substantial amount for one of the world's most destitute countries. Many suspect that the pirates now have links with the rad-ical Islamist group al-Shabaab, creating a pirate-fundamentalist nexus potentially capable of taking over the lawless country. But Islam and piracy aren't necessarily a deadly combination. When the Islamic Courts Union united Somalia's clans in 2006, piracy went down and the country witnessed the only brief months of stability it had experienced in twenty years.[2]

The fact that ransom money is divided up in equitable portions among clan members and that pirate attacks diminish when families of fishermen can take care of themselves tells us that Somalis are not driven purely by greed. Indeed, it seems that Somali grievances, like those of many current and would-be terrorists, have been more often exploited than addressed. Since the 1990s, international mafia have made the coastal waters of southern Somalia a favored location for the dumping of toxic—even nuclear—waste, while commercial Asian (particularly Chinese) trawlers have overfished Somali waters for tuna, leaving locals with little to catch, feed on, or sell. Somali pirates therefore claim they have no choice but to raid ships in order to demand their fair share. They see themselves as protectors of their waters against foreign intrusion.

Still, with shipping volumes and values so crucial to the global economy, the United States, European Union, India, China, and other strong nations are taking as tough a line today on piracy as America did more than two hundred years ago, their navies patrolling and killing pirates wherever possible as well as raiding onshore pirate hideaways (with some prosecutions in Kenya's courts). International vessels passing through the Gulf of Aden are pursuing a mixed strategy: using fire hoses to repel pirates, paying bribes and ransoms when necessary, and even arming themselves. Blackwater, the notorious private military contractor, has deployed a small flotilla to escort oil and cargo vessels, while other companies are offering electric fencing and stun guns to shipping companies.

Even though the gloves have come off, deploying expensive military convoys to float in the Gulf of Aden is hardly cost-effective. To avoid both an asymmetric arms race between Western navies and impoverished pirates, as well as potential friendly fire incidents among the dozen or more countries now patrolling the Arabian Sea, a more multidimensional strategy is required. On the other side of the Indian Ocean, Malaysia, Singapore, and Indonesia jointly patrol the Strait of Malacca, with Malaysia, Singapore, and Japan funding the improvement of Indonesia's coast guard capacity so that it can be a stronger participant in policing the waters rather than the weakest link. For the explosive Gulf of Aden, the money spent on perpetual naval patrols would be better spent on improving Somalia's ability to curb pirates from going offshore in the first place—for example, by strengthening the African Union's presence there.

The autonomous and dysfunctional Puntland region of northern Somalia is not only the source of most Somali piracy but also the area in which the underlying problems are being dealt with most promisingly. With its depraved coast guard of only three tiny ships, Puntland has been hiring private military companies since 1999 to harass Chinese trawlers illegally fishing in Somali waters, levying fines on them, and splitting the fees. Western governments are now offering to build an anti-piracy coast guard as well, while local Puntland sheikhs are cooperating with international agencies to offer jobs to young men to lure them away from a life of seaborne jihad. Like their land-based terrorist counterparts, pirates will keep popping up until they have incentives not to. Supplying Somali fisherman with new boats to boost their catch and fend off illegal competition makes more sense than trying to sink every pirate closing in on the horizon.

Nuclear Terror

Who wants to wake up in the morning and find out that Iran or North Korea has acquired sizeable nuclear arsenals capable of reaching their capital city? The fear of nuclear weapons spreading to rogue regimes or terrorists is particularly acute among the (nuclear-armed) great powers themselves, which are the most likely targets of nuclear terrorism. As President Obama said on NATO's sixtieth anniversary, "In a strange turn of history, the threat of global nuclear war has gone down, but the risk of a nuclear attack has gone up." Surrounding rogue regimes and threatening attacks on nuclear facilities seem only to accelerate proliferation, so how can diplomacy slow the spread of nukes?

The 1986 Gorbachev-Reagan summit at Reykjavík was a turning point in the nuclear arms race and the Cold War, the moment at which the superpowers pledged to cap and potentially reduce their arsenals. A quarter century later, the United States and Russia might finally complete this process as they embark on a series of agreements to cut their arsenals—together 95 percent of the world's total—and advance a global treaty to eliminate fissile material production. Not only will this liberate Russia from its current defense budget, which is half eaten up by the mere task of maintaining a redundant arsenal, but it allows the dynamic of disarmament to be taken seriously for perhaps the first time since the advent of the nuclear age. If Russia and America actually drop their existing arsenals to several hundred warheads each, declare no-first-use policies, and forgo ballistic missile defense programs and the weaponization of space, a credible movement toward a nuclear-free world could actually take root.

Until that time, however, most of the world considers the forty-year-old Non-Proliferation Treaty (NPT) a symbol of "nuclear apartheid," with the already nuclear-armed states in the West most loudly denouncing India, Pakistan, Iran, Libya, and North Korea for their nuclear quests. The NPT can't stop proliferation, particularly since it grants the right to nuclear enrichment and processing. States seek nuclear weapons to deter the United States and nearby enemies, to compel neighbors to accept their dominance, and to gain status in the world's nuclear club. In the Bush administration, disarmament disappeared from the diplomatic lexicon and proliferation increased. The rollback of Libya's nuclear program was achieved through secret negotiation, but that success was overshadowed by the U.S. invasion of Iraq, which, rather than scare Iran and North Korea, inspired the former to accelerate its centrifuge development program and the latter to kick out weapons inspectors and test a low-grade nuclear weapon. Scolding North Korea for "further isolating itself from the community of nations" doesn't seem to bother its leaders much, since they could not have been more isolated to begin with.

All the while, the nuclear issue grows ever more complex: weapons proliferation by states such as Iran, the risk of nuclear bombs or highly enriched uranium being stolen by terrorists, and the renewed prominence of nuclear power as an alternative to fossil fuels, making nuclear technology an increasingly sensitive and dangerous trade. Nuclear diplomacy has thus become a cat-and-mouse game in which nuclear cheaters manipulate reports, block inspections, and evade safeguards while continuing to build centrifuges, and nuclear sheriffs publish reports and intelligence, name and shame, hold international hearings, and threaten sanctions and military attacks. As more unstable countries from Egypt to Jordan to Pakistan expand their nuclear technology (or weapons) programs, the likelihood of nuclear theft and blackmail grows.

No issue blends such high tension with such low expectations. Many assert that America's approach to Iran and North Korea has been that of a reckless gorilla, but if anything it has been too narrow and cautious, focused on containment and isolation rather than on engagement and resolution. Each encounter between American and Iranian officials has been suffused with a significance rivaled only by an extraterrestrial encounter. Demanding that no negotiations would take place until Iran suspended its uranium enrichment program and allowed full inspections wasted three years during which enrichment accelerated. The so-called carrot-and-stick approach to Iran has been a self-serving euphemism for coercion, since the preconditions for negotiation are already too patronizing for the Iranians. As one Iranian scholar put it, "No more carrots and no more sticks—and please no more sticks in the shape of carrots either."

To confront the rogue nuclear trade and black market, the Proliferation Security Initiative (PSI) was launched in 2003 as a coalition of just eleven countries sharing intelligence on suspected transfers of nuclear material. Its signal success was the 2003 diversion of a ship bound for Libya carrying gas centrifuge parts, which led to the unraveling of the Pakistan-based A. Q. Khan nuclear network, which sold weapons technology to Iran, North Korea, and Libya. Now more than ninety countries participate in PSI—yet it has no secretariat. Its policing of nuclear trafficking is diffuse, difficult, and dangerous—and has no guarantee of success. Nor can PSI address Iranian motivations. An attack on any Iranian nuclear plants would paradoxically convince its people that they need nuclear weapons to defend themselves.

Preventing nuclear catastrophe—the most sensitive and high-stakes arena of diplomacy—very much requires a pairing of official and private approaches. The U.S. Nunn-Lugar program of the 1990s helped to locate and stockpile Russian fissile material, funded the conversion of defense industries into alternative businesses, and even retrained Soviet nuclear scientists. Today such technical assistance is needed in numerous other countries to tighten control over the globalized networks through which nuclear and other weapons materials and know-how spread. Companies and NGOs play crucial roles in making this happen. The Nuclear Threat Initiative (NTI), now overseen by Sam Nunn, the former U.S. senator from Georgia who undertook cooperative threat reduction in the early 1990s, is funded by Ted Turner and other concerned global philanthropists. It funds programs to boost nuclear security across eastern Europe and the Caucasus. The newly created World Institute for Nuclear Security, funded by NTI and the U.S. and Norwegian governments, is attempting to change the culture of the nuclear industry to focus on theft prevention. It encourages hundreds of companies to deepen partnerships with former Soviet chemical, biological, and nuclear weapons scientists to work on peaceful technologies.

Not sanctions and invasions, but more such mega-diplomacy can tip the scales in today's counter-proliferation race. The only way to stop Iran and North Korea from deepening their nuclear programs will be to convince their regimes that they don't need them—a strategy that has already proven successful with Brazil, Ukraine, Kazakhstan, and Libya. Iran's domestic upheaval of 2009 demonstrated how much its overwhelmingly young population seeks more open relations with the West. Iran should be flooded with contacts through commerce, media, and diplomatic channels that would force greater transparency on all its activities. Similarly, for North Korea, the only tenable solution is security guarantees from the United States (not to invade) and China (to protect North Korea), and economic incentives, which together might persuade the regime to allow inspectors to monitor weapons. In each case, it's not about the end state, which is unknown, but the next step, which could hardly take us farther back than where we have been. The path to making Iran and North Korea feel less secure is containment and deterrence, while the path to real regional security is engagement, investment, and exchange. The former is done with armies; the latter is done with companies. Both are essential in their own way, but neither will ultimately succeed without the other.

Chapter Seven

Getting Rights Right

Accountability is the DNA of civilized societies.

—Simon Zadek, founder, AccountAbility

The United Nations' Universal Declaration of Human Rights, adopted in 1948, was one of the earliest documents to embody the existence of an international community of values. The fact that it has almost no relevance in today's world, therefore, could be a good thing only if all of its tenets had been achieved. But that's not the world we live in. On paper, everyone in the world today has rights: citizens, taxpayers, corporations, immigrants, consumers, children, the elderly, disabled people, and refugees. Yet the contradiction between the notion of universal human rights and the reality of human wrongs has never been greater. Over the past three years, the number of countries that the NGO Freedom House has assessed to be, at best, "partly free" has risen to more than one hundred, while only ninety countries are fully "free." Another blunt reality is that in our neo-medieval world, neither America nor the United Nations has the moral authority to lead a new crusade for global rights.

The success of societies today is measured materially first, then justified ideologically. It seems most people in the world no longer care whether their system of government is a democracy or goes by

*some other label so long as it gets things done. The strong perfor-
mance of many non-democracies, such as China, Vietnam, and the
Persian Gulf states, has delivered a powerful wake-up call that good
governance can come in many forms. Similarly, there is also no single
rule book on how to promote justice across borders: The most effective strategies are now led by technology companies and street-smart
NGOs, both of which penetrate societies more deeply than government programs. But they all have their work cut out for them because, paradoxically, the wealthier many places become, the more
opportunities for corruption there will be. The fight for accountability requires mega-diplomacy from top to bottom.*

Democracy Über Alles?

There is no more tangible symbol of individual freedom today than
having your own mobile phone. In just a few years most of the
world's population will have one, each person feeling a unique sense
of empowerment. That's what makes Mo Ibrahim, Africa's first self-
made billionaire, so important. His business is telecommunications.
By spreading mobile phones around Africa faster than anyone else,
Ibrahim didn't intend to make a political statement. But recently, he
launched an annual $5 million prize for any African leader who per-
forms well on his "Ibrahim Index," whose benchmarks include providing safety, transparent government, and sustainable employment
to its people. Such is the state of African governance that in 2009 he
gave no prize at all. Still, most interesting about Ibrahim's metrics is
what is left off: democracy.

Winston Churchill famously claimed that democracy is the worst
form of government except for all the alternatives. Was he wrong?
Democracy is one of the most liberating burdens people can ask for.
It can mean freedom from oppression but also requires more trust
and self-reliance than some societies can muster. Progress is often
slow and tenuous, and rarely linear. Instead, democracy moves in forward and backward leaps and plateaus—Lebanon, Indonesia, and
Venezuela are just a few examples of haphazard democracies. Parlia-

mentary fistfights are an entertaining feature of democratic politics from Turkey to Taiwan to South Korea.

The democratic process can waste years emphasizing style over substance. Thailand has had six prime ministers and a coup in just three years. Even five years after pro-democracy revolutions in Ukraine and Georgia, genuine democracy takes a backseat to perpetual elite conflict. In Pakistan, the parliament is largely a mask for feudal interests. In Lebanon and India, democratic elections have devolved into auctions: Delivering security and welfare aren't just campaign promises, they are the campaign. And in Iraq, democracy is still a sectarian weapon of the majority against minorities. No system, democracy or autocracy, has a monopoly on quality control.

Is it worth promoting democracy in a world where so many democracies give the word a bad name, and where every society wants to run itself its own way? Between Islamist movements and authoritarian capitalists, democratization has slowed drastically since the mid-1990s, when a dozen ex-Soviet republics and satellites began their transitions toward membership in the European democratic club. Today's world features competing political and economic models, and the attractiveness of one over another is judged by the ability to provide material benefits for the people—not on how democratic it is.

When economies falter, democracy suffers, but when economies bloom, authoritarianism often does as well. Democracy requires capitalism to succeed, but capitalism doesn't require democracy. Emerging powerhouses such as Brazil under Lula help make the case that democracy—not just strongmen like Pinochet—can be fertile terrain for robust economic growth. But Russia and China are only the most prominent examples of a new state-capitalist alternative of open authoritarianism mixing economic and social liberalism with political centralization. They have deliberation but not democracy. If democracy is an end state and non-democracies would learn the virtues of democracy when they falter, then why do Russia's twenty-one-year-olds still strongly support the Putin-Medvedev team over the democratic "chaos" of the 1990s? Even if they turn revolutionary, it won't be because of outside inspiration but internal failure.

Iran's 2009 election demonstrates that more often than not, it is internal competition, not external meddling, that gets people excited about democracy. With four contenders for president, provocative TV debates, and the subsequent mass protests that brought hundreds of thousands into the streets to demand their votes be honestly counted, the revolution unfolding in Iran has been a homegrown enterprise. Most Iranians want to see direct democracy, even for the position of supreme leader—but they want it on their terms.

Democracy promotion is no longer a serious priority of American foreign policy. Neither China nor Russia, and not even strategic allies such as Saudi Arabia and Egypt, face real pressure from America to democratize, and the more the United States competes with China for influence in Africa and Eurasia, the less leverage it will have over others' internal politics. If democracy promotion were truly the centerpiece of foreign policy, then countries would receive support commensurate with measurable progress toward free elections, free media, impartial courts, women's rights, and market reforms. But mostly it is regional allies with questionable records, such as Yemen, Kenya, and Georgia, that are rewarded for such moves. Not surprisingly, then, Saudi activist Wajeha al-Huwaider now calls on American car companies as much as the American government to lobby for women's rights in her country— to sell women cars and liberate them in the process.

What is worth having is universal first and American second. If supporting democracy is to mean anything, then it has to transcend strategic interests and unintended consequences. Even if electoral winners are Shiite nationalists, Hamas, the Muslim Brotherhood, or Hezbollah, establishing a democratic ecosystem should be more important than who the winner is. The West must increasingly respect the political autonomy of nations to pursue progress however they choose.

Rather than judge a country's level of democracy, it is much more rewarding to observe its experiments with accountability. China, Singapore, and Arab monarchies aren't democratic in the Western sense, but they strive to be more responsive to their people through village councils and consultative forums that gauge the needs of their citizens in real time. Vietnam is evolving toward greater transparency, less corruption, and more economic freedoms—it is building the rule of law, not democracy. Malaysia's prime minister Abdullah Ahmad Badawi resigned in 2009 due to his unpopularity and perceived ineffectiveness, further showing how accountability doesn't require total democracy. In Dubai, Sheikh Mohammed used Facebook to ask citizens whether they wanted the start of the school year to be shifted to after Ramadan. (They did.) In Argentina, democracy hasn't changed the fact that tax evasion is a national pastime that weakens the state, but a reality show depicting tax collectors busting and shaming rich elites has brought greater transparency to politics. With decent leadership, the suggestion box can be as important as the ballot box.

For this reason, the notion of "good governance" is rapidly supplanting democracy as a global mantra. Leaders worldwide face growing pressure to provide economic freedoms, efficient services, and political transparency—but not necessarily democracy. In fact, good governance implies protecting and delivering on rights more than democracy alone does. China's Communist Party has a massively superior capacity to care for its citizens than India's Congress Party, but technology has enabled more than two million Indians to file electronic claims for rights to public information. In the Obama administration, the same bureaus and offices that used to issue rhetorical démarches about democracy are now focused on supporting enterprise funds that create jobs, establish public-private micro-credit programs through local banks, and use social networking technology to train journalists and encourage youth activism. This is the language of good governance and a better pathway to build democracy.

Human-Rights.com

Mo Ibrahim isn't the only cellular billionaire facing down dictators. Swashbuckling Irishman Denis O'Brien made his fortune selling cell phones to more than seven million people in the most corrupt countries, including Haiti and Papua New Guinea. His company, Digicel, sometimes cuts corners and plays dirty, building cell towers before receiving business licenses and heavily subsidizing phones to lure customers from state-run companies, but he embodies the mix of shrewd businessman and humanitarian that has inspired imitators as well as television shows such as *The Philanthropist*.[1] O'Brien didn't set out to meddle in third world politics, but he realized that making access to information a reality rather than a promise requires a pugnacious attitude. Our level of connectivity, not how much money we have or where we live, is becoming the most salient factor in determining the quality of citizenship. Cell phones improve information flow and transparency and are a vital business tool—but many governments can't be counted on to distribute them for precisely those reasons. This new human rights diplomacy could be the arena where dot-com really takes on dot-gov.

Mobile phones and the Internet are closing the gap between activism and uprising. In Xiamen, China, citizen groups armed only with cell phones and text messaging forced the local government and businesses to suspend construction of a harmful petrochemical plant. YouTube videos of Russian cops lamenting the obscene levels of internal corruption have embarrassed the Kremlin into cleaning up the police force. In Indonesia, tribal representatives were given GPS devices to stake out and mark their territory so that they could value it better when confronting mining giant Freeport-McMoRan. Twitter was essential to the coordination of Iran's anti-government protests in 2009, and was so vital for diplomats eyeing the situation that the U.S. State Department urged the firm to remain open despite its scheduled maintenance shutdown. In Nigeria and Egypt, students and human rights activists have been freed from incarceration because they managed to Twitter "arrested" before being dragged out the door by police, prompting colleagues and lawyers to spring into action to win their immediate release, denying governments their usual several-day period to have their way with agitators before concern is raised. A Facebook group in Colombia called "One Million Voices Against FARC" was able to rally more than twelve million people worldwide to march against the narco-terrorist group, leading to mass desertions from its ranks within days. If you have a mobile phone and can tweet, you can reach out and touch someone.

The usual suspect regimes are fighting back. During Iran's 2009 uprising, the clerical oligarchy widely blocked Internet access and began checking the Facebook accounts of Iranian diaspora members on arrival at the airport to make sure they weren't supporting the opposition. But technology finds a way. Across the Middle East, business and satellite television are perhaps greater threats to the stability of despots than radical Islamists.

Corporations and their software are now central to human rights diplomacy. Google, Yahoo!, and Microsoft were caught off guard when the Chinese government strong-armed them into providing user data to prosecute pro-democracy bloggers. Google regrouped and openly defied the Chinese government in 2010, declaring it would operate without stricture or pull out entirely. But Yahoo!'s Jerry Yang is still right that even partially censored access to China can do more for human rights than years of Western political pressure. When the United States sanctioned Syria, a move that included prohibiting its citizens from downloading Microsoft products, Syria's government responded by deleting its nationals' Facebook accounts—ordinary Syrians suffered a double whammy. By contrast, clever engagement can change policy even in China, the world's fastest-growing online market. For example, when China demanded that foreign PCs come preinstalled with software that would allow censors to block selected sites, the public outcry shamed the government to scale back its request, instead asking only to make the software optional. What if China tried to force ICANN to deregister certain domain names it had trouble blocking, and ICANN instead threatened to delist official Chinese servers? Eventually, the Chinese authorities may respect and even follow Google's unofficial motto: "Don't Be Evil."

Human-Rights.org

If global justice has a voice, its name is, appropriately, Avaaz, the word in many Asian languages for "voice." Avaaz is one of the largest online communities with more than three million members. Spearheaded by a lean team of social networkers, it has no use for national chapters, dividing its operations not by geography but by language—

currently thirteen of them (to the United Nations' six). Through viral petitions, Avaaz recruits thousands of signatories a day to lobby Western democracies to act on climate change and Darfur, and oppose the pope's stance on condoms. Through e-focus groups of thousands of people, it tests its campaigns in order to "keep pace with the pulse of the global demos," in the word of Avaaz founder Ricken Patel.

Avaaz gives a voice to the voiceless. If we actually want to empower human rights—and human will—Avaaz's linking of local grievances to global resources is the only way to go. The company's techo-activism not only provides real-time information to millions of people without waiting for media reporting or government statements, but it also gets the media and governments to focus on issues sooner than they otherwise might (if ever). It has unfurled giant banners above the disappearing Great Barrier Reef to cajole Australia's government into accepting binding reductions in greenhouse gas emissions and has taken out advertisements in Chinese media to signal the need for a shift in the party's hands-off policy toward the Darfur genocide. It's never quite clear what Western governments' Myanmar policy is—or if they even have one—but Avaaz pressured the Singaporean foreign ministry to close the Myanmar junta's bank accounts during its crackdown on monks in 2007, and within ten days of the devastating Cyclone Nargis in 2008, Avaaz delivered $2 million (from twenty-five thousand of its members) directly to the monks' relief effort.

Human rights are one arena in particular that must be contested from the bottom up, not the top down. The very notion of the United Nations as a central vehicle for promoting human rights is paradoxical: Because the United Nations is premised on national sovereignty, it avoids controversial cases such as Tibet. Almost all countries sign official UN human rights treaties, knowing that more attention is paid to whether they sign than whether they implement. Meanwhile, Amnesty International not only thrives on challenging government transgressions, but can even have more leverage than the United Nations within some countries. Given how reluctant authoritarian regimes are to listen to other governments, it is at least as likely that agile NGOs can slip under the radar in Belarus, Uzbekistan, and Myanmar as it is that intergovernmental diplomacy will put real pressure on such regimes. So the European Union and other governmental bodies increasingly fund NGOs that lobby to end the death penalty and curb torture, rehabilitate child soldiers, and advocate prisoner rights. These relationships between progressive governments and risk-taking NGOs are the key axis for improving human rights today, not the UN Human Rights Council.

"Torture is entirely man-made—it can be ended in the twenty-first century," declares Karen Tse, founder of the fledgling nonprofit organization International Bridges of Justice (IBJ). That would be a tall order given that there are more slaves in the world today than perhaps in any time in history, and torture is still the way of life and death for countless prisoners around the world. Democratic India allegedly has one of the highest custodial death rates in the world. In Cambodia, policemen even run brothels. Official human rights bodies launch fact-finding missions and prosecute Khmer Rouge henchmen from the country's brutal 1970s, but do little to shut down the torture chambers of today. Tse is adamant about the way forward: "You can't protect human rights through reports. The past six decades have been about declarations; the time is now for action."

So how do we actually create human rights, one victim at a time? Cambodia has had laws on the books since 1992 that allow for every citizen's right to a lawyer, but today few prisoners ever see lawyers, and if they do, it's only after police have beaten confessions out of them. "Most torture happens during ordinary criminal investigations. Compared to this, political torture is relatively insignificant," Tse explains. "For most of the rest it's just about lacking the resources to defend oneself." If public defenders don't get access to prisoners early, they will simply be considered "scum" who are "guilty by virtue of how long they've been locked up, no matter how arbitrary the arrest." Effective defense requires rapid response, so IBJ trains public defenders in as large a class size as possible, even in public squares in Cambodian villages, giving them the confidence to confront both police and prison officials. It publishes manuals (in local working languages) on how to uphold criminal law while respecting citizen rights—which are often more useful than the laws themselves. "The law can't be locked up in the president's drawer: It has to be in the hands of the judges or lawyers who are dealing with dozens of cases a day."

IBJ's toughest test has been China, whose official response to the U.S. State Department's 2009 report criticizing the country's human rights record was "Mind your own business." But here's what they told Tse: "If you're willing to work with us and not against us, then you're welcome here." China has proven more responsive to quiet dialogue and constructive, incremental recommendations than public shaming. Tse thus couches her work not as a moral crusade, but as an administrative upgrade, such as implementing habeas corpus rights so that the government at least publicly acknowledges when people are detained and informs their relatives. For this project she found the most credible and effective local partner on the inside—the Communist Youth League—which barged into police stations nationwide and demanded to hang up posters listing the rights of the accused (including the right not to be tortured and the right to counsel). As in Cambodia, the task was not to convene international workshops to draft a new code, but rather to make the existing one visible.

NGOs don't just promote human rights through dialogue with governments. Their shame campaigns can also turn sneaky companies into labor champions in short order. After Nike's shoe-making sweatshops in Indonesia were exposed, it quickly raised wages and implemented worker-training programs there. The same has happened with Monsanto after it was accused of covering up dioxin contamination in its products, leading the company to invest in genetically modified crop varieties that require no pesticides. To impact corporate behavior you have to work as fast as companies do. The Business and Human Rights Resource Center tracks the human rights impact of more than thirty-six hundred companies in 180-plus countries, updating its website every hour. Such real-time transparency can deter companies from making decisions that harm workers and the environment. When reputations and bottom lines are at stake, companies respond and change—and do so far more quickly than governments.

Human rights are adopted by example, not design. Even though naming and shaming is its modus operandi, Human Rights Watch (HRW) has made as much progress in recent years with difficult regimes as any Western government—while also proving how the two efforts can complement each other. When states such as Jordan and Libya want to get closer to the West, they need the public validation that comes from giving access and demonstrating progress to HRW. Companies now turn to HRW for guidance on how to manage the reputation fallout associated with doing business in countries with labor rights and torture issues—the United Arab Emirates, for example. HRW usually tells them to stay in-country rather than withdraw, but to improve conditions for their employees, including ensuring higher wages. This way, it is companies, not countries, that set the standards that others eventually follow.

The End of Corruption?

In a memorable scene from the Hollywood thriller *Syriana,* an American oil executive is outraged at being indicted for paying for the private school tuition for the son of a Kazakh government official in exchange for a lucrative energy contract. Flailing his arms and stomping his feet, he whines incredulously, "Corruption is what keeps us warm at night! Corruption is how we win!" It's easy to point to several high-profile cases of mega-corporations handing over briefcases of cash to government officials and declare all companies corrupt, but corruption is a two-way street. Corruption is as much a fact of life as birth and death, and almost requires no definition: You know it when you see it. In countries from Nigeria to India, the more ministers there are, the more corruption there is. The U.S. Foreign Corrupt Practices Act of 1977 has diminished American firms' ability to bribe foreign leaders, but it hardly stops anyone else. In a world desperately driven by profit at all costs, can shame curb this most universal social disease?

Enter Peter Eigen, a German lawyer with the audacity to take money from the world's governments and multinational corporations and then shame them for their misdeeds. After twenty-five years running World Bank programs in Latin America and Africa, Eigen in 1993 founded Transparency International (TI), a Berlin-based NGO perpetually collecting data from media outlets, businesses, governments, and civic groups that are compiled into its highly visible Corruption Perceptions Index report, the gold standard in the naming and shaming of countries. TI today remains so unimpeachable in its own credibility that it also bestows an annual Integrity Award, which in 2008 went to *Guardian* journalist David Leigh for uncovering British Aerospace Systems' murky weapons deal with Saudi Arabia— an issue Tony Blair would have preferred to sweep under the rug.

Eigen's formative experiences with the World Bank taught him that discussing corruption as an external official has little impact. Rather, TI needed to work from the bottom up to support local anti-corruption groups and accredit them as its national chapters. TI has also established websites for whistle-blowers from Nigeria to Cambodia to confidentially feed information. Such high-quality real-time data becomes an important signal to investors as well: When a country's ranking falls, it has to explain itself to those who hold the purse strings. Upon becoming the country's ethics and governance investigator, John Githongo, the head of Kenya's TI chapter, uncovered one of Africa's greatest looting schemes by Kenyan ministers. He then fled into exile in London to expose the charade—all while Kenya was earning top marks from bilateral donors and the United Nations.

Nothing holds a country back like audacious and endemic corruption, which eviscerates all efforts to provide public welfare. *Anti*-corruption efforts like those of TI are therefore a vital public service. But TI no longer works alone. Under its umbrella, companies such as mobile phone supplier Alcatel have preached reduced corruption from South Africa to Russia as a way to save money and gain a more predictable business environment. After being exposed for paying more than $1 billion in bribes in ten countries to gain preferential contracts, the engineering conglomerate Siemens agreed to spend $100 million on such anti-corruption training and education programs in emerging markets.

The opportunities for corruption only grow—not recede—as

many countries climb the development ladder and democratize. In Indonesia, local and provincial authorities have gained more and more autonomy from the central government, and everyone wants a piece of the action on oil and gas or mining deals. Indonesia's government can't force Sumatran politicians to abide by global standards of transparency and fair play—not that it would, anyway. Instead, one has to go inside the companies making investments to coach them in how not to cut corners.

This is what AccountAbility does. A British nonprofit founded in 1996, AccountAbility digs deep into its clients' culture to embed sustainable practices in a manner invulnerable to market whims and local conditions. Its experts go on-site with leaders and staff, mentoring from top to bottom, pushing tangible change from *within*. By working with the leadership of some of the largest companies, including Nike and Nissan, it kicks off a process of strategic sustainability that ripples through massive supply chains.

But AccountAbility is more than a corporate watchdog. Its Global Accountability Report evaluates UN agencies, development banks, and NGOs as well—all of whom have plenty of room to improve on measures such as whether their members control their budgets and how consultative they are with other stakeholders. Democracy cannot solve these problems, but collaborative governance can. This means leveraging private investment to build transport infrastructure and make water management more efficient, but in the context of partnerships in which business and government recognize mutual obligations and monitor each other.

Make no mistake: Corruption was not a big diplomatic issue between governments and companies before Transparency International and AccountAbility came along. It was TI that lobbied actively for the Organization for Economic Cooperation and Development Anti-Bribery Convention and the UN Convention Against Corruption—and to close loopholes in both. Now transparency has become a buzzword at both the IMF and the World Bank, and the U.S. Millennium Challenge Account uses TI criteria in determining which countries will receive American aid. Corruption is now on the diplomatic agenda, and diplomacy will be more effective as a result.

Part Three

A WORLD OF NEED

Chapter Eight

By Any Means Necessary

Poor countries are often rich in two things—people and natural resources—but most don't manage either of them well. To succeed, nations and their people must do something: Find a niche in the global marketplace. We have no global playbook to get countries on the path to success, but success has an essential ingredient: Doing one thing well. Right now there are quite a few countries with the potential to leap into the global economy. But rather than pretending to be disciplined enough to copy China, most of them would do better to look closer to home for the next best model they can actually emulate. In countries as diverse as the Persian Gulf states, Mauritius, Malaysia, and Vietnam, top-level public and private coordination, with both foreign and domestic investors and businesses, has proven to be the way to put people to work efficiently and extract resources profitably. For poorer countries, India's eclectic and experimental approach, which combines hybrid business-government commissions and philanthropic industrialists, is becoming a model of and for our anything-goes neo-medieval world.

Even across Africa, multinational corporations and China are raising the stakes, turning the continent from the final frontier to the hottest frontier market. Hundreds of millions of people in Africa could live better if China's hunger for natural resources could be mar-

ried with the West's concerns for good governance. What about countries that can't get even the basics right, squandering the one precious resource they may have? The world can no longer afford for them and their resources to go to waste—mega-diplomacy can make them run their countries right.

Nothing Succeeds Like Success

China is the world's factory floor, India its back office, Russia its gas station, and Brazil its farm. These are the "BRICs": Brazil, Russia, India, and China. You've been told already that if you're not invested there, you're missing the future. And yet they didn't get to this vaunted position by following Western prescriptions; they did just one thing well and have expanded from there. Brazil is now an industrial and energy power also; Russia is growing its agricultural production; India has become a major player in steel, manufacturing, and biotechnology; and China has moved up the value chain to semiconductors and satellites. The growing spending power of BRIC middle classes has Western retail brands scrambling, while the success of BRIC companies has blurred the traditional boundaries between North and South and realigned global economic relations faster than any multilateral negotiation. They are now part of every conversation about how to run the world.

Since Goldman Sachs first coined the term "BRIC," corporate labels have captured investors' imagination, reminding us that credit-rating agencies often have more influence over a country's prospects than the World Bank does. Indonesia, Egypt, and other countries now clamor to earn such labels that increase their visibility and attractiveness to investors from the United States, Saudi Arabia, and China. Malaysia's leadership explicitly brands its country "Malaysia Incorporated" to emphasize its fusion of public and private credentials. It takes its lesson from neighboring Singapore, the most respected government in the world—not least because it is modeled on and run like a company. In effect, it is not just companies, but also countries, that are represented on stock exchanges. Financial newspapers worldwide often refer to "Brand India" as if it is synonymous with the real thing.

Without capitalizing on a niche and growing from there, many economies will forever lie in the purgatory of underdevelopment. There is no one strategy for capitalizing on raw materials under the ground, the manpower of citizens, and the knowledge they possess. There are, however, certain common elements.* Successful countries manage to balance foreign and domestic priorities: giving access to multinationals while also catering to local businesses that want protection from outside competition so they can develop into a robust industrial base for the country. Often it just requires the confidence to invest in oneself. Brazil now issues local currency bonds—which have paid out handsomely in recent years—and provides a long-term capital lifeline to diminish the impact of financial crises.

Over the past decade, a string of Persian Gulf statelets and emirates has risen up to collectively function as a crossroads between Europe, Asia, and Africa. Surging ahead in sectors such as oil and gas exports, trans-shipment of goods, tourism, and Islamic finance, each is a model of public-private cooperation, both internal and external. Almost forty million passengers passed through the Dubai airport in 2008 (compared with sixty million at London's Heathrow), and it received seven million tourists in the same year (more than all of India). Hundreds of companies have their regional headquarters in the city's International Financial Center and Knowledge Village. In Qatar, Exxon is building the world's largest natural gas liquefaction terminals—boosting that country's exports and Exxon's profits. At the same time, it has become the hub for a growing number of Western universities that have established outposts in the Middle East. In Saudi Arabia, it was the national oil company Aramco, not the education ministry,

*According to the Legatum Prosperity Index, smart countries promote government efficiency, make starting businesses quick and cheap, expand education at all levels, invest in innovation, steadily open their economies, improve public health, and guarantee political and social rights. Australia, Austria, Finland, Germany, and Singapore are at the top of the list, while the Central African Republic, Mali, Zambia, and Yemen round out the bottom.

that partnered with foreign universities to build the King Abdullah University of Science and Technology, bringing global educational standards into the sheltered kingdom. The common denominator in the success of these Gulf statelets is that old and ossified bureaucracies have been bypassed by new parallel public-private authorities singularly focused on getting the job done.

The sensational allure of Gulf sheikhdoms, built on the back of third world Asian labor, has also perversely made their medieval stratification and hierarchy among citizens and foreigners acceptable to the world. Whether Riyadh, Doha, Abu Dhabi, Manama, Dubai—or any combination of them—becomes the economic engine of the Arab world, their success has inspired imitators to recognize the virtues of free trade, foreign investment, and lean bureaucracy. Special economic zones are popping up from North Africa to Southeast Asia, promoting their ironclad public-private synergy. The rival ports of Chabahar in Iran and Gwadar in Pakistan jockey to be called the "gateway to central Asia," while Tangier and Tunis contend to be North Africa's primary port of passage to Europe. Countries that want to catch up might have to set aside new physical spaces for high-productivity "charter cities" to be built from scratch, combining foreign capital and domestic labor. All of these experiments only reinforce our postmodern medievalism.

But most countries on the lower rungs of the global economy won't become the next Dubai anytime soon. What they should instead aspire to be is the *next best thing*. What is the most attainable or proximate model for them to emulate in the coming five to ten years? For largely mismanaged and teetering states such as Egypt and Syria, that means aiming for Tunisia, not Qatar. Tunisia has consistently been ranked one of the most competitive economies across Africa and the Mideast due to its solid infrastructure, comprehensive educational system, and transparent decision making. Numerous Arab countries could do far worse than to focus on these first steps, which might also earn them more breathing space on the authoritarian nature of their regimes (as Tunisia has done). Similarly, impoverished Tajikistan can at best over the next few years focus on copying Kyrgyzstan and Nepal, places where tour operators ferry in and out thousands of tourists seeking bracing mountain scenery. There is no Thomas Jefferson in Africa, but at least President Paul Kagame of Rwanda, who rigs elections and marginalizes opposition, also builds roads and boosts education. Afghanistan's best-case scenario is none other than Mongolia: poor and landlocked, but stable and profiting from taxing mineral exploitation. Countries can learn from those who have done it right and reached the next stage.

China has become the iconic example of a large, third world nation rapidly ascending the global economic and political ladder. Deng Xiaoping's policies—farmer subsidies, opening the economy to foreign markets, and limiting families to one child—combined to achieve the fastest decrease in poverty in history. China has also constructed about sixty-two thousand miles of highway per year, creating access to expressways for almost all its midsize and larger cities. Property rights are also increasingly widespread, allowing farmers to borrow against collateral, and China plans to have a medical clinic in every village by 2012. All of this may have the ring of a master plan, but the government explanation translates as "feeling the stones while crossing the river." Victor Chu, a prominent Hong Kong businessman, sums it up more bluntly: "Innovate or die. Do whatever works."[1]

But the China model is far more often discussed than successfully imitated. No other large country has anything like the capacity for sustained mass mobilization or the relatively unified vision of China. Instead, even the best parts of the developing world more often resemble the haphazard but frenetically high-energy India. Cities taking part in India's economic miracle—such as the Delhi suburb of Gurgaon—are a study in contrasts. Architecture of steel and glass is almost always juxtaposed with heaps of poverty and disavowed destitution.[2] India, South Africa, Nigeria, and other self-promoters tout their pulsing economic hubs but also have multiplying masses left behind by the elites who have bought their way to statelessness. India still ranks near the very bottom of the development ladder, has the world's highest number of child laborers and indentured servants, and is rife with caste and religious divides. Its democracy appears to be thriving, yet it suffers from a nearly total absence of governance. Its government is a gerontocracy in which incumbents win due to

good harvests rather than good policy. India's political slogans—
"Food, clothing, shelter" in decades past and "Roads, electricity,
water" today—should really be combined, since all of them are still
lacking for hundreds of millions of Indians.

In other words, India is a far more realistic portrait of the challenges of the developing world than China. Rather than futile at-
tempts to copy China, most countries way down the development
ladder should look to India's many idiosyncrasies as a useful collage
of possibilities for their own future. India spent two generations as an
aid and foundation super-project, but has since lifted perhaps three
hundred million people out of absolute poverty and gotten rid of
most foreign aid agencies. Its roaring information technology sector
supports several million citizens, while private investment has
boosted its manufacturing, textiles, auto-parts, pharmaceutical, defense, and telecom industries as well—all working to create gainful
employment for the world's second largest population. In one fundamental respect, India is the anti-China: It works best when the government gets out of the way.

India is a postmodern role model for the developing world because
all of its successes are attributable to a mix of entrepreneurial leadership and hybrid public-private governance. The Confederation of Indian Industry (CII), the country's premier chamber of commerce,
works in lockstep with the government to create a friendly business
environment for infrastructure investment. From tax policy to road
projects to career training, CII works with the Indian Planning Commission, and consults with relevant NGOs, on just about everything.
This multi-stakeholder consultation builds trust and encourages
openness amid competing agendas and cacophonous politics—and is
the real reason India is viewed as a country on the make today.

Public-private partnerships are the name of the game: Out with
the National Highways Authority, in with a new "Road Finance Corporation" that has boosted road construction from two kilometers
per day to twenty.

India's family-owned conglomerates are also role models for third
world industrialists. The Tata corporation all but owns the city of
Jamshedpur, which corporate founder Jamsetji Tata carved out of the

jungles outside Calcutta a century ago. It pays the health, education, and medical expenses for all employees of the town's steel factory. In Delhi, Tata Power helps the municipal government turn electricity thieves who tap into power lines into paying customers. Like Tata in Jamshedpur, Reliance Petroleum is building the world's largest oil refinery at Jamnagar in Gujarat, creating hundreds of thousands of jobs now and for decades hence. Big business doesn't have to put village entrepreneurs out of business. Bharti Enterprises makes sure not to destroy local retail operators when it enters a municipality, instead integrating them into larger supply chains that generate greater incomes, and ICICI Bank has bought large stakes in micro-finance bodies and funds local self-help groups. The development of the third world hinges on such elder corporate statesmen taking responsibility for their countries' bulging national populations. From community-level job creation to high policy, India's public-private and domestic-foreign governance represents the future of how most countries will be run.

Trading Up

In Voltaire's classic fable, Candide's most important lesson comes from a Turk who sends his fruit to be sold in Constantinople. "Work," the Turk says, "keeps us from three great evils: boredom, vice, and need." The people of the world need work on a scale so massive that all the governments in the world together cannot figure out how to do it—and they needed to yesterday. The World Bank estimates that 90 percent of the economic growth in the developing world is attributable to jobs created by small- and medium-sized enterprises in textiles, agriculture, steel manufacturing, tourism, and other labor-intensive, low-skilled areas. Almost none of these companies are listed on a stock exchange anywhere, yet they represent much of what most people in the world do every day. The construction sector alone generates the most jobs of any in the world. The only way to build and maintain a better life is to work for it.

Contrary to popular belief, poor countries have grown as fast as rich ones from the spread of free trade and open investment. In wealthy Sweden, Arctic towns would live off hunting and handouts were it not for the IKEA outlets that attract two million visitors a year. For underdeveloped countries, trade and investment have had the greatest impact on reducing poverty. NGOs that made headlines a decade ago for bashing globalization and trashing WTO summits have become vigorous champions of free trade. They've realized that a bigger problem than unfair trade is simply *not enough* trade. Indeed, global trade isn't really global. Ten countries alone account for 60 percent of the world's trade, while sixty countries make up 92 percent of it—so the remaining 130-plus other nations represent just 8 percent of global trade. While the WTO is perhaps permanently stalled, unable to force Europeans to reduce the two-dollar-per-day subsidy each of their cows receives (an amount greater than the daily income of seven hundred million Indians), targeted reductions in tariffs can help jump-start economies in need. The U.S. African Growth and Opportunity Act of 2000, for example, has boosted African exports to the United States multiple times over. Ghana has duty-free access to both Europe and America. Caribbean nations need the same deal.

But mandating free trade isn't enough; countries need to make things worth selling. That is why private investment remains the best and fastest hope for many countries. Mauritius is a shining example. The island nation was the first in Africa to abolish trade barriers, immediately attracting textile manufacturers from Hong Kong, but it also lowered restrictions for locals to start businesses so they could compete to become suppliers to foreign firms; it even expanded secondary education so that its workers would be worth higher wages. Eventually, local entrepreneurs acquired the know-how to get into the textile business themselves, and they lured Mauritian workers away from foreign-owned factories. By the late 1990s, indigenous investors owned more than half of the firms operating in the country's export-processing zones.

Yet even when local companies compete with the foreigners who have set up shop in their backyards, there are still benefits to be had. In Kenya, Tanzania, and Uganda, for example, foreign firms are more productive than local ones, but they have introduced valuable management skills to local markets, trained native workers, and invested in infrastructure. Most important, they have better access to global markets to stay afloat in good times and bad, providing consistent employment for local citizens.

To claim that foreign investment is bad for countries because it increases inequality is like saying no medicine is better than some. Globalization scholar Ulrich Beck said it best: "There is only one thing worse than being overrun by multinationals; that is *not* being overrun by multinationals." By changing the actual rules—or in some cases creating rules for the first time—of how economies are run, foreign companies create opportunities for countries to define their place in the global economy. Multinationals help countries deregulate stagnant financial sectors and even lobby heavily for debt relief as a way to earn goodwill with their supplier nations. International banks push for stable electricity supply in India, because without it their ATM machines would shut down and could be bashed open and robbed. Nepal's leadership is so incompetent that the Norwegian firm SN Power paid for lawyers to represent the government in negotiations for proposed hydropower projects that the country desperately needs.

Every country can have a niche in the global division of labor. In the Dominican Republic it's garments and footwear, Egypt is a leader in marble ceramics, and Kenya exports cut flowers. Vietnam has quickly become one of the largest exporters of both rice and coffee. Many experts fear that if economies are not diversified, they will become dependent on a single commodity or export, with all the exploitation and corruption that entails. But the sad fact is that many poor economies will never have the luxury of diversifying until they first get just one thing right, which usually means labor-intensive goods and services. If enough goes well, the poorest countries can become like Costa Rica, the Philippines, Malaysia, and Thailand, all of which not only export commodities such as coffee and rubber, but also manufacture a mix of auto parts, semiconductors, and circuit boards. It would be nice to see more African countries move up the value chain from raw materials to manufacturing, but they must get the former right first to prove themselves. Being part of the supply chain at all is an improvement for the poorest countries—even if they are the lowliest links.

It's pointless to talk about labor standards when people don't even have work. According to the International Labor Organization (ILO), our goal should not be just jobs, but also "decent work." How long could it take to achieve that? In ever-patient Chinese fashion, labor rights activist Han Dongfang argues that "respect for people's basic rights, limited work hours, decent compensation, better working conditions laws that are enforced—all these things will happen because it is natural that they do. That's just the process of civilization."[3] In the meantime, if the third world's unemployed are lucky they will be recycling tires and plastic bottles, dismantling laptops and keyboards, or picking apart discarded cell phones.

Penalizing countries for not complying with standards they can't yet reach makes no sense—but helping them implement such standards does. Rather than railing against poorly enforced labor standards, the NGO Ethical Trading Initiative works directly with the governments of Bangladesh and other countries. Social Accountability International (SAI), a multi-stakeholder nonprofit, has certified facilities in fifty-seven countries across seventy industries and funds itself through contracts with businesses looking for ways to improve labor conditions. SAI's certification and codes of conduct do far more for labor rights than empty appeals from the ILO.

Rather than "racing to the bottom"—always seeking the cheapest labor—more and more foreign companies are driving the "race to the top," spreading good management practices, training workers with new skills, and offering better salaries than what is offered domestically. Exporting good businesses is among the smartest diplomatic strategies the West can pursue to create tangible change worldwide. If we want to achieve "decent work" for the poor, then we must globalize the work. Because hundreds of thousands of small-scale enterprises in the world often go unscrutinized by labor activists, forging supply-chain connections between multinationals and local firms is the single greatest step to improving labor standards—and such joint ventures are also free of the odious colonial taint. A foreign-financed factory can contribute to income, women's rights, health care, and education all at once. As Leslie Chang describes in *Factory Girls,* the massive Yue Yuen factory in China employs seventy thousand workers and has its own kindergarten, hospital, and fire department; women earning a living there now play a stronger role in family financial decisions than they did before.

After China's successful hosting of the Olympic Games in 2008, foreign political leverage over the country on labor rights has dropped to virtually nil. But market pressure can be far stronger. Wal-Mart, whose $400 billion annual revenue dwarfs most countries' economies, currently employs more than two million people across seven thousand stores. The Chinese government doesn't enforce labor regulations tightly, but Wal-Mart can, with massive effects throughout its supply chain of more than fifty thousand factories. If Wal-Mart wants to support women's rights in Africa, all it has to do is open a store there and hire women. McDonald's already works with Chinese food producers, stores, and universities to devise and deploy a social compliance model into its operations that allows workers to individually voice concerns while requiring management to comply with high ethical codes at the factory level. Such practices have payoffs for a company's image, explaining why Wal-Mart, widely demonized in the United States, is welcome around the world.

Africa: The Final Frontier (for China)

Jonathan Auerbach doesn't throw rock concerts championing poor countries, but he's been to almost all of them, wherever in the world they may be. His purpose? To set up stock exchanges and find brokers to handle the billions of dollars in investment capital that an ever-growing number of American pension and mutual funds want to invest outside America. The firm of Auerbach Grayson makes their markets liquid, and the rest can take care of itself. It has built formal ties with stock exchanges in 128 countries, many of which have delivered impressive returns on index funds in recent years. Even when the worst news is coming out of countries—the Israel-Hezbollah war of 2006, the Kenyan riots of 2008, Israel's incursion into Palestinian

Gaza in 2008, and the Sri Lankan military campaign against the Tamil Tigers in 2009—Auerbach sees arrows pointing upward. "Even when they're bombing in Gaza, they're trading in Ramallah," he says. As conflicts in Iraq and Sri Lanka wind down, investors quickly move in. Indeed, Auerbach established relations with an Iraqi brokerage in 2009.

By providing access to capital where it is needed most, Auerbach is an agent of development for the connected age. In Zambia, where the U.S. Embassy mostly runs HIV/AIDS programs, Auerbach gets cash into the hands of farmers to help them upgrade to Caterpillar tractors. Because he shares commissions on investments fifty-fifty with local brokers, he provides a great incentive for them to act professionally. "In sixteen years in Africa I've never had a customer fail, a trade not fulfilled. They have the same Bloomberg terminals in Zambia and do the trades in real time like rich countries do." When the public sector alone ran the show in Africa, more capital fled out of Africa and into European banks than came into Africa in investment. Now, growth in Burundi and Tanzania has been greater than 7 percent for several years straight, savings rates are increasing, and cell phone and Internet usage have doubled every year. When Botswana's president Festus Mogae visits the United States, he courts private equity firms and hedge fund managers and reminds them that investments in Africa can return more than 300 percent, impossible anywhere else in the world. This is the Africa that is hungry for trade, not handouts.

Auerbach helps Africa brand itself as the final frontier of investment. In Kenya, he urged investors to take seriously the country's privatization of banks and extend credit. West African countries, which are rich in rubber, cocoa, palm oil, and coffee, are also good investments. The Ivory Coast's ports, run by the French Bolloré Group, can help boost West Africa's exports just as Dubai Ports World has for East African Djibouti. Zimbabwe's new investment laws have finally scrapped local ownership requirements in favor of joint ventures, and the agricultural sector desperately needs investment after Mugabe's land seizures. Someone has to move in, and Auerbach leads the charge. His investor conferences in South Africa are the financial equivalent of speed-dating: Portfolio managers from America and Europe sit for one hour each with CEOs from twenty African countries representing companies active in telecom, agriculture, consumer goods, micro-finance, and waste treatment; after an hour a bell sounds and they rotate.

Just as every company once rushed to create a "China strategy," then an "India strategy," today thousands of multinationals are demanding to know "What's our Africa strategy?" Despite the global economic slowdown, the circle of globalization has continued to grow, from the transatlantic economic expansion of the late Cold War era into the Far East and Latin America, to the rise of China, India, and the Persian Gulf over the past two decades—and now to Africa. Singaporean, Korean, and Indian investors are all over the continent, eager to replicate their own successes there.

China certainly is as well. In 2008, *The Economist* ran a cover story depicting a crew of diplomats and sentries riding camels across the African desert—with a giant Chinese flag waving in front. While G-8 countries' overall aid to Africa has diminished, China's has doubled in the past five years—as has China-Africa trade, which now reaches $100 billion per year. China bundles aid and investment in packages in ways Western donors abhor, but they have no say over China. The country has already hosted the largest summit ever of African leaders, with fifty-two showing up in Beijing in 2006. Unlike the World Bank, China imposes no environmental or human rights restrictions on investments, making it much more efficient to cut deals with China than negotiate strings-attached agreements in Washington.

If you didn't know that China has become Africa's top investor, alongside the United States and the European Union, you still wouldn't. There are no big CARE packages or sacks of grain painted with Chinese flags. Yet when one World Bank representative arrived in Guinea-Bissau in the early 1990s, he quickly found out that China was already there in a big way. It was Mao Tse-tung who initiated the current phase of outreach to Africa. The Chinese built Kinshasa's national assembly building in the 1970s and soccer stadiums in other countries through the 1990s. It has given $4 billion in aid and loans to Ethiopia, and established itself strongly in Addis Ababa to build relations with the AU diplomats based there—not least by building the new headquarters for the African Union itself.

Diplomats on both sides like to say "What's good for China is good for Africa." But is the reverse also true? It's not hard to decipher China's motivations, given that 85 percent of Africa's exports to China come from just five energy- and mineral-rich countries: Angola, Equatorial Guinea, Nigeria, Congo, and Sudan.[4] Western diplomats accuse China of bringing indebtedness and resource dependency back to Africa just when the West has finally offered debt relief and is encouraging political and economic transformation. China counters that Westerners only forgave debt in order to issue new loans, and is fearful of a new provider bringing competition to the continent. And, no less ironically than Western powers, China supports African peacekeeping efforts while selling weapons en masse to the continent's unprofessional and often rapacious armies. For Africa to benefit from China's presence, Africans will have to manage China better than they did the Europeans. China claims it is helping African nations find their niche: Zambia is China's "metals hub," Mauritius its "trade hub," and Dar es Salaam in Tanzania its "shipping hub." For better or worse, the cobalt and copper needed to manufacture everything from jet engines and cell phone batteries are found in anarchic African countries. Like European companies, Chinese corporations are willing to work through warlords to get tin ore, copper, cobalt, coltan, and zinc. Shutting down the mines—which is frequently attempted but always fails—doesn't do away with rebel armies and hurts workers who depend on them. Congo's mining minister denounces Chinese "exploitation," but if African leaders could take advantage of growing Chinese investment, they themselves could take over.

Rather than maligning China's presence in Africa, both Westerners and Africans should embrace the new competitive dynamic and make the most of it. Nigeria and Angola have explicitly devised oil-for-service barter agreements with China, awarding oil contracts to Chinese companies in exchange for infrastructure.[5] The giant road and rail projects China is building, as well as the free health clinics and doctors the country funds, are all opportunities for Africans to leverage new infrastructure and learn new skills. The Chinese may seem in control now—bringing in their own labor and refusing to teach the locals—but roads and railways can spark new jobs for Africans for decades to come, and competent African regimes can confidently ensure that they do.

This, too, is in China's long-term interest. Investors know that their assets won't be protected by states that don't exist. Negotiating with local warlords, criminal gangs, and protestors to secure facilities will be a permanently tenuous state of affairs unless China actually helps stabilize African states. In other words, China has become a part of African governance whether it wants to or not. That's why Hafsat Abiola of Nigeria has launched the China-Africa Bridge, an NGO that consults Chinese companies and diplomats on a case-by-case basis to boost the benefits of Chinese activity for Africans. If China doesn't get the message, there is still the power of shame. Thanks to the Internet and mass media, Africans are watching China with far greater scrutiny than they were ever able to monitor European colonizers. In Zambia, China is already so exposed that one party ran for parliament on the platform that it would recognize Taiwan. If China doesn't adapt, it could transition from being welcomed to resented faster than the amount of time it has taken for most of the world to even realize China was there. People are watching.

The list of countries where China, capital, and crude are coming together is growing—a trend that demonstrates how globalization can make implementing global norms harder, not easier. When Canadian-based Talisman Energy pulled out of Sudan, Chinese (and Malaysian) oil companies were happy to pick up the slack. If America and Europe want to stop China's cutting of exclusive, no-strings-attached trade deals across Africa, they will have to make their case in Africa, not Paris. One way would be to massively boost their investments in Africa, competing with but also setting a good example for China. Ironically, with newly built (often Chinese) infrastructure, there has rarely been a better time for African countries to pitch themselves as a manufacturing alternative to the increasingly expensive China. If Western donors and multilaterals can coach on environmental standards, while China continues investing in raw materials but hires more local labor under pressure from African governments, then the renewed great power interest in Africa can finally mean a race to the top, rather than to the bottom.

Reversing the Resource Curse

Were it not for De Beers, Botswana could very well have wound up like Sierra Leone. Like other postcolonial African states, Botswana is landlocked and suffered turbulent governance during its early independence years. But rather than engaging in a "blood diamond"–fueled civil war, Botswana's government auctioned off resource rights to get the best price for them, taxes corporate revenues rather than accepting personal bribes, and invests some of its profits in worthwhile national development projects. De Beers has been essential to Botswana's strategy of controlling diamond-export volumes to maintain a high price (which they split fifty-fifty with the government) and has also supported a domestic distribution plan for diamond wealth. Botswana president Festus Mogae now refers warmly to the "development diamonds" that account for 50 percent of the national budget and 70 percent of the country's exports. When you buy that diamond for your loved one, Botswana thanks you as well.

Sadly, Botswana is unique in Africa. Elsewhere, properly managing natural resources seems a hopeless task. Equatorial Guinea, one of the world's top oil producers, is often called "Africa's Kuwait," yet more than half the population lacks access to safe drinking water. Exxon pumps most of the country's oil, and the country's dictator siphons most of the profits for himself and his cronies. In Chad, Exxon attempted to make the largest single investment in Africa ever: $3.7 billion to develop an oil field and a six-hundred-mile pipeline to Kribi in Cameroon. The World Bank hoped to put a buffer between oil profits and the tin-pot regime of Idriss Déby by creating a panel of citizens who would steer the money toward health care, education, rural development, and a fund for future generations. What began as a model public-private partnership, however, quickly devolved into diplomatic disaster when Déby fabricated accusations that Exxon wasn't paying taxes so that he could threaten nationalization and cut a deal with a Chinese company that wouldn't scrutinize his spending: $30 million to buy weapons and a fleet of Maybach Mercedes.

Oil and mining companies want what's in the ground, not to interfere in what goes on above it, but over the past decades they have grudgingly become an integral part of the very governance of resource-rich African countries—corporate patrons are as vital a lifeline as superpowers were in the Cold War. But blaming oil companies for dictatorships is like blaming the future for the past. Many consider foreign investment in the extractive sector to be "bad FDI" (foreign direct investment) because it can skew economies and fuel civil wars. But there is no such thing as "bad FDI," only badly managed FDI. Keeping oil in the ground doesn't help Africa, especially since it presently accounts for 13 percent (and growing) of global oil output and represents a major energy exploration frontier.

Sir Mark Moody-Stuart is the best example of how African oil has turned corporate executives into CEO-statesmen. When he took over as Royal Dutch Shell's managing director in 1991, one of his main qualifications was a doctorate in geology, not political science. But in 1995, when Nigeria's maligned and disenfranchised Ogoni tribe of five hundred thousand in the Niger Delta region grew tired of protesting the military government's squandering of oil wealth, they turned their attention to Shell, which generated 15 percent of its global oil production in the country. Ken Saro-Wiwa, a noted Nigerian author, led peaceful mass protests with people chanting, "The flames of Shell are the flames of hell." Amnesty International, Greenpeace, and Friends of the Earth joined the Ogoni cause, but governments said nothing as the Nigerian military began a brutal crackdown. Even Nelson Mandela didn't intervene. After a 1993 coup that brought General Sani Abacha to power, Saro-Wiwa and eight other Ogoni were sentenced to death and hanged. Shell had already pulled its personnel out of the Delta, but its reputation was damned.

Today, Moody-Stuart has a new mantra: "If it is a problem for society, it is a problem for business." He made Royal Dutch Shell the first energy firm to combine its social and financial reports in one, believing that investors should see the full picture of the company's performance.

When Shell returned to Nigeria, it convinced the Nigerian government to spend more than 10 percent of its oil revenues on the communities in oil-producing regions. The Nigerian state of Akwa Ibom has been a prime beneficiary of this policy, its governor steering funds into job-creating infrastructure projects such as hotels, housing, and airports. But Nigeria isn't hovering around the bottom of Transparency International's corruption rankings for nothing—its kleptocrats work hard to maintain that dubious distinction. Since 1980, about $300 billion in donor aid—as well as half the country's oil revenues—have vanished, and rampant poverty and banditry mean that an estimated 10 percent of Nigeria's oil output is siphoned from pipelines and either locally consumed or sold on black markets each year. In 2009, Shell had to lend the cash-strapped Nigerian government $3 billion to help it sustain its commitment to oil-producing communities, beyond which Shell also funds schools—from buildings to textbooks and teacher training to adult literacy programs—and awards one thousand annual university scholarships. Since Nigeria remains Shell's second largest source of oil and gas after the United States, Shell needs Nigeria, and Nigeria needs Shell.

Many hope that Angola could serve as a better model for Africa's new energy powers. After three decades of civil war in which a half-million people were killed, the country's infrastructure destroyed, and the countryside littered with land mines, Angola is becoming the Nigeria of sub-Saharan Africa and even a potential export hub rival to South Africa. The country's unemployment rate still hovers at 50 percent, its infant mortality rate is still among the world's highest, and dreadful slums surrounding Soviet-like block apartments tell the story of Angola's ideological history. Yet today Luanda is considered Africa's Dubai: flashy cars, cranes and construction, and new bank branches opening daily as oil and diamond money seems to spill onto the streets, as it does in Baku on the Caspian Sea. China has won big infrastructure contracts and is a major oil buyer; Portuguese, Dutch, and Brazilian companies run flourishing financial and retail businesses; and agribusiness giants are negotiating to gain access to the country's fertile soil to produce coffee, bananas, and sugar. An estimated one hundred thousand Portuguese have moved to their former colony in the last five years for high-paying jobs. Gun buyback programs have collected more than one hundred thousand AK-47s, giving people some confidence that the country is getting safer.

Because so much rides on Angola's success, the government can't be left to its own devices. Instead, the country is becoming a vital test case for the Extractive Industries Transparency Initiative (EITI), which brings together NGOs, the World Bank, donors such as the United Kingdom's Department for International Development, and the government to make public and monitor the spending of resource revenues. EITI also brings in the expertise to coach governments in setting up futures funds (like Norway's or Kazakhstan's) and other vehicles that ensure that oil money isn't squandered the moment it comes in. Given the country's legacy of civil war, Chevron has partnered with USAID and the conflict-resolution group Search for Common Ground to work in oil-producing areas to satisfy community needs. It will take all of these efforts and more to ensure that Angola doesn't return to its own bloody past or Nigeria's present scenario of constantly kidnapped police and oil workers.

The conditions for a Magna Carta–style revolt of barons against the king aren't visible in most African states, but the people of Angola, Chad, and Nigeria shouldn't have to wait for the day their countries become democracies to enjoy the bounty under their soil. Where governments can't be trusted to represent their people, investors and donors can require multi-stakeholder committees to submit aid requests and budget proposals. If governments don't play along, the only solution might be to halt production or even pursue direct distribution schemes that challenge the government itself. When poor and corrupt countries can't govern their own resources well, companies will have to play a part in doing it for them.

That is certainly the case in the mining industry, where the next great finds of uranium and other minerals are in places such as the Andes Mountains and Siberia, regions so poorly governed—or simply ungoverned—that mining companies might make more reliable governors than governments. Indeed, in Bolivia, citizens are accustomed to lobbying multinational corporations for services their governments don't provide. But rather than return to the nineteenth-century mining town model, Newmont Mining and Barrick Gold locate their staff directly in mining communities to coach local mayors in fiscal management (since the average mayor in Peru has about a sixth-grade education). They also hire part-time workers to spread the wealth to more citizens, source drinking water locally, and train locals to operate the mines.

Not surprisingly, companies are often mistaken for governments— or at least are held responsible for what governments should do. To whom should the Kalahari turn when African governments threaten to cut off their water and send militias to intimidate them if they don't vacate their land? What about the Tuareg of northern Niger, who remain destitute while the army seizes the uranium supplies on their land? It is very often NGOs who fight to turn resource curse into resource cure. Taking advantage of legal instruments such as the U.S. Alien Tort Claims Act, the International Labor Rights Fund sued Unocal in the 1990s on behalf of impoverished Burmese villagers for abuses committed by the ruling junta during the construction of the $1.2 billion Yadana pipeline, where villagers were paid little or nothing, and shot if they moved too slowly.

While legal tactics have evoked reflex benevolence from companies, NGOs also actively lobby the same corporations to reshape their policies on the ground prior to getting sued. Rather than continuously publishing damning reports on blood diamonds, Global Witness decided to sit down with De Beers to forge what became known as the Kimberly Process for monitoring and certifying the origin of diamonds being sold worldwide. Now more than one hundred diamond companies, monitoring groups, and regional organizations are involved. The worldwide governance of natural-resource wealth is now emerging through such public-private networks.

Naming and shaming can stop bad practices, but nothing works better to promote good ones than globalization. Ninety percent of the world's private sector is made up of small- and medium-sized enterprises and state-owned firms that lack sophisticated management and are rarely subject to scrutiny—and have the worst track records of inefficiency and pollution. The UN's Global Compact—which has eleven companies and six NGOs on its board—reaches this deeper, thicker layer of business worldwide by setting up national business chapters and workshops to promote sustainable supply chains the way Transparency International does for corruption. Long before most governments figure out how to regulate multinational corporations, multi-stakeholder programs such as the Global Compact are improving the state of their nations for them.

The man tasked with bringing corporate ambitions and global ethics into harmony is John Ruggie, the UN's special representative on business and human rights. A mild-mannered Canadian, Ruggie takes a psychological approach to explaining the corporate citizenship life cycle: "First, they ignore the problem. Then they deny it. Eventually they pretend they're doing something about it, and finally they comply. Ultimately, they do get there." Shuttling between Harvard's John F. Kennedy School of Government and the United Nations, Ruggie has become a middleman among dot-gov, dot-com, and dot-org, hearing NGO demands for corporate accountability, developing countries' pleas for fairer deals, and heeding companies' warnings to respect the narrow limits of international law. It's one of the most delicate assignments in diplomacy: Overreach with expansive norms and companies walk away; let companies off the hook and they walk away with all the booty. "It's the most complex game I've ever played," he says.

None of this would be necessary if governments respected their own laws and international obligations—but that world is a long way off. In the meantime, more and more companies—both local and global—are moving beyond the trite Hippocratic Oath to "do no harm." Ruggie's efforts to construct "soft law" is therefore the real stuff of global governance today: not just grand declarations of principles but also audits, information disclosures, community petition channels, human rights impact assessments, and social reporting. There is no universal international law regulating corporate behavior, and certainly not in war zones, but such innovations fill the gap— perhaps permanently. A corporate superego is an essential part of a global superego.

Chapter Nine

The Case Against Poverty

Poverty is the greatest of evils and the worst of crimes.
—George Bernard Shaw,
Major Barbara

*Don't patronize the poor. They are not dumb,
and most of them work harder than we do.*
—Bill Clinton

I t's the best of times and the worst of times. The world has never been so rich, but has also never been so poor. Population growth, financial crises, and political instability all but guarantee that the world will continue to have perhaps two billion or more extremely poor people for decades to come, with many societies suffering from the vicious circle of poor health, minimal disposable income, and economic unrest. For the "bottom billion" there has been very little change between the first and second Middle Ages. Whether you view the world's poorest as a security hazard, a moral blight, or a vast marketplace, they are a permanent feature of the global agenda and a standing test for whether human civilization has any meaningful solidarity.

Global goals and statistics—and even money—often matter little in states with extreme poverty, which is why we should focus on their citizens' basic needs: food and water, health care, shelter, and education. Designing systems to meet the needs of these societies isn't about revising the existing architecture but rather building a new one altogether, one focused on empowerment at the community level first and foremost. Forget stale debates about "trade versus aid." What countries want is "aid for trade": assistance that directly helps them ramp up their own exports. And forget nation building: Community building is nation building done right. In millions of small communities worldwide, micro-credit operations, new donors, diasporas, and social entrepreneurs are treating the causes, not just the symptoms, of social problems better than most of the world's governments put together. They also prove the axiom that the best global governance is local governance. The global village would mean more if it helped these individual villages.

Show Me the Money

In 2008, twenty-five years of poverty-reduction efforts were wiped away through food and fuel price spikes. Riots broke out in Egypt, Indonesia, Myanmar, Nigeria, and Haiti. Now close to two billion people live below the World Bank's $1.25-a-day poverty line. The number of hungry people also increased by forty million in 2008, bringing the estimated total number of people—especially women and children—suffering from malnutrition to about one billion. The poorest have also been perversely slammed by financial tsunamis: collapsing banks in New York mean shrinking credit for exporters in Mexico and Africa. Just as grain prices were going up, garment workers in Uzbekistan were laid off, remittances dropped from Pakistan to the Philippines, and falling copper prices led to thousands being fired from Zambian mines. When revenue is tight, social spending is always the first to get cut. The global economy slowed so precipitously in 2008 that millions of Chinese factory workers were laid off and wandered home to rural villages. One migrant returning from Shang-hai wrote, "It was a leap from post- to pre-modernism, from the 21st century back into the medieval world."[1]

Statistics actually matter little amid such volatility. As Mark Twain said, "There are three kinds of lies: lies, damn lies, and statis-tics." Touting economic growth percentages, for example, without taking into account population growth and resource consumption, makes a mockery of any meaning numbers might have. Trickle-down economics doesn't work in third world–sized populations. Ethiopia has eighty-five million people today but is growing by al-most two million per year. Many Arab and African states have little idea how to manage populations that are so much larger than only several decades ago, so they barely even try. The only sure thing about the future of the developing world is that it will contain about one billion more people thirty years from now. As famed Indian jour-nalist Khushwant Singh once wrote, "As we multiply, so do our problems."

Pretending the world should be equal—or even can be equal—harms development. Such is the state of global disparity that while more than one billion people go hungry, another billion now suffer from obesity and other lifestyle diseases. Chanting about "global poverty" is useful as a moral outcry, but doing something about it is not as simple as pointing out that the assets of the world's top three billionaires—just three people—are greater than the world's poorest six hundred million people. Thomas Pogge of Yale University makes a moral case that even though sins cannot be inherited from our fore-fathers, the fruits need not be enjoyed so unevenly. And yet they always will be. The G-20's collective $2.3 trillion in stimulus pack-ages in 2008–9 didn't even include $50 billion to help cushion the poorest.

So let's stop talking about inequality as if making the rich poorer would actually make the poor richer. We will always have disparity, but we need not always have such vast poverty. In fact, rather than even talk about poverty, we should focus on need. Poverty is amor-phous and sounds incurable, but needs are specific: food, water, shelter, medical care, and education. There are an estimated one billion urban squatters, twenty-seven million slaves, and two billion small farmers; the only question we should be asking is this: Who needs what to survive without excessive dependence on others? Extending opportunity—not sexed-up campaigns to "make poverty history"—is the right and realistic way to improve lives.

In the 1970s and '80s, aid agencies focused on basic needs and contributed to marked economic and social progress in Latin America and Southeast Asia. But since that time they have become largely ossified bureaucracies. Their stale laundry list of unmet goals—boosting aid to 0.7 percent of rich-country GDP (five times more than the United States currently gives), rooting out corruption, building social safety nets, creating a global free/fair trade regime—is a near carbon copy of the World Bank's 1965 strategy document. The more political and less functional these bodies have become, the more they produce lowest-common-denominator rallying cries, such as the Millennium Development Goals (MDGs), which have already been nicknamed the "Most Distracting Gimmick." The poor cannot eat reports.

One thing no underdeveloped country needs is more official aid programs—at least not the way they are currently designed. Uganda had more that 1,050 aid programs between 2003 and 2006, and tiny Eritrea has twenty-one official and multilateral donors. In Ghana, there are seventeen major donors operating in the health sector, with the government reporting to each of them. The United Nations provides just 2 percent of the aid Vietnam receives yet has eleven active agencies there. Thirty-eight individual countries each host at least twenty-five or more active donors.

It's enough to make one's head spin and enough paperwork to keep government officials chained to desks rather than doing their jobs. The 230 official aid agencies in the world are actually greater in number than the total number of countries in the world—both donors and recipients—combined. And while the number of donors is growing, the size of the projects is shrinking—but, of course, overhead costs rarely get cut. No wonder most Africans view aid as a cow to be milked—but not by them. As American comedian David Letterman joked, you know you work for an international aid agency if "you tell yourself it's not failure if you turn it into a lessons-learned document." The poverty trap is also an aid trap.*

Rather than flocking to the flavor-of-the-month program—girls' education or postconflict reconstruction, for example—and then claiming to suffer from "responsibility fatigue," the UN Development Program and other agencies should learn to do just one thing well. It's widely known that low inflation, sound financial markets, a stable foreign exchange, openness to trade, a solid rule of law, adequate public services, modern infrastructure, a robust tax base, and protection of minorities are good for development, growth, and stability— no country needs the World Bank to tell them that. Entrenched bureaucrats holding tight to tax-free salaries should instead be sent out into the field—armed with a shovel. In particular, World Bank economists who hail from the third world should return home and work in the governments they have spent years paternalistically advising from afar, start businesses that will attract foreign investment, pay taxes to their home countries, and crusade for accountability from within.

In other words, they should be measured by their promotion of *human will*: How many factories did they help start? How many jobs did they create? How many doctors did they train? So often aid bureaucrats talk about the need for a new "Marshall Plan" for Africa or other poor regions, but the Marshall Plan was decentralized and implemented at the provincial level. Why should we pour money into such centralized and inefficient funds when we can support these causes directly? Do we really need an "African Solidarity Fund" to help Africa?

Rather than contributing to the glut of funds that don't take nec-

*Debt relief also shouldn't be allowed to masquerade as aid. A decade ago, the IMF, the World Bank, and the "Paris Club" of creditors slashed $45 billion in debt for twenty-three countries in Africa and Latin America, and in 2005, G-8 countries canceled another $42 billion. For all these seemingly generous gestures, creditors have known for decades that they would never have gotten paid back, so the cycle of granting more loans to pay interest on loans has been little more than a pointless shell game.

essary risks on the poor, a better plan is to constantly run experiments at the local level and scale up only what works. This is, of course, what entrepreneurs do. The Philippines, South Africa, and other countries have become the world's liveliest laboratories for the interplay of remittances, micro-credit, FDI, bilateral donors, and new public-private partnerships—with results tracked and measured on websites such as AidData.org. Stories of success inspire replication and scale. Small models that work are far more useful than failed big ones. In Nepal, the Asian Development Bank runs a performance-based grant system: Local constituencies that spend money wisely get more as a reward. Members of the public are informed about which districts are getting what resources, so they have started to lobby hard for better local governance. This is a good model for better global governance as well.

Caring for Orphans

There are certainly countries in the world—dozens of them—where aid still makes the difference between life and death. They don't show up in emerging markets investment funds, so few people can name their currencies. No donor agency official wants to devote his or her career to unsexy countries such as Burkina Faso, Central African Republic, Gambia, or the Republic of the Congo (Brazzaville). Often they don't even live there, but shuttle in and out from Paris. Tuvalu, East Timor, Haiti, São Tomé and Príncipe, Kiribati, the Solomon Islands, Liberia, and Sierra Leone are yet more countries who seemingly have no choice but to live off international life support.

These are the orphans of international relations, places where aid makes up at least half the annual national budget; most of their citizens earn less than $500 per year. For orphan states, diplomatic paternalism is a like-it-or-not scenario; they are micro-trusteeships of the international community, with their budgets, spending, and even political system managed as much from the outside as from within. Imposing any political conditionality on orphan states would be a kiss of death, since revoking aid would mean the immediate collapse of what little economic and social order exists. It would mean bureaucratic genocide.

Given that there are so many orphan states in the world—and people orphaned by natural disasters, geography, or nonexistent infrastructure—the World Bank and most UN agencies should make it their singular focus to adopt the world's orphan countries and help them stimulate domestic and foreign investment so that they can one day stand on their own feet. This means most of all supporting infrastructure investments (roads, hospitals, irrigation, sanitation, electricity) with loan guarantees and supporting medium-sized enterprises. Building capacity has to mean more than neat org charts in capital cities. Public-private partnerships are the only way to save even the most forsaken societies.

Capital used to be a coward: Companies were interested in infrastructure investment only if it was a safe thirty-year bet. But in today's competitive global market, if corporations don't take risks in far-off places, they may not be in business in thirty years. Former Afghan finance minister Ashraf Ghani likes to say, "The difference between rich and poor countries is not money but mechanisms." Reinsurance is perhaps the most important of these because it lowers the price of risk. Private reinsurers such as AIG, Swiss Re, Lloyd's of London, and Axe determine the cost of entering a foreign market—and the cost went up substantially in the years after 9/11.

Two special agencies of the World Bank Group can bring that cost down, encouraging investors to enter the adoption market for orphan states. The Multilateral Investment Guarantee Agency (MIGA) offers political risk insurance, credit guarantees, catastrophe bonds, and first-loss protection to investors, helping overcome first-mover fears and liquidity shortfalls. MIGA's American counterpart, the Overseas Private Investment Company (OPIC), also helps generate foreign investment for the places that need it most. In Zambia, OPIC helps small banks provide mortgages so that locals can purchase land and build homes. Swiss Re and the World Bank together now offer low-cost catastrophe insurance to poor, hurricane-prone countries in Central America, transferring risks to capital markets while delivering support at prices that don't break the budget. The International Finance Corporation (IFC), whose explicit mission is to partner with corporations to invest in infrastructure, already has an excellent track record in out-of-reach and often dangerous places. In 2006, the IFC sponsored Iru-pana, a small Bolivian organic food maker, to send three Bolivian women—along with a dozen others from Afghanistan, Gambia, Sierra Leone, Mali, and Cameroon—to Barefoot College in the Indian state of Rajasthan to learn how to assemble, install, and repair solar power units in a manner simple enough for middle-age village women to understand. From that one visit to India, one thousand households across the participating countries launched themselves into the solar power age. In 2009, the IFC partnered with Citigroup to offer $1.25 billion in trade financing to poor countries trying to keep factories open and increased its annual lending to agribusiness companies to more than $2 billion to combat hunger.

African farmers often walk twenty-five miles to the nearest village. They cannot go and "get" development; it has to be tailored for them. In the small communities of orphan states, traditional aid packages are often too large to even be absorbed. In such places, assets aren't measured in dollars, but can be a pile of wood, a cow, a garden, a fish pond, or a bicycle. For farmers on tiny plots of land, a pig is one of the highest interest-bearing assets since it takes up little space and thrives on scraps, and an average sow can give birth to sixteen piglets a year. That's why Heifer International, a charity based in Little Rock, Arkansas, calls its animals "living savings accounts" and raises and donates them around the world. Trickle Up, a foundation that has worked in more than one hundred countries over the past thirty years, focuses only on the rural destitute, providing them with grants to build skills such as fixing shoes, sewing, or raising goats. Almost all of the private donations Trickle Up receives go straight to villagers in Mali, Burkina Faso, Ethiopia, Uganda, Nepal, Guatemala, and Nicaragua. Just $100 can turn a collective of twenty to twenty-five women into a credit union of their own for their village, a phenomenon reinforced by CARE and the Gates Foundation, which is piloting community-based and child-focused savings accounts in a dozen similar countries.

The key is to focus on the resources at hand, start small, and spread good practices widely. In Ethiopia, dairy and other farming cooperatives are ideally suited to the micro-structure of tribal society. Unions of coffee cooperatives have come together to export hundreds of tons of coffee annually to the United States and Europe with the support of certification by the Fairtrade Labeling Association. Because these cooperatives are locally owned and run, they not only help build business and management skills but are also small enough to be scaled, restructured, and redirected as the economy demands. In this way, more Africans could grow rather than import fruit, bottle their own water rather than buy it, and set up their own diaper factories and start exporting worldwide.

These needy communities also need micro-insurance from the global marketplace. LeapFrog Investments, which Bill Clinton has recognized as the leading "insurer to the poor," has a staff that combines veteran social entrepreneurs from Ashoka and senior executives from pharmaceutical giants such as GlaxoSmithKline, resulting in investor-adviser hybrids. It provides insurances for farmers against price shocks or crop failures, and its expertise and loans together help farmers buy better technology.

The billion people at the bottom of the world's economic pyramid are as far from middle class as one can get, yet they represent a massive market that the smartest companies in the world would be wise to capture. As Muhammad Yunus, founder of the Grameen Bank in Bangladesh, argues, "The poor are as capable of doing their own business as anyone else. All Grameen has done is come in to release the existing energy." Grameenphone, now in seventy-five thousand villages, has boosted the income of its "phone ladies" to about $1,000 per year, and now Grameen is putting people to work making a $1 pair of shoes for Adidas. Yunus's micro-finance model no longer even captures the hunger for moving beyond loans in the poorest countries, which is why he has partnered with the Micro Equity Development Fund to cater to the many investors who want to buy stakes in the small enterprises that employ most of the world's population.

Bangladesh's 160 million people are part of the staggering South Asian population mass of 1.5 billion that increasingly defies meaningful central governance. Through persistent natural disasters, emergency rule, and military coups, Bangladeshi society effectively runs it-self while its government perennially scrapes the bottom of Trans-parency International's Corruption Perception Index. By contrast, the Bangladesh Rural Advancement Committee (BRAC) reaches three-quarters of the country's population with its micro-finance and vil-lage school programs.[2] Such groups reinforce good governance without being captured by corrupt governments. They emphasize common purpose over clientelism, society over bureaucracy, and tan-gible belonging over abstract citizenship.

Around the world, the community is taking center stage in devel-opment and politics. Israelis have long practiced the art of kibbutz living, and today Chinese and Japanese people are moving back to the land in droves in search of stable and sustainable community living. The Self-Employed Women's Association (SEWA) in India has its own community-level banks, health clinics, child-care programs, legal ser-vices (such as sexual harassment and workers' compensation), and re-tirement accounts. SEWA doesn't just champion women's rights; it *provides* those rights through its own quasi-economic and political communities across India. The so-called informal economies of com-munity cooperatives often go unregistered in economic statistics, yet they are a legitimate mode of economic and social survival for hun-dreds of millions of people worldwide.

What is crucial to understand about Grameen, BRAC, SEWA, and other such organizations is that their primary unit of organization is not the town or village but the *community*. Community building *is* nation building done right.

Supporting such community-level entrepreneurialism was the founding vision of the micro-lending website Kiva.org. Kiva connects the local to the local: It's not B2B, but P2P (person to person). It's about more than just the first world helping the third world—it pro-motes what its name means: unity. Kiva has zero interest on capital—people lend for the emotional satisfaction, and they keep on lending, rarely pulling money out of the Kiva system as outstanding loans are repaid. Kiva employees work there for the same reason. Its head-quarters in the Mission district of San Francisco resembles a dormi-tory common room. All but one world map are upside down—the symbol of solidarity with the global "South"—and rooms are named after third world capitals such as Kabul and Dili (of East Timor).

A digital ticker on the wall counts the number of loans disbursed through Kiva—more than one hundred thousand by mid-2009—to everyone from Afghan carpet weavers to Ugandan goat herders. The ticker flashes to another statistic, the loan repayment rate: over 97 percent, higher than Americans' credit card debt payment rate. The global poor are a more credible investment, and enough Americans know this that they make up four out of every five lenders on Kiva. In fact, as of 2009, Americans now lend to one another through Kiva as well.

But what about the financial crisis? In February 2009, the same month that Deutsche Bank, a major shareholder in micro-finance institutions (MFI), froze new disbursements in the sector, Kiva had its biggest month to date. It continues to ramp up partnerships with new MFIs at a rate of three per month (though there are more than ten thousand in the world). And Kiva will work with many MFIs that Deutsche Bank doesn't have the appetite for, ones that haven't yet been operating for a few years and don't offer the high rates of return that investment banks are looking for.

If NGOs such as CARE represent a significant gain in efficiency over the World Bank and USAID, then Kiva is a quantum leap. Its leverage ratio—meaning the amount it loans out versus its costs—is approaching ten to one. One reason for this is that Kiva is a model public-private partnership: Google gives it free ads, PayPal allows free usage, and law firms do its legal work pro bono. Kiva not only has a real-time feedback loop to provide transparency on projects—like an eBay for development finance—but Ernst & Young performs due diligence on almost all Kiva projects worldwide at reduced cost. Additionally, at any given time, up to one hundred Kiva fellows are embedded with field partners from Sierra Leone to Sudan to Afghanistan, snapping photos and filing reports on project status to verify their credibility. Hundreds of volunteers who work as translators and editors for Kiva's website wind up also spotting inconsistencies and raising flags, accelerating the correction rate on errors even further. Today Kiva literally comes closest to the cliché of not wasting a single cent.

No organization has a monopoly on putting together people, ideas, and investment. Like Kiva, GlobalGiving.org has enabled over one hundred thousand people from American students to Fortune 500 companies to directly lend to worthy projects across the world. USAID and other inefficient aid agencies act indifferently toward the Grameen and Kiva models despite their success in places such as Afghanistan, where USAID struggles the most. "We've bumped up against Washington bureaucrats so many times. They treat us like mosquitoes," recalls Kiva cofounder Premal Shah. And yet loans to American-occupied Iraq are the most popular on Kiva.

Entrenched habits and inertia may prevent the establishment from embracing Kiva, but time is on Kiva's side. For decades graduate students have sought internships and jobs with the World Bank as a stepping-stone to a career in international development. Now they flood Kiva's in-box with their CVs—they want to commit "sweat equity," not just reap financial equity. Seeking greater authenticity in their lives, even ex-investment bankers, tired of the uncertainty and moral void of Wall Street, are willing to volunteer for months to be Kiva fellows. Kiva alumni quickly join the boards of MFIs and go on to work for the World Bank and traditional donors, gradually reshaping their policies from the inside out.

There is nothing wrong with aid being handled like a business marketplace. To the contrary, that is precisely what will bring it greater transparency and efficiency. Devex—a firm whose motto is "Do Good. Do It Well."—calls itself the "Bloomberg of foreign aid" because it provides an online clearinghouse for development tenders beyond the usual cliques of donors and their pet projects. But more than just providing data, Devex now also actively consults for companies. In countries from Angola to Kazakhstan, oil giant Chevron knows its operational stability may depend on building quasi-cities of schools and clinics for local villages. Devex helps them do it well.

Today's new social entrepreneurship universe embodies an economic culture that is radically different from what the developing world is used to seeing. So-called philanthropreneurs, or impact investors, bridge pride and profit and take bold risks on innovative projects. Bill Gates, Bill Clinton, Warren Buffett, George Soros, Richard

Branson, and foundations including Ashoka, Schwab, Skoll, and the Omidyar Network (the latter two named for eBay's founders) all provide a steady flow of capital to ventures that aim to level the economic playing field. Led by Gates and Buffett, forty billionaires have pledged half their net wealth to charity during their lifetimes. Synergos, the Global Philanthropy Forum, and other groups turn high-net-worth individuals and dot-com billionaires into social entrepreneurs with portfolios of progressive activities. Today's students of the Skoll Center for Social Entrepreneurship at Oxford's Saïd Business School learn to be social *intrapreneurs* as well: going inside large corporations and changing their psychology and mission from within.

The best thing these new social investors can do is—like celebrity actors—inspire their counterparts in other parts of the world. Jack Ma, the founder of Alibaba.com (China's version of eBay) has given millions to seed a Chinese version of Grameen Bank. He says, "When you have several hundred million or even several billion, then that money is no longer your money. Rather, it is a resource that belongs to society." More and more Asian billionaires have started family foundations, especially as younger generations take the helm. The Chen family of Hong Kong not only builds community libraries across China but is also funding R & D investment into lowering the per-unit cost of adaptive eyeglasses that help young people learn better and older men and women work more productively, whether they are chopping vegetables in Ghana or sewing fishing nets in Thailand. Selling the glasses to rich Japanese helps cover the cost of donating them to the poor in Africa—but once the production cost comes down to two dollars a pair, they can be sold even to the poor, meaning the market, rather than charity, will sustain the innovation. James Chen has already sponsored the "Vision for a Nation" program in Rwanda, claiming, "If we succeed, Rwanda will have the best vision in the world—now that's leapfrogging!"

Technological leapfrogging—from no phone to mobile phone, and no power to solar power—used to be a small niche of development strategy; now it is the dominant paradigm to advance social empowerment, job creation, and environmental sustainability at the same time. A study by the consulting firm Deloitte found that a 10 percent increase in mobile phone penetration raises GDP by 1.2 percent. Nokia has smartly targeted even areas with little or no electricity supply by creating cheap phones that power themselves simply by being spun around; now the World Bank follows Nokia's lead in a partnership to support tele-banking across Africa. There are already five billion mobile phones in the world and about two billion computers. Worldwide, the number of people with access to cell phones now surpasses the number with safe drinking water. If anything shows the power of the market to deliver services, that is it.

Just like the IFC and MIGA can provide risk insurance to help build infrastructure in orphan states, the financial sector can embrace socially responsible investing (SRI), which already represents about one-tenth of funds professionally managed in the United States.[3] Goldman Sachs and other major investment banks now integrate social and environmental factors into their equity research, pushing "triple bottom line" reporting up high on the agenda for many companies. Social investment funds such as Calvert and Underdog Ventures now provide an important alternative to the typical market psychology of running for the exits at the hint of risk. Instead, they lock in money, sometimes for ten years, precisely because such capital guarantees help to reduce risk. Such social funds have provided backing to African micro-credit operators including Nigeria's Blue Financial Services, which has more than two hundred branches in a dozen sub-Saharan countries (excluding South Africa). Capitalism is creative enough without needing the "creative capitalism" Bill Gates has called for. What he really means is Kantian capitalism, which sees people as ends in themselves. Even in hard times, there is no better strategy than helping others help themselves.

Need-Based Design

Who owns Earth? The question has fresh relevance in the new Middle Ages. Largely under the radar, a vanguard of private equity firms backed by investment banks, pension funds, and university endowments is leading a speculative frenzy to buy up or lease millions of hectares of farmland to grow and export food for profit, underpaying already underfed locals in Kenya, Sudan, and Ethiopia. Rich Arab and eastern Asian states use their own state-backed firms to do the same thing. They not only want fertile cropland but also access to the water underneath it—which can be pumped out and shipped overseas while locals die of thirst. Corporate farmers are becoming the new feudal overlords.

Political will and a wave of the pen aren't enough to redesign a global food system precariously based on abundant water and cheap energy—both of which are gone for good. Eighty percent of Africa's hungry live on small farms, as do two-thirds of southern Asia's and China's populations—in other words, about half the world's population continues to live in agricultural medievalism. Agricultural policy *is* development policy, yet for years the two have worked at cross purposes. American and European Depression-era subsidies to big farmers and biofuel industries have not only raised food prices by diminishing food production, but continue to block access for the world's poorest farmers, forcing them to depend on food aid rather than feeding themselves—but just-in-time food assistance often comes too late. America's $2 billion in annual food aid long carried the odious caveat of spending on American grain, which meant most of the funds went to shipping and overhead costs rather than food itself.*

Partnerships among lean international agencies, food companies, and NGOs have become a powerful axis in improving global food policy, spreading food wider and earlier to where it's needed, and helping the rural impoverished grow more food themselves. UNICEF and the World Food Program, which shun top-heavy bureaucracies, devote most of their resources to delivering food to hungry women, children, and orphans in neglected pockets of the world such as central Africa—and they partner with major logistics companies such as Dutch TNT to build a network of emergency food banks and depots. The WFP now helps peanut farmers generate revenue by producing

*By contrast, Canada and European donors give their food aid either totally untied or through the WFP.

and selling vitamin-fortified peanut butter that nourishes children during food crises. When U.S. policy finally changed in 2009 to allow aid groups to purchase food from local suppliers, International Relief and Development (IRD) partnered with Indonesian food companies to boost their production of rice, egg noodles, and wheat biscuits and to improve their logistics network to distribute the food nationwide, a program being replicated in Cambodia, Niger, and Sri Lanka. IRD even builds small feeder roads in Iraq and Afghanistan to help restart agricultural businesses. With smart assistance from the United Kingdom's Department for International Development to subsidize one-hundred-pound sacks of fertilizer for one-third the market price, Malawi went from bad harvests and starvation in 2005 to producing more than three million metric tons of corn in 2007 and selling the surplus to the WFP.

The race continues between Malthusian predictions of a growing world population without enough food and promises of a global "green revolution" that can feed us all. India's 1960s Green Revolution brought new strains of wheat, seed subsidies, and infrastructure to grow and distribute more food. But today, after decades as a food exporter, India is competing to buy food on the world market. It needs a second green revolution—this time aided by global genetically modified seed giants such as Monsanto and Syngenta, and food companies such as PepsiCo that fund contract farming ventures that boost output while paying good prices for potatoes. If Africa is to have its own green revolution, it, too, will have to be a commercial one that scales mass agriculture. The Gates Foundation, G-20, and World Bank have pledged billions of dollars for an African agriculture development fund, while the Rockefeller and Gates foundations subsidize Monsanto to invest in developing high-yield strains of the seeds Africans need most—cassava, sorghum, and millet—and give credits to ten thousand African agro-dealers to upgrade small-scale rural food storage centers. Proving Malthus wrong is still possible if global food production and policy are actively devolved to the world's farmers themselves and to science rather than special interests.

• • •

We should think in terms of technology rather than technocracy to get the world's poorest the basics they need. As freshwater supplies dwindle, rich Persian Gulf countries pay a steep price for energy-intensive desalination plants; but, for the poor, Seattle-based World Wide Water sells a solar-powered micro-desalinator that works even with brackish saltwater and can be deployed all over desertified Africa and central Asia. The American nonprofit KickStart has sold its low-tech and low-cost water pumps to more than eighty thousand small-scale irrigation businesses from Mali to Tanzania. Water authorities in the developing world can't control growing consumption and dwindling supplies—it's up to innovation and activism to promote efficiency and conservation.

The same is true for basic health care, which has become diplomacy's most active arena of public-private partnerships. Alejandro Jadad of the University of Toronto uses cell phones to capture and share photos for analysis, to store medical data, and to relay guidance from doctors. Through such "point-of-care diagnostics," Jadad can treat patients in Colombia, Nigeria, and Sri Lanka. He couriers prescription medications and bills them nothing. Similarly, delivering hand sanitizer and oral rehydration therapy to elementary schools around the world would cost almost nothing and prevent close to five million deaths per year from diarrhea, parasitic worms, and other infections.

Left to their own devices, governments are often obstacles to public health rather than enablers. Take the reaction of Indonesia and India to the outbreak of H5N1 avian flu in 2008: Indonesia's health minister ordered a joint U.S.-Indonesian medical research laboratory NAMRU-2 shut down, while Indonesia, India, and Thailand convened the Non-Aligned Movement to declare "viral sovereignty" to protect against Western encroachment and Western ownership of disease strains for profit. International agencies aren't much better, running programs "more like a lemonade stand than like Google."[4] For decades the World Bank actually insisted that poor people pay for medical services they simply couldn't afford, perversely incentivizing them not to seek medical care at all. It's hard to imagine any such bureaucracy operating like the Clinical Directors Network, which constantly tests models for community-based health centers and spreads best practices worldwide. With leaders such as former South African president Thabo Mbeki denying the existence of AIDS and its impact, it's no wonder that foreign mining companies and other multinationals partner directly with labor unions and NGOs to offer workplace AIDS testing and treatment to keep South Africans alive and working.

The need to tackle HIV/AIDS and other global plagues has given rise to entirely new kinds of mega-diplomatic institutions. The Global Fund to Fight AIDS, Tuberculosis, and Malaria has such a unique structure that the Swiss government had to create a special legal status for it. Its board is made up of donors, NGOs, and companies; half its funding comes from governments and half from foundations. The fund is more a financing instrument than an organization. It has raised more than $10 billion to date to sponsor one million–plus antiretroviral HIV/AIDS treatments and two million tuberculosis treatments, distribute eighteen million insecticide-treated bed nets and twenty-three million anti-malarial medications, and train four million people in health service delivery. The Gates Foundation has also pioneered new models. It not only funded the highly successful Global Alliance for Vaccines and Immunization a decade ago, but more recently founded the Institute for OneWorld Health, the first nonprofit pharmaceutical company devoted to health and vaccine research for poor people, and has spent more in the past decade on neglected-disease research than all the world's governments put together.

Some believe that direct interventions like those of the Gates Foundation don't add up to systemic transformation, but is there really another way to achieve the latter without the former? The Gates Foundation has such a staggering budget—$3 billion per year and $67 billion in total assets—that its staff members act like private health diplomats, engaging directly with national ministers of health, commerce, and foreign affairs, while also funding and running local projects within countries worldwide. Botswana was a pioneering case. Thanks to a partnership between Gates and pharmaceutical giant Merck, the country's population was saved from near extinction through the rapid deployment of more than eighty thousand antiretroviral treatments. Today the Gates Foundation spends over 80 percent of its budget on public-private partnerships. Such partnerships aren't a substitute for government policy—they are the new public-private way of *doing* policy.

The same strategy is essential for delivering another human basic: a roof over one's head. In a rapidly urbanizing world, civil society and social entrepreneurs are the reasons millions of people have homes at all. Habitat for Humanity built 250,000 homes in five years—but could put up one million in the next five with the help of construction companies. It has partnered with InnoVida, an American firm specializing in using nonflammable and hurricane-resistant materials for simple residential properties—even with solar panels—that can be put up in seventy-two hours. It not only sells these homes to companies employing south Asian laborers in the Persian Gulf, but has also donated thousands of them to India while training hundreds of unskilled laborers to erect them on their own. Forty miles outside Nairobi, the Acumen Fund, the world's first nonprofit venture capital firm, has turned the village of Kaputei into an eco-friendly model town. Acumen confronts the lack of rural housing, urban congestion, and pollution all at the same time by underwriting the construction of modest homes and giving residents jobs in wastewater treatment and recycling plants that serve nearby cities. Acumen is spreading this process to Pakistan, providing loans to investors to develop low-cost housing for the country's estimated thirty million squatters. When affordable technology, social entrepreneurship, and underutilized citizens come together, far fewer people in the world need be homeless for much longer.

Just like arguments over housing and health care, debating whether the public or private sector should be providing basic education is futile in places where it is hard enough just to legislate universal primary schooling, let alone achieve it. Even with billions of dollars in official commitments, international campaigns such as UNESCO's "Education for All" have not come anywhere near their goal of universal literacy. Today more than two billion people in the world cannot read. Poor women and children spend hours each day finding and carrying their meager daily water supply, leaving them little time for formal schooling. And the ABCs and 123s aren't useful if children catch diseases from unsanitary latrines, are malnourished from the lack of nutrient-enriched foods, or contract HIV. Education, in other words, is a health and poverty problem as well—and even a security problem, given the need for secular schooling as a path away from extremism for hundreds of millions of Arab and Pakistani youth who have little or no economic prospects.

The U.S. government has regularly considered abolishing the penny—and if all the pennies currently in circulation were channeled through grassroots education programs, it would be enough to provide basic education for the one hundred million children in the world who don't get it. It costs less than fifty dollars to provide books, stationery, and pencils for a third world primary school student for a year. Across Africa and southern Asia, private citizens spend up to fifty times per capita what the government does to put their kids in school. In Pakistan, a full one-third of all primary and secondary schools today are privately funded and run, and private schools cost half as much as public ones, so even unskilled laborers can afford them for their children.[5] Pratham, an Indian NGO, conducted a survey showing how even most of the children classified as literate still couldn't read their own languages; now it is responsible for the country's largest education campaigns.

Again: The best outcomes don't come from a false choice between public or private, but rather through the union of public and private. Numerous Latin American countries now follow the model of Colombia, where so-called concessional schools (which are private) receive tuition payments from the government in order to educate more students from overcrowded and failing public schools. Arab countries worried about their masses of unemployed youth have partnered with HSBC on a Pan-Arab Youth Training Program to train young people in skills necessary for the region's manufacturing-starved labor market. Uruguay was the first country to purchase "$100 laptops" for every school-age child through the One Laptop Per Child Association, and Rwanda's adolescent "Cheetah Generation" is getting there thanks to a similar program by President Paul Kagame. Under the leadership of Ellen Johnson Sirleaf, Liberia has partnered with Nike and the World Bank to set up girls' vocational schools. And after Google set up a development center in Nairobi to get more Kenyans online, CEO Eric Schmidt mused, "The creativity of the people will take care of the rest."[6]

How to Adopt a Country

Get in a taxi in Washington, Frankfurt, or Dubai, and chances are your driver is from Somalia, Nigeria, Turkey, India, or Pakistan. Tip him generously, because you're paying for his family's well-being as well as his own. Migration has always been the most visible face of globalization. Three percent of the world's population (about two hundred million people) are migrants—and there is as much migration between poor countries as there is between poor and rich. Even where migrants live in ghettos, tent cities, or container villages, they still manage to send remittances home in excess of $500 billion per year, more than five times the collective rich world's foreign aid budgets combined.

As with agriculture, migration policy *is* development policy. A 3 percent increase in labor mobility to Organization for Economic Cooperation and Development countries would be worth another $300 billion per year to the poor on the other end of the remittance chain, and a mere 10 percent increase in per capita remittances would decrease poverty by over 3 percent across seventy-one countries.[7] Encouraging sensible migration policy, however, falls on the shoulders of the voluntarily underfunded International Organization for Migration (IOM), which has no more clout than the hodgepodge of NGOs that make recommendations to rich countries on dealing with legal and illegal migrants, guest workers, refugees, and highly skilled workers. Businesses, labor unions, assimilation facilitation groups, and diaspora lobbies are just some of the players that also have a stake in one of the most sensitive and fundamental aspects of globalization.

Archbishop Desmond Tutu called migration caps "apartheid on a global scale." But not all rich countries fear hordes of illegal migrants, such as the United States from Latin America or Europe from Africa. In fact, Japan uses free-trade agreements to lure Indonesians and Filipinos to move there to compensate for its dwindling population. Italy is easing dual citizenship for Brazilians of Italian origin to compensate for its demographic demise as well. The movements of Chinese underscore just how strategic migration can be: With the United States monitoring China's ports more closely, illegal Chinese migrants now flood into America via Mexico.

Migrants are very smart about financial trends affecting their lot: When the dollar is too weak, they pass straight through the United States to Canada, or head across the Atlantic to earn euros. The reliability of remittance flows has been so substantial that some Brazilian banks use them to underwrite greater capital lending. However, global migration dropped in 2009 for the first time in decades, plunging remittances by up to 30 percent or more from many rich countries. Amazingly, the global financial crisis proved just how important remittances are to the poor. When Indians in the Persian Gulf, Tajiks in Russia, and Nepalis in America lost their jobs, their families at home actually sent them money to help them ride out the recession and hopefully find work again. For good times and bad, some migration relations have become all but permanent. Kharian, a village of thirty thousand near Lahore in Pakistan, is also called "Little Norway" since one-third of its families have at least one member living in Scandinavia, working as repairmen or taxi drivers and sending home up to $1,000 per month, a huge amount for ordinary Pakistanis.

Diasporas represent diplomacy *within* an ethnic universe. We tend to think of immigrants as struggling to adopt the culture of their new homes, but remittances are the best example of immigrants readopting their native lands: providing continuous help to their families and communities back home. And the easier it gets to care for people overseas, the more likely it is to continue in perpetuity. The emotional durability of kinship and cultural ties makes it a far more reliable vehicle for delivering aid than faddish ideas such as the "vulnerability fund" proposed by the World Bank. Instead, we should take advantage of the *spheres of responsibility* diasporas represent. What better country to adopt than your own?

Dollar for dollar, remittances have the most direct impact on the quality of life of the poor. Every remitted dollar to Bolivia, Haiti, Somalia, Sri Lanka, Bangladesh, or the Philippines keeps families afloat, and when natural disasters strike Latin America or elsewhere, remittances arrive instantly. Beyond funding basic survival, remittance money has a multiplier effect at home, especially when it's used to buy goods, pay for school fees, or start small businesses. Over one or two generations, remittances help not just families but entire communities rise out of poverty, as has been the case in Turkey, thanks to its many *Gastarbeiter* in Germany. Perhaps this is the least that can be offered back to the developing world in exchange for the brain drain of its able-bodied skilled workers and educated elite. Higher up the value chain, diasporas also repatriate first world knowledge around the world as returning migrants replicate their success from their new homes to the old. Taiwanese, Indians, and Israelis who have returned from Silicon Valley to seed high-tech centers are called the "New Argonauts"; China calls them *hai gui,* or "sea turtles," who have swum home, reversing brain drain in the process.

India is the world's top recipient of remittances, which provide 3 percent of its GDP. Especially in the southern state of Kerala, almost every single family is tied to someone in the Persian Gulf. Nonresident Indians are also the leading investors in India, pumping in more capital than foreign investment and portfolio capital combined.[8] The Ministry of External Affairs has set up a special Overseas Indian Facilitation Center with a website to ensure hassle-free investment from the diaspora as well as to offer special diaspora passports. With support from the Confederation of Indian Industry's Indian American Council, a quasi diaspora "peace corps" is emerging whereby young Indian Americans constantly rotate in and out of Indian villages to provide management and technical help in health care, education, micro-finance, and entrepreneurship.

Whether through low-tech *hawala* or high-tech electronic banking, the remittance market has captured the attention of and sparked competition among banks and credit unions to smooth remittance transfer. Western Union, the telegraph operator many thought would go bankrupt with the rise of the Internet and PayPal, is now a $5 billion company that tracks migration faster than any census bureau, advertises in dozens of languages including Tagalog, and offers discounted rates during holidays in Fiji. The company's slogan is "If you can't be there, your money can." In the Philippines, understanding Western Union's procedures is as important as having a passport.[9] With support from Vodafone, Kenya's Safaricom has become a mobile banking leader, making lending, borrowing, and receiving remittances virtually free, especially compared to the $700 it can cost to open a bank account in sub-Saharan African countries.

The Philippines and Mexico are the most evolved examples of how remittances are already interwoven into the national political fabric. "Leaving in order to live" has become a way of life, expanding over generations as Filipino sons and daughters follow in their parents' footsteps—and often change places with them—as expatriate workers in America and the Persian Gulf states. Ten percent of the country's population lives and works abroad, sending home about $1 billion per month. Not surprisingly, Philippines president Gloria Macapagal Arroyo calls the country's diaspora members "modern heroes" and welcomes them home with open arms each time they return.[10] Similarly, one-tenth of Mexicans live in the United States, often working several jobs to send money home, making migration—and the fences put up to prevent it—one of the top issues (next to drugs) on the U.S.-Mexican agenda. The United States doesn't give aid to Mexico as such; rather, their "Partnership for Prosperity" program relies heavily on the private sector. Bank of America eliminated all currency exchange and wire-transfer fees for customers with checking accounts, and on Mother's Day in 2004, Wal-Mart reduced its money-transfer fee by 50 percent.

At the other end of the spectrum is the world's most notorious failed state. Somalia's collapse in 1991 meant an abrupt end to simple luxuries such as banks, schools, hospitals, and law enforcement. Infrastructure crumbled and emigration soared. With the country still in a perpetual civil war, remittances from Somali taxi drivers in Minneapolis to students in Finland (where Somalis are one of the largest ethnic minorities) remain a major lifeline for the people—72 percent of Somali GDP in 2006. Almost all reconstruction projects in the country have been privately launched and financially supported by the Somali diaspora. Private remittance companies in Somalia issue ID cards to their customers, serving as registrars for communities in the absence of a government; they even cooperate with anti-money-laundering and anti-terrorist-financing initiatives. It may be years before multilateral organizations know who they're dealing with in Somalia, but they could already leverage Somalia's extensive diaspora and remittance networks to rebuild parts of the country not at war.

One of the shining exemplars of adopting communities is the Aga Khan, spiritual father to the fifteen million Ismaili Muslims. The Aga Khan is as much entrepreneur as religious figure. Through the Aga Khan Development Network (AKDN), Ismaili wealth is invested in poor and dangerous areas from East Africa to Tajikistan—wherever Ismailis are—in the name of preserving and protecting their threatened communities. The Aga Khan is perhaps the largest single investor in all of Afghanistan, and he encourages members of the Ismaili diaspora to invest there and in other hotspots. AKDN increasingly partners with official aid agencies around Europe to coach them on small-scale community projects. Most important, perhaps, the Aga Khan's work is an important role model for the growing Islamic Development Bank based in Jeddah, Saudi Arabia, whose lending is increasing 30 percent per year.

The postcolonial world is full of interesting examples of lingering suspicions turning into fruitful and lucrative partnerships. Italy and Libya have buried their hatchet, with Italy promising $5 billion in compensation for colonialism—but earmarking the money for counter-migration programs—and Libya's Muammar Gaddafi using his $70 billion sovereign wealth fund to buy up shares in Italian telecom, construction companies, and football clubs. Former Portuguese colony Brazil has joined with its former master to launch medical exchanges to train doctors in numerous former Portuguese colonies such as Angola and Mozambique. Portugal's main legacy in Angola today is an estimated ten thousand businesses that have been an important force in reviving the country's post–civil war economy. Such productive postcolonial relationships abound in today's world. Spain is the most popular business partner in Latin America, and London-based Standard Chartered Bank earns 90 percent of its profits in former British colonies in Africa, Asia, and the Middle East, where it also supports sixty micro-finance institutions with $500 million in capital. In East Africa, Indians have returned not as British colonial laborers, but as major investors in construction and real estate. The Tata corporation describes its work in Africa as that of a "for-profit development agency." The new postcolonial adoption is mutual.

Some countries can't sell anything to the world, so they have to bring the world to them as much as possible. Tourism is thus a kind of short-term adoption—and a longer-term one as well when visitors bond with, return to, and sponsor the economies of places they visit, such as Nepal and Cambodia. Tourism accounts for 10 percent of global GDP and employs more than 250 million people. In Africa, tourism has grown faster than other sectors and benefits particularly women. As ecotourism grows, game reserves in South Africa and Botswana give special benefits to local tribes. The best thing a country can do to attract tourists is simply to be a safe place. Even after a year of riots and unrest, Kenya got lucky with the U.S. presidential election of 2008, after which tourism jumped 15 percent as the country began to offer "Obama's roots" tours.

While Western diplomats and scholars are busy dreaming up grandiose new "Marshall Plans" for Africa, a more practical reality is emerging as migration-driven remittances expand, historical allegiances rekindle, new trade and investment partners rise, and Asian tourists flood the world. Micro-credit operations, social investment funds, family foundations, and social entrepreneurs are not ethereal, flash-in-the-pan phenomena on the margins of the "real" global governance of governmental institutions. Rather, they are the talisman of the emerging world order in which the local *becomes* the global faster than the reverse.

Chapter Ten

Your Planet, Your Choice

Don't throw it away. . . . There is no "away."
— Shell advertisement

*The green business of the future will no longer
be called green, it will just be business.*
—VIJAY VAITHEESWARAN,
The Economist

Al Gore's 1992 book *warning about global warming was titled*
Earth in the Balance. *If there were a sequel two decades later, it
would have to be called* Earth Out of Balance. *Most people are aware
that climate change is happening, but few think they can do anything
about it. That is the problem. Like the economy, the environment is a
truly global issue that impacts our industrial viability and geopolitical
stability. Every individual, company, city, and country can take steps
to protect, ensure, adapt, and mitigate climate change before it's too
late—which is what it will be if we leave it to the world's governments
to negotiate for us.*

*No issue has greater potential for dot-gov, dot-com, and dot-org
collaboration to tip the balance back in favor of sustainability. Getting on the right path isn't about bashing Mideast despots but mak-*

ing the most efficient use of the resources we already have. The eclectic experiments under way from Brazil to India in alternative energy, water sharing, and emissions reductions hold the greatest promise for sustainable living, and the new partnerships emerging among cleantech companies, mayors, and conservation groups are the real story of climate diplomacy today. Diplomats often aspire to save the world—this is your chance to actually do it.

All Politics Are Ecological

The following headlines are coming to a newspaper near you: "Indonesian Rain Forest Dwindles to Few Million Hectares," "Nile River Flow Reduced to Silt Sludge," and "OPEC Pushes Pedal, but Oil Gushers Gone." The only question is when—ten years, twenty years, or thirty years—but each scenario is all but inevitable given present trends in deforestation, overconsumption of water, and demand for oil.

Yet imagine this scene: A half-mile-long super-cargo ship pulls into port, hulls painted deep blue with bold white inscriptions, its deck covered bow to stern with shiny new electric-powered automobiles whose lithium-ion batteries can carry four passengers more than 185 miles before recharging at stations already installed on the country's highways. Thousands of eager citizens have already prepaid for the cars, and even dropped off their gas-powered vehicles in a special recycling lot near the harbor. Behind the cargo ship is another one, and another one, and another one. The country that manufactured the car has captive export markets worldwide and has earned hundreds of billions in hard currency, while the countries buying the cars are cutting their greenhouse gas emissions and dependence on unstable oil supplies. Which country is the seller and which is the buyer? We don't know yet, but both will be winners.

The environment insinuates itself in all of the neat lenses we falsely use to prioritize human activity, such as security or economics. Take geopolitics: Controlling natural resources—particularly oil, gas, timber, uranium, gold, and other precious metals—is the new environmental "Great Game." And there are no nice guys: democratic India and authoritarian China are both in the hunt, from East Africa to Myanmar. In the oil-rich Middle East, nuclear power likely also means nuclear proliferation. Global warming could even give birth to an independent Greenland, replete with gold, diamonds, and zinc buried under melting glaciers—and access to the potentially ninety billion barrels of oil and 1,670 trillion cubic feet of natural gas under the Arctic Sea.[1] Russia, Canada, and America are already fortifying bases, operating stealth submarines, and flying bombers over the Arctic to stake their claims. As Canada's premier, Stephen Harper, said during an Arctic visit in 2009, "Use it or lose it."

But making the climate a security issue—as Tony Blair did by raising it at the UN Security Council—doesn't impress poor countries that resent any potential excuses for Western interventionism within their borders and prefer to retain the focus on poverty. And yet poor countries, which contribute little to climate change, are sure to be the biggest losers from it. Among rising temperatures, soil erosion, deforestation, desertification, melting glaciers, pollution of freshwater, depletion of fisheries, and changing disease patterns and oceanic currents, the unpredictable flux of the environment will force a mixture of adaptation and suffering on almost all countries, but certainly not equally. Rising sea levels are sinking small island nations in the South Pacific, the increasingly frequent droughts of northern Kenya have led to what some call a "permanent emergency" for a growing number of nomadic farmers squeezed into smaller and smaller plots of arable land, and Bangladesh's monsoon flooding now comes every five years instead of every twenty, drowning entire villages and turning the country into a perma-swamp in which communities cluster along the sides of higher roads to escape rising tides.

Humans live where they do—along coasts and rivers—because of the climate, and yet increasingly they cannot live in these areas because of the climate. Absent an integrated view of climate, health, food, and energy, sustainability is the victim of perverse and naïve thinking. Environmental decay is not merely an "externality," an unintended consequence of the greater goal of economic growth. It can, in short order, destroy that growth. Just look at how America's biofuel subsidies led to diminished food production and thus contributed to food price surges that have forced worldwide belt tightening. Similarly, China's main obstacle to superpower status isn't the United States but rather the ecological and health costs of reckless industrialization. Its labor force is stricken with lung cancer and other diseases that not only cut 3–4 percent off its GDP but ruin families and morale.

Imagine measuring income not just in GDP terms, but also weighing a nation's health and environmental stress factors; or a standard for calculating the carbon emissions consequences of deals between firms that regulators could use in determining the legality of mergers; or credit-rating agencies taking a firm's sustainability score into account in its investment grade. This may seem like hard work, but we should know better than to live behind the lies of numbers divorced from the ecosystem.

When it comes to the environment, there is an element of personal responsibility that people don't feel with other issues, a sense that particularly a younger generation has innately grown up with. Many seventh graders in America log on to CarbonRally.com as part of a nationwide competition to reduce their carbon footprint. Citizen activists promote causes town by town, from flushing toilets less frequently to Paul McCartney's "Meat Free Monday" campaign in favor of vegetarianism—a "low-carbon" diet—to preserve forests slashed for cattle grazing in Brazil. In New Delhi, the paper versus plastic debate in supermarkets and bazaars has been settled in favor of cotton: keep and reuse. And in Hong Kong, an NGO recycles rice sacks into sturdy grocery bags labeled "re-sack-le" and makes them available across the densely populated city. Sustainably transitioning the economy will take what former White House environmental adviser Van Jones calls "thousands of heroes at every level of human society."

A hero in this sense is someone who realizes that simple, individual steps matter as much as high-level negotiations—the latter is, in fact, meaningless without the former. For rich people that means triple-layer windows, LED streetlamps, inflating car tires regularly, upgrading to hybrid cars, teleconferencing and reducing air travel, and using solar-powered lawn mowers. For the poor, the mundane strategies include water harvesting for agriculture, fixing leaky pipes that waste up to half of irrigated water—which can lead to "more crops with fewer drops"—and using fuel-efficient and biogas-powered stoves. And for oil exporters such as Mexico, Russia, and Iran, this means greater foreign investment in their energy sectors to improve their antiquated and inefficient technologies. Energy guru Amory Lovins says, "Increasing energy efficiency is the largest, least expensive, most benign, most quickly deployable, least visible, least understood, and most neglected way" to meet future energy demand.

We can't negotiate with nature. Solving the world's environmental problems has so little to do with the diplomacy of setting targets and caps and so much to do with scaling these prosaic behavioral changes. The planet doesn't care if targets are set for 2015 or 2020 if energy consumption will double by 2030. What matters more than the fancy language of "ecological debt" are meaningful initiatives that tackle the principle sources of emissions: electricity generation, home heating, automobiles and airplanes, mineral and oil extraction, and deforestation. The real story of sustaining human life is thus about private-sector innovators and motivated citizens more than international regulations. Even if governments muster the political will to agree on targets, achieving any of them requires an even greater dose of human will.

Supply and Demand

Sinopec, Petrobras, Exxon Mobil, Gazprom—these and the world's other energy giants live and die by one rule: supply and demand. Public or private, they comb the world in search of oil, gas, uranium, coal, and other raw materials. Like water for humans, energy is a matter of national survival: Hungary has appointed a special ambassador just to handle the Nabucco gas pipeline project, which would ensure a steady gas supply evading Russian control. The International Energy Agency can't govern the competition for energy in a world in which the national oil companies of Russia, Iran, Venezuela, and Saudi Arabia have captured the high ground in the world's highest value business. But even these single-minded titans can still be steered down the path of sustainability and diversification, mitigating dangerous rivalries in the process.

Coal, oil, and uranium are the world's three main sources of energy, with China most reliant on coal, America the largest consumer of oil, and Europe the leader in uranium-fueled nuclear power. But as oil peaks, coal wreaks atmospheric havoc, and uranium remains expensive, dangerous, and narrowly located, we have to rethink both how much and how we use these energy sources. If the people of China and India drove cars at anything approaching the rates of Westerners, OPEC would need to produce twice the amount of oil it does each day. But such projections are actually farcical: OPEC countries know—and fear—the limits of their supply. There can't be a worldwide middle class on this earth living the way the West does.

The geography of geology is unfair. Most of the world's oil, gas, coal, and metals lie in what *Commanding Heights* coauthor Joseph Stanislaw calls the Saudi-Caspian-Siberia-Canada corridor. These resources do more than just satisfy energy demand; they bring poor and landlocked countries such as those of oil-rich central Asia into the global economy and give them a fresh identity. For Brazil and Indonesia, deforestation for timber and agriculture are economic pillars but the cause of 70 percent of their carbon emissions. As their rain forest resources dwindle, they must be careful not to reap what they sow: Industrial development generates employment but also rapidly absorbs precious arable land. We are running out of other resources that are just as important as oil.

It's become a cliché that the Stone Age did not end because we ran out of stone, and the fossil fuel age will not end because we run out of fossil fuel. After a decade of drought, Australians began to grow less water-intensive fruit while constructing desalination plants for Sydney and Melbourne. Kevin Rudd, the country's prime minister, actually campaigned on the climate change issue and has announced a multibillion-dollar public-private proposal to build the world's biggest solar power plant (even though the country is a massive coal producer). Diversifying energy supply has all sorts of positive spin-off effects. Shifting away from coal improves public health, shifting away from oil can ease geopolitical tensions while relieving economic pressures, and slowing deforestation can restore biodiversity and its many medical benefits. If just one company, Asia Pacific Resources International Limited, carries through with its plan to create a ring of tree plantations around one of Indonesia's densest forest peninsulas, it would curb Indonesia's emissions by 5 percent.

Like oil, water is unevenly distributed around the world, and so much of the supply—ocean water—is undrinkable in its present form. Swirling around in the Pacific Ocean currents is a giant blob of discarded plastics and zooplankton allegedly twice the size of Texas. This "Great Pacific Garbage Patch" is perhaps the best metaphor for how far along we are in the quest to sustainably manage the global commons. Two-thirds of the planet's surface is covered by oceans, yet oceanic governance is at best in its infancy. The Law of the Sea Treaty demarcates oceanic zones, but who will enforce its provisions for protection of marine life? Right now it's NGOs from the San Francisco Bay Area that are working with marine scientists to figure out how to recycle the oceans' gathering plastic heaps before they leak back onshore and pollute our food cycle. The world's major river systems—the Amazon, Nile, Mekong, Yellow, Indus, and Tigris-Euphrates—are being dammed and polluted, their drying causing water tables to drop and lakes to disappear. Global drying means that tropical heat spells will spread disease faster and lower agricultural productivity. The drylands belt of North and East Africa, the Middle East, and central Asia is the worst-affected region—and the recent famines in Niger, Malawi, and the Horn of Africa may be an unfortunate sign of things to come.

Most countries depend on others for their oil and water, making these resources either the greatest impetus for future conflict or its greatest opportunity to transcend borders. The population of the Middle East is expected to reach four hundred million by 2020, with about two-thirds of the currently low level of freshwater available per person. Along the way, the strategic value of the Golan Heights has shifted from military to environmental as it provides about one-third of Israel's water supply. In southern Asia, India and Bangladesh have already declared that China is engaged in a "water war" against them due to its hydroelectric dam and water diversion projects of the

Brahmaputra toward China's northern plains. Receding glaciers in Kashmir have made India's own Ganges River one of the world's most endangered sources of freshwater even as five hundred million people depend on it for drinking and irrigation. The Indo-Pak rivalry over Kashmir's strategic headwaters is increasingly a sideshow compared to the necessity of sharing what is left.

There are many opportunities to barter resources to rectify the imbalances inherent in our increasingly arbitrary borders. In central Asia, tiny Tajikistan has bet its future on producing and selling hydroelectric power to Kazakhstan and Uzbekistan, which sell it oil and gas. Rather than the fruitless summits they regularly hold to condemn one another for damning rivers upstream and raising electricity prices downstream, the three countries could set a price relationship for the resources they control and promise adequate supply in all directions. Saudi Arabia pumps water north into Jordan, while plans are moving forward to construct a Red Sea–Dead Sea canal that would replenish the latter's dwindling waters while desalinating it at the same time. Whether oil or water, there is still enough supply to meet demand, but only if we think in terms of channels, not borders, between countries.

The Climate Olympics

October 17, 2009, was no ordinary day in climate politics. Instead of putting on their suits and going to the presidential office in Male for their daily meeting, eleven cabinet ministers of the Maldives islands in the Indian Ocean put on scuba gear, took a twenty-minute boat ride, and dove sixteen feet underwater. Amid soft brown coral and zebra-striped fish, they sat at a rectangular table and passed around a laminated document calling for the world to cut greenhouse gas emissions. Using hand signals to communicate, they each voted and signed the declaration. During an underwater interview, Maldives president Mohamed Nasheed said, "This is what will happen to the Maldives if climate change is not checked. . . . And if the Maldives cannot be saved today we do not believe there is much chance for the rest of the world."

Environmental diplomacy is like the Olympics: many events, variable numbers of players, some games long and others short, some high-tech and others not. Climate debates also break down North-South divides. Brazil, China, and India often speak for the world's poor, but they are also among the world's largest carbon emitters. Poor countries don't want to hear about the primacy of environmentalism over economic growth since they are achieving the latter but claim they can't yet afford the former. India, with four hundred million people living in the dark with no access to electricity, won't sign emissions cuts until it finally caters to those in need.

Just because environmental solutions are needed globally doesn't mean there is one global solution. International organizations have fared no better in promoting environmental sustainability than they have in ensuring universal human rights: It's all talk and very little action. The United Nations deserves credit for convening the 1972 Stockholm Conference on the Human Environment, but since then there have been no less than five hundred multilateral environmental agreements, almost all nonbinding and implemented by only the wealthiest European nations and Japan, who kick the role of summit host back and forth from Kyoto to Copenhagen. Advocates of beefing up the United Nations' ability to manage the commons have proposed a "Global Environment Mechanism"—to do what, exactly?

The Montreal Protocol is widely cited as a model of successful international environmental diplomacy because it reduced chlorofluorocarbon emissions that were damaging the earth's ozone layer. Although the process of debating the science, proposing frameworks, and bringing governments and industries to an agreement on regulation required a dozen treaties over fourteen years, ozone damage was finally brought under control. Yet in the same amount of time, the Kyoto Protocol on greenhouse gas emissions has achieved virtually nothing. Kyoto took so long to negotiate that China and India, which were effectively given a pass in the treaty, have quickly risen to be among the world's top emitters, and its Byzantine complexity involving buying and selling credits and emissions-trading mechanisms has come to look like the environmental equivalent of financial engineering. Offering countries the option to buy "pollution allowances" is hardly evidence of moral courage.[2] Poor countries love the "polluter pays" principle, whose "you broke it, you fix it" logic requires rich countries to accept responsibility for climate change proportionate to the damage they've done over the course of history. African nations have demanded $40 billion in compensation from the wealthier countries causing climate change. But lawsuits are also not meaningful vehicles for reducing emissions.

The problem with all governmental negotiations is that they function according to countries rather than sectors. But such a substantial share of China's massive greenhouse gas emissions stems from catering to the world's largely non-Chinese-owned manufacturing industry that China itself can't be fully blamed for not taking precautions its foreign investors won't pay for. If climate change strategies are to work, they have to think as much in terms of supply chains as nation-states. Indeed, the common language for successful climate diplomacy will not be targets but technology. As Jorgen Berson of the Norwegian firm Point Carbon says about the Copenhagen process: "It was the same protracted, prolonged, and harsh negotiations. Blocks emerged and debates were repeated ad nauseam while forests burn. Emerging markets have a low appetite for global regulation and targets they can't measure, but a far larger appetite for technology and innovation if it's affordable."

Since the 1992 "Earth Summit" in Rio de Janeiro, global civil society has been a constant feature at environmental negotiations, storming the gates and making noise while also watching its bold proposals be watered down by timid governments. Multi-stakeholder bodies such as the World Water Council grew out of Rio to corral NGOs, UN agencies, governments, and engineering companies to address the freshwater crisis. By the 2002 Johannesburg summit, two parallel conversations had emerged: a dynamic and productive dialogue between business and civil society, and a stagnant intergovernmental track. The summit's final declaration named the guidelines produced by the nongovernmental Global Reporting Initiative as a leading benchmark for eco-compliance, and more than 330 multi-stakeholder partnerships were launched covering emissions reductions, biodiversity protection, energy provision, and water management. Rather than confrontational international negotiations, what we need are new *facilitators*, such as the Global Water Partnership, which links two thousand water experts, development agencies, and private companies to share best practices.

International organizations that want to make an impact on the environment need to put their money where their mouths are. They should stop trying to supervise the world and throw themselves into real programs. The UN Environment Program, for example, has launched efforts such as the "Billion Trees Campaign" and a Renewable Energy Enterprise Development project to help countries make and profit from green investments. The World Bank's Clean Development Mechanism, which approves projects after third-party vetting, has given $200 million to Indian companies to upgrade their power plants, while the International Finance Corporation has boosted funding for gas refinery projects that are compliant with its eco-friendly Equator Principles. Progress in climate negotiations actually depends on emerging markets confidently adopting the technologies that will allow them to even bother showing up at summits. Until then, climate conference should be put on ice, and all the money put into clean-tech transfer funds.

Were it not for the scientific community housed at major universities, diplomats would be pushing their target dates back for centuries to come. The Intergovernmental Panel on Climate Change has global credibility most of all because it has among its members scientists and scholars, not diplomats defending national interests. And its strength lies in being able to recommend strategies and investments that can be made by nations and companies individually without the need for an overarching bureaucracy that wastes valuable funds.

This free-for-all approach to climate diplomacy—in which all are expected to do their part and none escape scrutiny—is an approach more likely to succeed than grand summits, even as it is amorphous and confusing. Vague and cowardly intergovernmental dialogue cannot substitute for active competition and collaboration among governments, NGOs, and businesses. Some NGOs train the media to be climate savvy, some water engineers bring their best practices to the developing world, and some stock exchanges give special listing to green companies. By late 2010, business groups swarmed the United Nations demanding a transparent climate treaty that will facilitate balanced competition. So far, governments have been reluctant to ratify it. All of these actions are as much a part of the climate remedy as summits in Kyoto, Bali, and Copenhagen.

A World of Experiments

As with reducing poverty, for real progress on the climate change issue, we need learning across borders more than we need global institutions. The European Union has been an environmental leader from the get-go. It pushed for inclusion of cap-and-trade schemes in the Kyoto Protocol and went ahead with them even after the United States rejected Kyoto. European governments have sustained high fuel surcharges, making their nations the most efficient energy consumers in the world: EU citizens have half the per capita emissions output as Americans but a better quality of life. Even in the absence of global standards, the European Union sets them through its regulatory mechanisms. It is forcing power generators to pay for all of their emissions by 2013 but funding the policy through revenues from the European carbon market. It has pledged to calculate similar costs for non-European countries as well, and tax their imports accordingly, forcing upward compliance toward EU standards.

The European Climate Exchange even creates a value for rain forest land preserved for "carbon ranching" in places such as Madagascar, pricing it higher than if the trees were chopped down and sold off. EU legislation now calls for massive investments in carbon capture and storage. European energy giants such as Vattenfall are testing everything from pumping coal emissions into the ground above oil fields to add pressure for oil extraction to burying it several miles below the earth's surface, where it will harden into limestone. Most of the world's most profitable solar and wind power companies are publicly traded in Europe; Spain's Vestas provides 35 percent of the world's wind turbines and installs a new one every four hours. German engineers have designed "passive homes" that are so well insulated that they use almost no energy for either heating or cooling; Norwegian start-ups have invented an electric car that is 95 percent recyclable, and Volkswagen has a sleek new coup that plugs into an electric socket. Lufthansa and other European airlines now put carbon dioxide emissions data on e-tickets as matter-of-factly as calorie labels on a candy bar.

Just because Europeans aren't fighting in the new "Great Game" doesn't mean they haven't already won. Europe has ramped up the transition toward natural gas, which is cleaner-burning than oil and in abundant supply. American companies are taking their business to Europe, where cities such as Lisbon, Birmingham, Hamburg, and Madrid welcome Cisco's Connected Urban Development project to monitor and even eliminate traffic through smart traffic signals. In any case, European cities were designed before the car, so will outlive the end of oil through their electric trams and swarms of healthy cyclists. China and America don't need global codes—they just need to become more European.

At present, however, the American government alone—from government offices to navy aircraft carriers—is by far the largest energy consumer in the world, and thirty of the world's seventy-five largest emitters of greenhouse gasses are U.S. states. America's voracious energy consumption habits are deeply ingrained in its national character, meaning green living will only work in America if it's made easy. Google, for example, subsidizes employees to buy electric cars, and even provides them free of charge for running errands during the day. Its California cafeteria serves only organic food grown within 150 miles of headquarters. These are the steps companies across America can take to forge the transition toward community-based sustainability. Google is in the lead, and maybe the Pentagon will follow.

Because short-term financial considerations often trump long-term common sense, saving nature requires to some extent commoditizing it—pricing it according to its value to users. Both oil and water should cost more than they do. Once gas prices fall, many Americans suddenly think they don't need fuel-efficient or hybrid cars. The United States could tax carbon consumption, penalize oil speculators, and eliminate subsidies for fossil fuels—putting those funds into alternative energy research and development instead. But implementing any of these schemes will require a new level of public-private collaboration. President Obama's plan to reduce emissions in the United States was announced in partnership with car companies and labor unions, and coupled with $6 billion in subsidies to Nissan, Ford, and Tesla to develop hybrid cars. Nissan CEO Carlos Ghosn has put it most bluntly: "We must have zero-emissions vehicles—nothing else will keep the world from exploding." If hybrid cars powered by bio-fuels, batteries, and hydrogen can flourish, oil will lose its captive transportation market.

In tackling both financial and energy crises simultaneously, the Obama administration is planning everything from a "green bank" to a clean energy development agency to provide more than $100 billion to fund clean-tech research and create jobs in solar cell installation (which takes more hands than running a power plant), to build commuter railways and smart grids, to expand the country's natural gas infrastructure, and to reinsulate houses and buildings. The United States has at least 250,000 square miles of land in the Southwest alone that are suitable for solar plants. America's high-tech and clean-tech communities are now coming together to design green infrastructures for the common man. Shai Agassi's company Better Place has been designing an electric car infrastructure since well before Obama was elected, while local entrepreneurs and utilities are combining to make a thirty-foot-tall windmill with seven-foot blades the new must-have backyard accessory in as many as fifteen million homes.

Initially, however, America's "green collar" revolution may really be a European and Japanese one. The United States can invest billions of dollars in high-speed rail, but Obama officials had to travel to Spain and Japan to learn how such systems actually work. In fact, America presently runs a "green trade deficit" of $8 billion, importing vastly more clean energy goods than it exports. Toyota's hybrid Prius has been a bestseller in the United States, prompting its higher-end Lexus line to pitch Americans the "hybrid lifestyle" as it rolls out a fleet of new cars built largely from recycled or recyclable materials from its new green complex in California.

California's experiments with energy efficiency—which make it more like Sweden than the rest of the United States—demonstrate that the real action on climate change, like so many other issues, is taking place at the periphery, not the center. Like Brazilian cities or European countries, American states can be laboratories for innovation. In Florida, a planned coal plant in the Everglades was rejected in favor of a solar cell farm, oil heavyweight Chevron is also the largest installer of solar cells in California, and in New Mexico, a symbiosis is forming among solar cell companies, conservation biologists dedicated to protecting wildlife, and universities training graduates in environmental science.

In a world where less than fifty cities cause most of the greenhouse gas output, curbing emissions is as much the job of mayors and governors as presidents. Stockholm and London began congestion pricing earlier this past decade, while Copenhagen has steadily removed parking places in the city center to encourage people to take buses, ride bicycles, or walk. Berlin has contracted companies to green fifteen hundred buildings, reducing the city's carbon footprint by 25 percent. The greening of the Empire State Building presently under way in New York City is self-financing through savings in utility bills and will achieve the emissions reduction equivalent of taking nineteen thousand cars off the street. Even poor cities can change citizen and consumer behavior, leapfrogging to low-carbon, off-grid solutions such as distributed power networks that draw from multiple sources of energy. In Mexico City, the World Resources Institute ran a program mostly funded by the Shell Foundation to retrofit diesel metro buses with catalytic converters.

All the efforts under way to control Western emissions will be a quaint sideshow if they aren't copied in China, where hundreds of state-owned companies shun environmental regulations and are impervious to external scrutiny and shame as each year they build enough coal-fired plants to power Italy. Yet precisely because these state-run companies are literally public-private ventures, the country is actually well-placed to orchestrate a transformative shift in its national energy policy—a "Green Leap Forward." Indeed, the share of China's 2009 stimulus package devoted to greening its economy is the largest in the world. Its new corporate tax policy takes direct aim at the country's top one thousand companies to incentivize a switch to alternative energy, a consumption tax targets those disposing rather than recycling chopsticks, and the government has seeded at least five eco-investment funds. Thanks to a start-up loan given by the local party boss of Wuxi to Shi Zhengrong in 2001, China's Suntech Power has become one of the world's largest solar power firms and raises hundreds of millions of dollars on the New York Stock Exchange. China's State Grid Corporation, the world's largest public utility, has undertaken massive investments in wind and hydroelectric power, promising to generate 30 percent of its energy from renewable sources by 2030, and offered subsidies to cities to switch their taxi fleets to electric cars—of which Shenzhen-based BYD has already rolled out a fully Chinese-made line. The city of Baoding has declared itself a renewable city, sponsoring local firms to build wind and solar-cell farms.

The diplomacy of curbing Chinese emissions is all about mayors, factory owners, party officials, and American clean-tech companies—all brought together by a nonprofit called the Joint U.S.-China Collaboration on Clean Energy, which knows that the supposedly insurmountable problem of reducing China's emissions comes down to convening these players to find win-win deals. Even at the factory level, where owners are often in bed with local politicians, old and inefficient plants are being replaced with new ones equipped with CO_2 scrubbers.

Like China, India's challenge is to generate enough power for its people, but to do so in a way that reflects the ecologically conscious spirit of the times. India has an Energy Conservation Act that mandates that states set aside funds for clean energy. New Delhi has enforced strong regulations requiring buses and scooters to run on natural gas, while planting thousands of trees to make the city's air breathable again—a rare success for a poor-country mega-city. Its accomplishments are the results of both a progressive high court and a persistent lobbying from India's rambunctious civil society, particularly the Center for Science and the Environment, which sends representatives from village to village to teach people to harvest as much as

60 percent of the rainwater that falls on their properties using a system of rooftop gutters and ground trenches.

Most of India still lives in the villages, where the Small-Scale Sustainable Infrastructure Development Fund acts as a social merchant bank to provide locals with modern lights, pressure cookers, and water purifiers. Though it reaches a scale international organizations commonly neglect, it receives funding from a staggeringly diverse set of donors, such as the British Foreign Office, the Shell Foundation, the Blue Moon Fund, the Yahoo! Employee Foundation, and Électricité de France. Tulsi Tanti, once the owner of textile factories and frustrated by the intermittent local power supply, was inspired to set up two wind-power turbines. The result grew into Suzlon, a global wind-power giant that is buying entire energy grids across India and overseas to green their energy production.

Clearly there are two climate conversations going on. While Asian politicians act defensive at international gatherings, their businesses are angling to gain an edge in the global markets for solar power and micro-cars. China and India have also quickly become among the largest markets for clean tech. Vattenfall hopes to sell its CO_2 capture and storage technology in China, without which China would never sign emissions reduction agreements. BASF has figured out how to recycle emitted heat from its European factories, cutting its emissions in half while saving $300 million per year, a technology it now exports to China. Commercial real estate firms planning billions of square feet of office space in China now put forward green building plans rather than offering to retrofit later. India's burgeoning second-tier cities like Gwalior are buying energy-efficient fluorescent lighting as well as load-monitoring systems that distribute electricity where it's most needed. And First Solar of Arizona is building a solar field larger than Manhattan—in Mongolia.

Even oil-rich countries are investing in a non-oil future. Abu Dhabi's Masdar City, a joint venture with General Electric, MIT, and numerous other international partners, aims to create a $22 billion, fully carbon neutral eco-city to be ready by 2016, complete with fifty thousand residents. All power will come from photovoltaic cells and hot-water collectors, cars will be banned, electric-powered shuttles will ferry citizens around, and waste water will irrigate biofuel farms.

Africa is another emerging market for clean energy, and a continent that could literally grow its own power. In Mali (as in the Asian countries of India, China, and the Philippines), a low-maintenance plant called jatropha is being planted widely, and modified generators that run on oil from its seeds are being distributed hundreds of miles from any electricity grid.[3] In Malawi, the Dutch mail delivery company TNT has planted biofuel beans, creating a market for twenty thousand farmers. And in Ethiopia, the French firm Vergnet is building the continent's largest wind farm.

Biofuel cars in Brazil, CO_2 scrubbers in China, electric cars in India, and crop power in Africa—these are the signs of progress on climate change, not goals set for 2050. A treaty is just the icing on the cake after innovative firms have done the real work.

Eco-Crusaders

Some people go to great lengths to protect the environment when no official authority will. Ted Turner and other philanthropists have bought up chunks of Montana and now Argentina in order to protect its wilderness—while also keeping in mind that if the rest of the forests don't survive the ax, their plots will be the most valuable to turn into eco-resorts. Then there is Anthony White, a wealthy Australian painter who offered Blackwater millions of dollars to protect whales from Japanese harpoons since the Australian coast guard won't. Since trees and tribes lack a political voice, representatives of the UK-based NGO Survival International and the World Rainforest Movement laid down their bodies to block two major Brazilian logging companies from destroying a major section of the Paraguayan Amazon inhabited by indigenous peoples. NGO pressure has resulted in more than a third of the Amazon now being self-governed by local tribes.

The role of NGOs in transforming the world's economy and consciousness in an eco-friendly direction cannot be understated. In 1995, Greenpeace spent $1 million to prevent Shell's sinking of the Brent Spar oil rig in the North Sea, setting a precedent whereby all out-of-use rigs are now disposed of on land. No company wants to be named one of the notorious "Toxic Ten" in the categories of air pollution or chemical waste either, so they often comply to get NGOs off their backs. After the Brent Spar incident, Shell seeded a foundation with $250 million, much of which is distributed in loans to African small- and medium-sized enterprises and invested in infrastructure services for poor communities in Africa and Asia. One signal success has been Zingisa Coal, a small mining firm started by just five women in South Africa. After the women were turned down by dozens of banks, Shell loaned them $70,000, enough to grow and even expand their operations across Africa.

Shell and other companies have learned that NGOs aren't all out to get them, but can help their image and their bottom line. Companies don't want their personnel to be attacked and held hostage by tribes in protest of their disposal of arsenic and mercury into local waters, as happened to Denver-based Newmont Mining in Indonesia. Nor do they want to contribute to deforestation and soil erosion to such an extent that locals are driven into the arms of insurgencies that block their access to mines, as was the case with BHP Billiton in the Philippines. NGOs can help enhance their local credibility. Yes, certain NGOs are made up of hysterical activists, such as those who blocked the opening of a Romanian gold mine that would have provided thousands of jobs for poor locals. But increasingly they follow the savvy model of Fred Krupp, who as head of the Environmental Defense Fund (EDF) was not only a chief architect of America's Clean Air Act but also a pioneer of coalitions with Fortune 500 companies to coach them in reducing emissions. When private equity giant Kohlberg, Kravis, Roberts & Co. partners with EDF to evaluate all its investments for eco-compliance, you know something has changed in corporate-NGO relations.

NGOs set the very standards governments and companies use to measure their own environmental policies. The World Business Council for Sustainable Development (WBCSD)—whose unofficial motto is "Business cannot succeed if society fails"—has two hundred members whose combined economic value is $8 trillion. Its Greenhouse Gas Protocol is the most widely used international accounting tool for both governments and businesses to quantify and manage their emissions. WBCSD specializes in working by sector as well. Its cement initiative represents almost half the world's cement industry and helps construction giants such as Lafarge of France consume less energy in cement production and building construction. The Access Initiative, Climate Action Network, and Carbon Disclosure Project are other networks of hundreds of NGOs who each provide tailored guidance to companies and gather disclosures from them one by one.

The future of managing the environment can be seen in multistakeholder initiatives that often have NGOs as their hubs. For example, the Forestry Stewardship Council (FSC), launched by the World Wildlife Fund, takes no funding from the timber industry but manages the de facto standard codes for timber-harvesting operations and allocates the coveted FSC logo, which certified companies can label on their products. When the American Forest and Paper Association and other industry groups countered with their own voluntary and more lax codes, NGO pressure through the Rainforest Action Network forced Georgia-Pacific, International Paper, and retailers such as Home Depot to drop the ruse and elevate to the FSC standards. To protect their brand, Office Depot and Staples have ended their relationship with Asian Pulp and Paper, whose practices plundered the Indonesian rain forest. The Marine Stewardship Council plays a similar role for fisheries, 70 percent of which are being harvested to below replacement levels, using the power of its labels to certify seafood producers. It even uses real-time Google Earth maps on its website to track and promote sustainable fisheries and their techniques. In Alaska, the privatization of fisheries incentivized fishermen to catch halibut only when prices are high, saving the fish from overexploitation. For both forests and fisheries, a sense of local ownership is the key to building community-level sustainability.

Protecting natural habitats can go hand in hand with tourism. In Brazil's Amazonian state of Pará, the minerals conglomerate Vale operates a massive open-pit iron ore mine but also partners with local government and NGOs to preserve one million acres of forest around the mine. Rather than chop the trees down, the group instead runs a guesthouse to show tourists how such a partnership has resulted in greater community revenues while preserving huge natural habitats. In New Caledonia, Vale cooperates with local authorities to hire people from tribal communities and train them as environmental technicians to protect plant species. NGOs have also convinced Vale not to mine in areas designated as UNESCO World Heritage sites. Marriott, too, has partnered with the provincial government of Amazonas to protect 1.4 million acres of endangered forest, where it promotes sustainable tourism, while UNESCO and Expedia have combined to rehabilitate war-ravaged forests in Congo and hurricane-devastated communities in Mexico, opening them both to ecotourists.

NGOs are also the key drivers of government policy in the environmental arena. Conservation International spends more than $100 million per year in forty-four countries to protect endangered species, something few governments bother to advocate for, while the International Union for the Conservation of Nature (IUCN) directly advises seventy-five countries on biodiversity strategy and runs online training programs for environmental management professionals. The Russian government commissioned IUCN to conduct an impact assessment on its $20 billion Sakhalin II gas project, leading to a sound strategy for managing the local habitat. Governments may hold legal responsibility for protecting the planet, but it is mostly NGOs that show them how to do it.

The Business of Business Is Sustainability

The sustainability movement has advanced through waves, starting with the green movement in the 1960s and '70s, which led to Western governments ramping up regulations and putting businesses on the defensive. The 1984 Union Carbide disaster in Bhopal, followed by the Chernobyl accident in 1986, sparked the 1980s and '90s environmentalism of citizen activism. The increasing intensity of globalization in the late 1990s, and the so-called antiglobalization movements it inspired, generated a third wave of sustainability thinking focused on strengthening international regulations, such as the Kyoto Protocol, and demanding more responsible corporate governance. The fourth wave has now begun. Blending NGO activism, corporate innovation, and the role of emerging economies, this is the first truly global and inclusive effort.[4]

Environmental innovation is a process, not an event, and it is best embodied in the work of SustainAbility. A mix of think tank and consultancy, SustainAbility counsels chemical, energy, and finance giants on managing their environmental risk and integrating reporting procedures into their operations. It actually pioneered the "triple bottom line" concept in the early 1990s to explain how companies should measure performance based on social and environmental criteria, in addition to financial. Corporations are paying top dollar for such insight today. SustainAbility recently helped DuPont start to transition beyond hazardous chemicals toward products and services with a greener footprint. SustainAbility is also a discreet broker among corporations, watchdog NGOs, and academic experts. It provides politics-free analysis of the environmental impact of everything from fuel cells to nanotechnology, and gets behind hortatory declarations to uncover whether the Chinese government is moving toward efficient technologies, and what impact urbanization is having on that country's water supply. In this fourth wave, corporate statesmen have become environmental brokers as well. Acting in his private capacity as Goldman Sachs's chief in China, John Thornton proposed that the China Yangtze River Three Gorges Project Development Corporation retain the Nature Conservancy, an American NGO, to consult on making the dam more efficient and erode less soil, a relationship that has stuck as the dam proceeds to completion.

One of SustainAbility's principal backers, the reinsurance giant Swiss Re, shows how regulation within the private sector can move faster than any government. Upon realizing the impact of climate change on its own risk exposure, Swiss Re demanded that all of its clients perform climate assessments, as two-thirds of the FTSE 100 and Fortune 500 have now done. Swiss Re even invested $3 billion in wind and biomass power research. Given its client base of the world's largest firms, the company can be as powerful a climate regulator as almost any world government.

Globalization makes government regulation of corporate activity far more complicated than it seems. Governments fear that corporations will run off to regulation-free zones, resulting in a loss of tax revenue for them. Yet a mix of regulation, shareholder activism, consumer boycotts, and other forms of leverage have steered many multinationals toward high environmental standards, even in developing countries where rules are lax or nonexistent. The same cannot be said of state-owned Chinese, Malaysian, or Russian companies. Chinese authorities have allowed lead-poisoned baby formula to circulate on the world's grocery store shelves, but multinational corporations can almost never get away with such egregious actions due to the ISO standards, a set of thirteen thousand codes for product development and safety that apply much more to Pepsi and McDonald's than to nameless state-owned firms with opaque or nonexistent standards.[5] Globalization seems to allow for the regulation of everyone but the state itself.

In a world in which the mining multinational Rio Tinto has higher emissions than the country of Ireland, getting the largest companies to think in terms of the "triple bottom line" of people, planet, and profits simultaneously is more important than any international environmental convention. Even in the absence of strong regulations, and despite the financial crisis and volatility in oil prices, major energy-related firms are innovating internally to reduce their greenhouse gas emissions. BP, GE, Toyota, DuPont, and Michelin have all used their own equity to keep renewable projects going. UPS and FedEx are quickly converting fleets of thousands of vehicles to hybrid electro-diesel or other alternative fuels. John Browne's efforts to reduce BP's emissions cost the firm $20 million per year, but have saved more than $1.5 billion. The company continues to invest substantially in renewable energy, such as solar panel businesses and sustainable biomass, indicating a potentially long-term shift in the company's acronym toward "Beyond Petroleum."

Every industry can improve its environmental performance. Every year, 1.3 billion tires are shipped to third world countries to be burned or discarded in giant heaps into the oceans, polluting air, sea, and land equally. Green Rubber, a company based in rubber-rich Malaysia, has pioneered the science of devulcanizing tires and recycling them into new products. Paradoxically, the information revolution has not only failed to deliver the paperless office, it has also vastly increased electricity consumption. The world's data centers consume more energy than all of Sweden. Air-conditioning accounts for 96 percent of the electricity that data centers use, with only 4 percent needed to actually store data. More efficient data center cooling, placing servers closer together, and making computers out of recyclable material are all steps the IT industry could take to live up to its aspiration to be a realm of abundant information without destroying nature's abundance.

As in the arena of labor rights, perhaps no entity in the world can influence the global economy's eco-footprint like Wal-Mart. The firm spends $500 million of its own every year to implement renewable energy in its supply chain, and it is moving toward a "zero waste" policy globally as well, requiring environmental reporting from all its suppliers—everywhere, with no exceptions. At its Sustainability Summit in Beijing in 2008, it announced that suppliers must make cuts of at least 20 percent in their energy usage to maintain their contracts. The NGO Environmental Defense no longer demonizes Wal-Mart but instead works with it to green its stores, improve conditions at the fish farms that provide its seafood, minimize its packaging waste, and improve the environmental performance of the thirty thousand Chinese factories that supply its stores.

Launched in 2005, GE's Ecomagination initiative represents another blockbuster commitment by one of the world's largest companies toward an alternative energy future. The project's seventeen major products include the GE90–115B aircraft engine, which in a twin-engine plane emits 141,000 fewer tons of greenhouse gasses than competing four-engine planes, or enough CO_2 to be absorbed by thirty-five thousand acres of forest. Ecomagination's sales are reaching 10 percent of GE's overall portfolio while making the company's worldwide customers more energy efficient. Ecomagination is now reaching beyond its Masdar City work in Abu Dhabi. Together with the emirate's Mubadala sovereign wealth fund, it has announced venture funds of a combined $40 billion to invest in pursuing renewable energy in Africa and Asia and has signed an agreement with China's National Development and Reform Commission to advance renewable energy in two hundred second-tier Chinese cities. Between Wal-Mart and GE, the private sector is doing more to elevate China's environmental policies and standards than any vague treaty could.

What remains is to ensure that more efficient and accessible technologies emerge for rich and poor nations alike. American and European venture capital funds pour $6 billion per year into clean technology, and institutional investors such as pension funds, endowments, and sovereign wealth funds represent by far the largest pool of capital taking an interest in clean energy. Whereas there used to be an unbridgeable "valley of death" between public and private-sector support for renewable energy research, the two now cooperate to commercialize risks from the earliest stages. Governments alone could never identify, fund, and scale up proven biomass, wind, hydro, geothermal, methane capture, and nitrogen-free fertilizer projects as quickly as those who want to profit from these innovations, including Kleiner, Perkins, Caufield & Byers; RNK Capital; and Global Change Associates. Clearinghouses for clean energy trends such as the Climate Group and New Energy Finance have become a vital resource for investors lining up to enter the alternative energy market. The goal is not to find a single breakthrough, but to create an innovation space such as the GreenXchange, in which Nike, Best Buy, Yahoo!, and Salesforce operate an online commons to track and share eco-innovations seeking investment.

Nobody holds a monopoly on providing incentives to those interested in saving the planet. Companies and charities together fund huge competitions such as Coke's clean water prize and the X-Prize, which awards $250 million in prizes across fifteen areas but has inspired $2.5 billion in investment among the competing teams to find solutions to cancer, emission-free driving, and human genome sequencing. Richard Branson has put $25 million into a "Carbon War Room" to fund emissions reductions in "battle theaters" such as industrialization, transport, electricity, and deforestation. Where else would we get ideas such as using ocean waves to generate electricity, feeding atmospheric CO_2 to algae to produce biofuel, floating sulfur-dioxide balloons into the stratosphere to reflect more sunlight, and engineering giant parachutes to pull supertankers across the ocean? Competitions like those sponsored by the X-Prize Foundation are not a silver bullet but a symbol of the revolution in incentives under way to innovate solutions to problems that world leaders could never otherwise solve. We need more X-Prize competitions and fewer proposals for a toothless World Environment Organization.

One of the enduring images frequently deployed to capture the planetary crisis is of a lone polar bear stranded on a tiny floating ice patch. No government in the world has rescued that polar bear or devised a plan to save his species from drowning or extinction. You will have to do it.

Chapter Eleven

The Next Renaissance

Philosophers have all interpreted the world differently.
It now depends on changing it.

—Karl Marx

If it's fair, it's good.

—Amartya Sen

More than two hundred years ago, Immanuel Kant claimed, "The history of the human race as a whole can be regarded as the realization of a hidden plan of nature to bring about an internally perfect political constitution as the only possible state within which all natural capacities of mankind can be developed completely." If there is such a hidden plan, it is unlikely to emerge during our current period of global uncertainty—even if now is when we need it most. Instead we are headed into the "turbulent teens," a decade (or more) of confusion, disorder, and tension between tradition and modernity. How can we steer mankind from the new Middle Ages into the next Renaissance?

Typically books on global politics end with bromides about how the world needs more rationality, creativity, common sense, generosity, kindness, cosmopolitanism, democracy, or humanism, and calls for new super-organizations to instill these virtues. But as H. L. Mencken famously remarked, "For every complex problem there is a solution that is simple, neat, and wrong." Antiquated debates about whether America can lead the world—or whether any single power or institution can—no longer meet even the most basic test of taking place in reality. For those who prefer some centralized, overarching governance with values shared by all, the writing is on the wall: It isn't going to happen.

Traditional models of diplomacy hold only one lesson for how to manage this world: that they are themselves totally insufficient. Rather than finding common projects through which to transcend their differences, the few leading powers of the world, from America and Brazil to China and Japan, are still feeling one another out about which red lines should not be crossed in one another's affairs. Any time we turn to them for leadership—whether at the UN Security Council or the Copenhagen climate summit—we are let down. Where governments fail, great powers come to prop them up, not to reinvent them. Where people clash, they send peacekeepers, not peacemakers. And so we accelerate into a perfect storm.

All grand global schemes miss the point that representation—democratic or otherwise—is not enough to satisfy our visceral need to be in control of our own affairs. Today, for the first time, the under-represented and disenfranchised have access to information, communication, money, and the tools of violent revolution to demand and effect real change, not just new variations on the status quo. They will constantly pressure the system to evolve. Out-of-touch governments and international organizations are already feeling the heat from a bottom-up awakening: labor unions and coca farmers in Latin America, the Arab underclass in the Middle East, the Pashtuns of south-central Asia, Maoists and Naxalite tribal groups in India, and migrant laborers in China. International bureaucrats should expect nothing less than a technologically empowered revolt against their plans—or perhaps they will simply be ignored altogether. It would be too easy to suggest that all states must be strengthened and that the world of strong sovereign nations should be re-created. That world never really existed. We should embrace the next one.

The same continent that brought us medievalism also brought us a road map toward the next Renaissance: Europe. Indeed, the most inspirational figure for twenty-first-century diplomacy shouldn't be balance-of-power statesmen such as Henry Kissinger and George Kennan, but rather Jean Monnet, the architect of European unity after World War II. Monnet was the original shuttle diplomat. Named deputy secretary-general of the League of Nations after World War I, he used his family's financial business to stabilize eastern European currencies in the 1920s, then in the 1930s worked with Chiang Kai-shek to reorganize China's railway system. As the drumbeats of war sounded, he shuttled between Paris and London to help forge an anti-Nazi alliance, and then shifted to Washington to purchase war supplies for Europe. He also cajoled President Roosevelt to undertake the Victory Program that brought America into World War II.

Monnet, in other words, was the first multistate diplomat, a global statesman for our postmodern times. Having experienced two great European wars, he realized that rebuilding Europe on the basis of national sovereignty was a recipe for deferred disaster. Instead, Monnet devoted most of the next three decades to promoting first the 1950 Schuman Plan, which created the European Coal and Steel Community, and gradually other pan-European institutions such as the European Economic Community ("Common Market"), European Commission, European Monetary System, and European Parliament. Within the European Union he inspired, diplomats don't really represent their countries to one another so much as co-govern a common space alongside transnational networks of farmers, industries, regulators, unions, and other groups. The European Union spends massively on "cohesion funds" to raise living standards in poorer regions, turning medievalist disparity into postmodern solidarity.

Today Europe has countries but virtually no borders, making it a hopeful metaphor for our neo-medieval universe of linked but autonomous communities. Importantly, the European Union is not an end state but a constant process and an experiment. As two scholars recently wrote, "Europe does not exist, only Europeanization."[1] The ever thickening integration of Europe is a successful end in itself and a model for other regions. From Morocco to Azerbaijan, laws are evolving toward European standards even as such countries may never become full EU members. Monnet believed that such dynamic European solidarity was "not an end in itself, but only a stage on the way to the organized world of tomorrow." To have such solidarity beyond the state on the global level is both the most—and the best—toward which we can aspire.

The transition from the late Middle Ages to the modern era began unexpectedly with the existential calamity of the Black Death that ravaged much of Europe's population in the mid-fourteenth century. In a moment of turbulence among Italian city-states, the same Medici family of Florence that had risen to prominence and power in the papal era came to be counseled by the founding father of secular rational governance, Machiavelli, and sponsored two of history's greatest artists and inventors, Michelangelo and Leonardo da Vinci. The Renaissance's rediscovery of classical scholarship, coupled eventually with the invention of moveable type and Gutenberg's printing press, paved the way for the Protestant Reformation, which culminated in the bloody Thirty Years' War of the mid-seventeenth century. We cannot forget that the Renaissance was a politically volatile era even as it bred some of mankind's greatest cultural accomplishments. If we are on the path to another Renaissance, it will be a similarly uneven and tumultuous time.

Yet the pillars of the next Renaissance—intellectual humanism, the rediscovery of ancient wisdom, and the rise of vernaculars—can now flourish on a global scale. Giovanni Pico della Mirandola, the early Renaissance champion of human freedom, sought to re-center discussions of the divine around the individual. Even as his *Oration on the Dignity of Man* was taken as a secular manifesto, in fact his true effort was to reconcile the church with classical strains of logic such as Aristotle's. His lesson for today's age is that our fruitless debates between the West and Islam should instead become a more inclusive discourse on achieving spiritually and morally informed governance.

Similarly, the Renaissance witnessed innovations such as double-entry bookkeeping and large-scale credit, bringing new commercial opportunities to Europeans whose geographic and cultural horizons were gradually opening as Crusaders returned home. The manner in which the current economic turbulence has shaken up our financial architecture could do the same. Chastened bankers from Lehman Brothers are actually leading an effort to revise models of financial analytics to emphasize value creation, not just wealth creation. At the invitation of French president Nicolas Sarkozy, the Nobel Prize–winning economist Joseph Stiglitz is reinventing the notion of GNP to include measures of sustainability. Just as great companies like Google and PayPal took off after the late 1990s dot-com bubble burst, new innovators are emerging from the recession. They are focusing on serving ordinary people, including the world's poorest, wherever they may be.

The next Renaissance, then, is about universal liberation through exponentially expanding and voluntary interconnections. We are in the early phase of a new era in which each individual and collective has the ability to pursue its own ends. The information revolution has empowered individuals to claim their own authority, leading us into a world of mutuality among countless communities of various sizes. This unfolding epoch will force us to appreciate the second law of thermodynamics: the inexorability of universal entropy. Complexity is our permanent reality. The future will be about multiple sovereignties, not exclusive ones.

We must pursue an active evolution toward this more networked order. "Active" means not waiting for a more capable America, China's adaptation to global leadership, or more blue-ribbon panels to reform the United Nations. In their own spheres of activity, governments should focus on internal stability and delivering the basics to the populations within their borders, NGOs should devote themselves singularly to empowering local communities, companies should view their employees and supply chains as their citizens and infrastructure, and religious groups should practice the Golden Rule themselves to be considered legitimate. Importantly, all of these actors should allow organic alliances to emerge to solve the problems at hand. We can admire the boundless creativity of human ingenuity all we want. Better diplomacy is how to harness it. If you can afford to buy this book, or have the technology to order it, you have no excuse not to contribute to the new mega-diplomacy.

The future of global governance is not as simple as talking about the "BRIC" countries. Instead, it is a bricolage of movements, governance arrangements, networks, soft law codes, and other systems at the local, regional, and global level. Some experts are skeptical that a world of connected but self-governing communities of various sizes—and many more transcending space altogether—can be more than the sum of their parts. But we don't have to be skeptics to apply skepticism to evaluate what works in diplomacy today. Witness how central mechanisms have ceased to be useful proxies for human progress, and how it progresses nonetheless: The WTO is stalled, but global trade is carried on by merchants at the top and bottom of the global economic food chain; the Copenhagen process did nothing for the climate, but clean-tech companies forge ahead with innovation undeterred; the UN Security Council may never be reformed, but regional organizations are picking up the slack. Each of those local experiments holds greater promise than banal global org charts. Compliance with weak treaties is not a measure of our collective evolution; increasing participation in the actions that produce global solidarity is.

If a new global social contract is to emerge, it will be as a result of the communities of the world—whether nations, corporations, or faiths—sharing knowledge and cooperating, but also learning to respect one another's power and values. As they practice mega-diplomacy, they leverage each other's resources and hold one another accountable. In a world in which every player has a role in global policy, the only principle that can reliably guide us is pragmatism: learning from experience and applying its lessons. The dot-gov, dot-com, and dot-org worlds are converging toward such pragmatism. How will we know when we have succeeded? By lives saved and improved, crises averted, and networks built. This networked world need not be a tribal one. Webs of interdependence among diverse enclaves are the logical extension of globalization, not a break from it. The local to the local is still global.

Interdependence is one of the buzzwords of our age, but it is an observation, not a strategy. Perpetual resilience, not stiff governance, is the strategy that nations, economies, and communities must pursue irrespective of their degree of interdependence with the rest of the world. A world changing so quickly needs to be run in real time, and even anticipate the future. It has to be made up not of rigid states, but rather of networks of resilient systems. Resilience is about local stability rather than centralized dependence, a diversity of approaches rather than reliance on any one solution, flexibility of institutions to change as the tasks shift, and transparent collaboration to build trust and generate maximum resources.[2] Resilience means Africans don't have to wait for the United Nations to approve military interventions or for the World Bank to provide them loans; it means Europeans and Australians don't wait for the United States to sign climate treaties before turning global warming into a commercial opportunity; and it means emerging markets don't wait for G-20 meetings to launch stimulus packages or issue local-currency bonds. Resilience is how the local thrives amid the global.

We need risk management systems more than we need—or will ever have—powerful global institutions. Our goal should be an autopoietic world: self-regulating and re-creating. We must be vigilant, recognizing the fact that contagions can spread rapidly in networks, so we must code an operating template that builds immunities after failure and learns with each cycle of reproduction. Think of it like a world of wikis that everyone can access and navigate, and if one link breaks, there are alternative paths. If you poke a spiderweb, it doesn't fall apart.

A hybrid, diffuse, public-private world is not flawless and is certainly far more complex than our existing order, but it is an improvement rather than a step backward. If the diverse groups populating the world can feel that they have a direct or indirect say in global policies, the next phase of diplomacy will be better than the last. It is said that the pessimist sees difficulty in every opportunity and the optimist sees opportunity in every difficulty. Winston Churchill was a pragmatist. He said, "I'm an optimist—it doesn't seem of much use to be anything else."

Acknowledgments

Over the past decade I've been privileged to sit at many of the crossroads of global thinking on how we run the world, from the United Nations to the World Economic Forum to Washington think tanks to closed-door foreign ministry discussions to the world's leading NGOs. I deeply appreciate the support of so many individuals who have shaped my thinking on global governance, while taking full responsibility for the arguments and claims in this book.

I would like to thank the members of the 2005 Low Level Panel on UN Reform and the 2007 Next Generation Fellows of the American Assembly, and participants in the March 2007 InWent conference in Berlin on "Global Governance in Flux," the April 2008 NGO Leaders Forum in New York, the October 2008 Geneva High-Level Symposium on Global Health Governance, the August 2008 Global Institutional Reform workshop at Princeton, the February 2009 International Studies Association Annual Convention in New York, the March 2009 Bertelsmann Global Policy Council in Berlin, the April 2009 Center for Post-Industrial Studies roundtable in Moscow on "Democracy in a Changing World," and the April 2009 Georgetown Global Forum on "Profits, Philanthropy and Development."

I hope this book lives up to the reputation of the New America Foundation as a hub for the next generation of policy innovation. My colleagues there once again provided a steady stream of fresh ideas and constructive feedback. I am indebted to Steve Coll, Steve Clemons,

Sherle Schwenninger, Maria Figueroa, Michael Cohen, Peter Bergen, Priscilla Lewis, Janine Wedel, Doug Rediker, Flynt Leverett, Sean McFate, Nick Schmidle, Ray Boshara, and Jamie Zimmerman, and researchers Jeff Meyer, Katherine Tiedemann, Ben Katcher, Faith Smith, and Jeremy Strasser. I would also like to thank Bonnie Jenkins, my program officer from the Ford Foundation, which generously supported research for this book. Colleagues from fraternal think tanks have also been enormously helpful: Ben Barber, David Callahan, Miles Rapoport, and Michael Edwards of Demos; David Devlin-Foltz and Peter Reiling of the Aspen Institute; Stewart Patrick of the Council on Foreign Relations; and Joerg Husar, Guenther Maihold, and Ulrich Schneckener of the Stiftung Wissenschaft und Politik.

Numerous experts in global affairs have provided wisdom and insights over the course of my research: Kishore Mahbubani, Barry Carin, Gordon Smith, Steve Weber, Ely Ratner, Bruce Jentleson, Nazneen Barma, Alan Alexandroff, Andy Cooper, Jonathan Hausmann, Stephen Stedman, Thomas Wright, Vladislava Inozemtsev, Daniele Archibugi, John Dunn, Natan Sharansky, Amitai Etzioni, Ekaterina Kuznetsova, Jim DeWilde, Janice Stein, Paul Mayer, Rana Sarkar, Thierry Malleret, Chandran Nair, Barry Buzan, David Held, Danny Quah, Tyler Brule, Peter Marber, Raymond Saner, Lichia Yiu, Iver Neumann, James Der Derian, Lora Viola, Vikram Raghavan, Pamela Mar, Francisco Martinez Montes, Simon Maxwell, James Traub, Ethan Burger, Fouad Ghanma, Neemat Frem, Pete Singer, Ali Wyne, Nadia Sood, Paul Romer, Sara Agarwal, Joel Harrington, and Philip Zelikow.

From the World Economic Forum, I am grateful to Klaus Schwab, Rick Samans, Kevin Steinberg, Paul Smyke, Fiona Paua, David Aikman, Michael Seo, and John Moavanzadeh; and from the WEF's Global Governance Initiative, I am indebted to Ann Florini, Sartaj Aziz, Joachim von Braun, Gareth Evans, Al Sommer, Jonathan Lash, Chris Colclough, Mirai Chatterjee, Moisés Naím, and Mary Robinson. WEF senior advisers, including Sean Cleary and Subi Rangan, also provided valuable insights.

Many current foreign service officers, State Department personnel, and other distinguished American diplomats have provided valuable insights for this book. I'd particularly like to thank Richard Holbrooke, Helena Finn, Rudi Lohmeyer, Farah Pandith, Bill Whelen, Steve Hill, Greg Behrman, Ashley Bommer, Jared Cohen, Nazneen Ash, Adnan Kifayat, Amar Bakshi, and Tad Brown.

The following experts on the role of corporations were extremely helpful: John Ruggie, Georg Kell, Marketa Evans, Clare O'Brien, Raj Kumar, Diana Farrell, Christine Bader, Salil Tripathi, Earl Dos Santos, Sara Agarwal, Eric Nonacs, Brad Ryder, Peter Kellner, Jonathan Auerbach, Hans Vries, and Pamela Hartigan.

On civil society matters, I received exceptional insights from Ricken Patel, Daisy Khan, Paul Reynault, Karen Tse, Premal Shah, Henrik Lund, Bill Abrams, Mark Suzman, Peter Bell, and Tony Pipa.

For their expertise on India-related trends I am grateful to Kiran Pasricha, Anwarul Hoda, Ashok Ummath, Jayanta Roy, T. Vishwanath, Ajay Khanna, Shashi Tharoor, and Ameet Mehta.

On the issue of conflict management, particularly related to Afghanistan, I am grateful for the insights of Stan McChrystal, Carne Ross, Paul van Zyl, Rick Ponzio, Barney Rubin, Ellen Laipson, Clare Lockhart, Seema Patel, Joshua Gardner, Chris Hanson, Mary Ann Callahan, John Schweiger, Michelle Parker, Chris Eaton, Brian Fawcett, Christine Fair, Anja de Beer, Hamish Nixon, Paula Kantor, Meloney Lindberg, Joanna Nathan, Tilly Reed, Rory Stewart, Masuda Sultan, Humayun Hamidzada, Saad Mohseni, Aaron Tallaferino, Ashok Parameswaran, Cathy Silverstein, Espen Eide, Robert Kaplan, Carter Page, Jonathan Paris, Greg Mortenson, Christiane Leitinger, Paula Newberg, Verena Ringler, Srilal Pereira, David Hoffman, Ramesh Thakur, Melissa Payson, Mosharraf Zaidi, and Matthew Arnold.

For their insights on matters relevant to the environment, global public health, poverty, and human rights, I am indebted to Jose-Maria Figueres, John Hafner, Ulrich Adamheit, Vijay Vaitheeswaran, Terry Taminen, Bill Hinchberger, Kate Taylor, Esha Chhabra, Paul Meyer, Laurie Garrett, Alejandro Jadad, Ilona Kickbusch, Devi Sridhar, K. J. Singh, Emilie Filmer-Wilson, Joerg Schimmel, Sanjay Reddy, Nenad Rava, David Morrison, and Sarah Leah Whitson.

As before, I have been guided by a dream team made up of my editor, Will Murphy, at Random House and my agent, Jennifer Joel, at International Creative Management. I am forever grateful for having them in my corner for this second book and hopefully for many projects to come.

Without my family I could never run my own world. My father, Sushil, once again deserves special thanks for reading and editing the entire manuscript several times, as do my mother, Manjula, brother, Gaurav, and sister-in-law, Anu, for their constant love and support. Much of this book was written in the presence of my two constant companions, both at home and abroad: my lovely and brilliant wife, Ayesha, and our adorable baby daughter, Zara.

Notes

Chapter One: Mega-diplomacy

1. Toynbee, *Civilization on Trial*, 23.

2. Ridley, *The Origins of Virtue*, 264.

Chapter Two: The New Diplomats

1. John Newhouse, "Diplomacy, Inc." *Foreign Affairs,* May/June 2009.

2. Bono, Speech to Global Business Council for HIV/AIDS, Berlin, Germany, April 21, 2004.

3. George Soros, "The People's Sovereignty," *Foreign Policy,* January/February 2004, 66–67.

Chapter Three: The (Fill-in-the-Blank) Consensus

1. C. K. Prahalad, "Twenty Hubs and No HQ," *strategy+business,* Spring 2008.

2. WTO Statistics Database, available at http://stat.wto.org/Home/WSDBHome.aspx?Language=E; UN Conference on Trade and Development (UNCTAD) 2008 World Investment Report, available online at http://www.unctad.org/en/docs/wir2008_en.pdf.

Chapter Four: Peace Without War

1. Greg Mills and Jeffrey Herbst, "There Is No Congo," *Foreign Policy,* March/April 2009.

Chapter Five: The New Colonialism: Better Than the Last

1. "A Plan for Action: A New Era of International Cooperation for a Changed World: 2009, 2010 and Beyond" (report of the Managing Global Insecurity project, Brookings Institution, Washington, D.C., September 2008).

Chapter Six: Terrorists Pirates, Nukes

1. Jones and Libicki, *How Terrorist Groups End.*

2. Jeffrey Gettleman, "The Most Dangerous Place in the World," *Foreign Policy,* March/April 2009.

Chapter Seven: Getting Rights Right

1. Bernard Condon, "Babble Rouser," *Forbes,* August 2008.

Chapter Eight: By Any Means Necessary

1. BBC World Debate, Tianjin, China, October 2008.

2. Jan Ross, "Ein Stossdaempfer mit tausand Federn," *Die Zeit,* March 26, 2009.

3. Jehangir S. Pocha, "One Sun in the Sky: Labor Unions in the People's Republic of China," *Georgetown Journal of International Affairs,* Winter/Spring 2007, 11.

4. Harry G. Broadman, "China and India Go to Africa," *Foreign Affairs,* March/April 2008.

5. Michael Ross, "Blood Barrels," *Foreign Affairs,* May/June 2008, 7.

Chapter Nine: The Case Against Poverty

1. Tom Mitchell, "An Army Marching to Escape Medieval China," *Financial Times,* April 16, 2009.

2. Sixty-five percent of BRAC's revenue is generated from its own programs and 30 percent from direct private support.

3. "Just Good Business: Survey of Corporate Social Responsibility," *The Economist,* January 19, 2008, 4.

4. Josh Ruxin, "Doctors Without Orders," *Democracy,* Summer 2008.

5. Tahir Andrabi, Jishnu Das, C. Christine Fair, and Asim Ijaz Khwaja, "The Madrasa Myth," ForeignPolicy.com, June 2009.

6. G. Pascal Zachary, "Inside Nairobi, the Next Palo Alto?" *The New York Times*, July 20, 2008.

7. Pritchett, *Let Their People Come*, 85.

8. Mukul G. Asher and Amarendu Nandy, "Remittances: Maximizing India's Strategic Leverage," *Pragati*, June 2007.

9. Jason DeParle, "Western Union Empire Moves Migrant Cash Home," *The New York Times*, November 22, 2007.

10. Ibid., "A Good Provider Is One Who Leaves," *The New York Times Magazine*, April 22, 2007.

Chapter Ten: Your Planet, Your Choice

1. Scott Borgerson, "Sea Change," *Atlantic Monthly*, December 2008, 88–89.

2. Ted Nordhaus and Michael Shellenberger, "Scrap Kyoto," *Democracy*, Summer 2008.

3. Lydia Polgreen, "Mali's Farmers Discover a Weed's Potential Power," *The New York Times*, September 9, 2007.

4. Adapted from SustainAbility, http://www.sustainability.com.

5. Benedict Kingsbury, Nico Krisch, and Richard Stewart, "The Emergence of Global Administrative Law," *Law and Contemporary Problems* 68 (Summer/Autumn 2005).

Chapter Eleven: The Next Renaissance

1. Beck and Grande, *Cosmopolitan Europe*, 2–10; Charles Sabel and Jonathan Zeitlin, "Learning from Difference: The New Architecture of Experimentalist Governance in the EU," *European Law Journal* 14, no. 3 (May 2008): 271–327.

2. Jamais Cascio, "The Next Big Thing: Resilience," *Foreign Policy*, May/June 2009.

Bibliography

Abu-Lughod, Janet L. *Before European Hegemony: The World System A.D. 1250–1350*. Oxford, UK: Oxford University Press, 1989.

Adamson, Daniel de Faro, and Joe Andrew. *The Blue Way: How to Profit by Investing in a Better World*. New York: Simon and Schuster, 2007.

Ali, Saleem H. *Treasures of the Earth*. New Haven, Conn.: Yale University Press, 2009.

Anheier, Helmut, Marlies Glasius, and Mary Kaldor, eds. *Global Civil Society 2001*. New York: Oxford University Press, 2001.

Archibugi, Daniele. *The Global Commonwealth of Citizens: Toward Cosmopolitan Democracy*. Princeton, N.J.: Princeton University Press, 2008.

Ashdown, Paddy. *Swords and Ploughshares: Bringing Peace to the 21st Century*. London: Weidenfeld and Nicolson, 2007.

Ayoob, Mohammed. *The Third World Security Predicament: State Making, Regional Conflict, and the International System*. Boulder, Colo.: Lynne Rienner, 1995.

Barnett, Michael, and Martha Finnemore. *Rules for the World: International Organizations in Global Politics*. Ithaca, N.Y.: Cornell University Press, 2004.

Barrett, Scott. *Why Cooperate? The Incentive to Supply Global Public Goods*. Oxford, UK: Oxford University Press, 2007.

Barry, Christian, and Sanjay G. Reddy. *International Trade and Labor Standards: A Proposal for Linkage*. New York: Columbia University Press, 2008.

Bartelson, Jens. *A Genealogy of Sovereignty.* Cambridge, UK: Cambridge University Press, 1995.

Bass, Gary J. *Freedom's Battle: The Origins of Humanitarian Intervention.* New York: Alfred A. Knopf, 2008.

Bates, Robert. *When Things Fell Apart: State Failure in Late-Century Africa.* New York: Cambridge University Press, 2008.

Baumol, William J., Robert E. Litan, and Carl J. Schramm. *Good Capitalism, Bad Capitalism, and the Economics of Growth and Prosperity.* New Haven, Conn.: Yale University Press, 2007.

Baylis, John, and Steve Smith, eds. *The Globalization of World Politics: An Introduction to International Relations.* New York: Oxford University Press, 1997.

Beck, Ulrich. *Power in the Global Age: A New Global Political Economy.* Cambridge, UK: Polity, 2006.

Beck, Ulrich, and Edgar Grande. *Cosmopolitan Europe.* Translated by Ciaran Cronin. Cambridge, UK: Polity, 2007.

Bishop, Matthew, and Michael Green. *Philanthro-capitalism: How the Rich Can Save the World.* New York: Bloomsbury Press, 2008.

———. *The Road from Ruin: How to Revive Capitalism and Put America Back on Top.* New York: Crown Business, 2010.

Booth, Ken. *Theory of World Security.* Cambridge, UK: Cambridge University Press, 2007.

Bradford, Colin, and Johannes Linn, eds. *Global Governance Reform: Breaking the Stalemate.* Washington, D.C.: Brookings Institution Press, 2007.

Bremmer, Ian, and Preston Keat. *The Fat Tail: The Power of Political Knowledge for Strategic Investing.* New York: Oxford University Press, 2009.

Brendon, Piers. *The Decline and Fall of the British Empire, 1781–1997.* New York: Alfred A. Knopf, 2008.

Brenkman, John. *The Cultural Contradictions of Democracy: Political Thought Since September 11.* Princeton, N.J.: Princeton University Press, 2007.

Brest, Paul, and Hal Harvey. *Money Well Spent: A Strategic Plan for Smart Philanthropy.* New York: Bloomberg Press, 2008.

Brown, Chris. *Sovereignty, Rights, and Justice: International Political Theory.* Cambridge, UK: Polity, 2002.

Brown, Lester. *Plan B 2.0: Rescuing a Planet Under Stress and a Civilization in Trouble*. New York: W. W. Norton and Co., 2006.

Bull, Hedley. *The Anarchical Society: A Study of Order in World Politics*. New York: Columbia University Press, 1977.

Buzan, Barry, and Ole Wæver. *Regions and Powers: The Structure of International Security*. Cambridge, UK: Cambridge University Press, 2003.

Caplan, Richard. *International Governance of War-Torn Societies: Rule and Reconstruction*. Oxford, UK: Oxford University Press, 2005.

Chayes, Sarah. *The Punishment of Virtue: Inside Afghanistan After the Taliban*. New York: Penguin Press, 2006.

Chesterman, Simon. *You, the People: The United Nations, Transitional Administration, and State-Building*. Oxford, UK: Oxford University Press, 2004.

Clark, Ian. *Globalization and International Relations Theory*. Oxford, UK: Oxford University Press, 1999.

Clarke, Duncan. *Crude Continent: The Struggle for Africa's Oil Prize*. London: Profile Books, 2008.

Clinton, William J. *Giving: How Each of Us Can Change the World*. New York: Alfred A. Knopf, 2007.

Cohen, Raymond. *Negotiating Across Cultures: Communication Obstacles in International Diplomacy*. Washington, D.C.: United States Institute of Peace, 1991.

Collier, Paul. *The Bottom Billion: Why the Poorest Countries Are Failing and What Can Be Done About It*. Oxford, UK: Oxford University Press, 2007.

———. *Wars, Guns, and Votes: Democracy in Dangerous Places*. New York: HarperCollins, 2009.

Cooper, Andrew F. *Celebrity Diplomacy*. Boulder, Colo.: Paradigm Publishers, 2008.

Cooper, Andrew F., John English, and Ramesh Thakur. *Enhancing Global Governance: Towards a New Diplomacy?* Tokyo: United Nations University Press, 2002.

Cutler, A. Claire, Virginia Haufler, and Tony Porter, eds. *Private Authority and International Affairs*. Albany: State University of New York Press, 1999.

Devarajan, Shantayanan, David Dollar, and Torgny Holmgren, eds. *Aid and Reform in Africa: Lessons from Ten Case Studies*. Washington, D.C.: World Bank, 2001.

Dezalay, Yves, and Bryant G. Garth. *The Internationalization of Palace Wars: Lawyers, Economists, and the Contest to Transform Latin American States*. Chicago: University of Chicago Press, 2002.

Dhillon, Navtej, and Tarik Yousef, eds. *Generation in Waiting: The Unfulfilled Promise of Young People in the Middle East*. Washington, D.C.: Brookings Institution Press, 2009.

Diehl, Paul F., ed. *The Politics of Global Governance: International Organizations in an Interdependent World*. Boulder, Colo.: Lynne Rienner, 1997.

Dobbins, James. *After the Taliban: Nation-Building in Afghanistan*. Washington, D.C.: Potomac Books, 2008.

Dorman, Andrew, and Greg Kennedy, eds. *War and Diplomacy: From World War I to the War on Terrorism*. Washington, D.C.: Potomac Books, 2008.

Drezner, Daniel W. *All Politics Is Global: Explaining International Regulatory Regimes*. Princeton, N.J.: Princeton University Press, 2007.

Duffield, Mark. *Global Governance and the New Wars: The Merging of Development and Security*. London: Zed Books, 2001.

Dunne, Tim, and Nicholas J. Wheeler, eds. *Human Rights in Global Politics*. Cambridge, UK: Cambridge University Press, 1999.

Durkheim, Émile. *The Division of Labor in Society*. New York: MacMillan Co., 1893.

Easterly, William. *The White Man's Burden: Why the West's Efforts to Aid the Rest Have Done So Much Ill and So Little Good*. New York: Penguin Press, 2006.

Eberly, Don. *The Rise of Global Civil Society: Building Communities and Nations from the Bottom Up*. New York: Encounter Books, 2008.

Edwards, Michael. *Just Another Emperor? The Myths and Realities of Philanthrocapitalism*. New York: Demos, 2008.

Edwards, Michael, and John Gaventa, eds. *Global Citizen Action*. Boulder, Colo.: Lynne Rienner, 2001.

Elkington, John, and Pamela Hartigan. *The Power of Unreasonable People: How Social Entrepreneurs Create Markets That Change the World*. Boston: Harvard Business Press, 2008.

Emmerij, Louis, Richard Jolly, and Thomas G. Weiss. *Ahead of the Curve? UN Ideas and Global Challenges*. Bloomington: Indiana University Press, 2001.

Esty, Daniel C., and Andrew S. Winston. *Green to Gold: How Smart Companies Use Environmental Strategy to Innovate, Create Value, and Build Competitive Advantage*. New Haven, Conn.: Yale University Press, 2008.

Evans, Gareth. *The Responsibility to Protect: Ending Mass Atrocity Crimes Once and for All*. Washington, D.C.: Brookings Institution Press, 2008.

Falk, Richard. *Law in an Emerging Global Village: A Post-Westphalian Perspective*. Ardsley, N.Y.: Transnational Publishers, 1998.

Fisman, Raymond, and Edward Miguel. *Economic Gangsters: Corruption, Violence, and the Poverty of Nations*. Princeton, N.J.: Princeton University Press, 2008.

Florini, Ann. *The Coming Democracy: New Rules for Running a New World*. Washington, D.C.: Brookings Institution Press, 2005.

———, ed. *The Right to Know: Transparency for an Open World*. New York: Columbia University Press, 2007.

Foley, Conor. *The Thin Blue Line: How Humanitarianism Went to War*. London: Verso, 2008.

Frank, Thomas. *Fairness in International Law and Institutions*. Oxford, UK: Clarendon Press, 1995.

Gannon, Kathy. *I Is for Infidel: From Holy War to Holy Terror*. New York: PublicAffairs, 2005.

Gearty, Conor A. *Can Human Rights Survive?* Cambridge, UK: Cambridge University Press, 2006.

Gellner, Ernest. *Plough, Sword, and Book: The Structure of Human History*. London: Paladin, 1988.

George, Rose. *The Big Necessity: The Unmentionable World of Human Waste and Why It Matters*. New York: Metropolitan Books, 2008.

Gerencser, Mark, Christopher Kelly, Fernando Napolitano, and Reginald Van Lee. *Megacommunities: How Leaders of Government, Business and Non-Profits Can Tackle Today's Global Challenges Together*. New York: Palgrave Macmillan, 2008.

Ghani, Ashraf, and Clare Lockhart. *Fixing Failed States: A Framework for Rebuilding a Fractured World*. New York: Oxford University Press, 2008.

Giddens, Anthony. *Runaway World: How Globalization Is Reshaping Our Lives*. London: Routledge, 2000.

Goldsmith, Jack L., and Eric A. Posner. *The Limits of International Law*. New York: Oxford University Press, 2005.

Goldstein, Judith L., Miles Kahler, Robert O. Keohane, and Anne-Marie Slaughter. *Legalization and World Politics*. Cambridge, Mass.: MIT Press, 2001.

Grande, Edgar, and Louis W. Pauly, eds. *Complex Sovereignty: Reconstituting Political Authority in the Twenty-First Century*. Toronto: University of Toronto Press, 2005.

Green, Duncan. *From Poverty to Power: How Active Citizens and Effective States Can Change the World*. Oxford, UK: Oxfam International, 2008.

Hancock, Graham. *Lords of Poverty: The Power, Prestige and Corruption of the International Aid Business*. New York: Atlantic Monthly Press, 1992.

Handy, Charles. Introduction to *On the Manner of Negotiating with Princes: Classic Principles of Diplomacy and the Art of Negotiation* by François de Callières. Boston: Houghton Mifflin, 2000.

Hart, Stuart L. *Capitalism at the Crossroads: Aligning Business, Earth, and Humanity*. Upper Saddle River, N.J.: Wharton School Publishing, 2007.

Held, David. *The Global Covenant: The Social Democratic Alternative to the Washington Consensus*. Cambridge, UK: Polity, 2004.

Held, David, and Anthony McGrew, eds. *Governing Globalization: Power, Authority, and Global Governance*. Cambridge, UK: Polity, 2002.

Henderson, David. *Misguided Virtue: False Notions of Corporate Social Responsibility*. London: Institute for Economic Affairs, 2001.

Higgott, Richard A., Geoffrey R. D. Underhill, and Andreas Bieler, eds. *Non-State Actors and Authority in the Global System*. London: Routledge, 2000.

Homer-Dixon, Thomas F. *The Ingenuity Gap: Facing the Economic, Environmental, and Other Challenges of an Increasingly Complex and Unpredictable World*. New York: Vintage, 2002.

Jackson, Robert H. *The Global Covenant: Human Conduct in a World of States*. Oxford, UK: Oxford University Press, 2000.

———. *Quasi-States: Sovereignty, International Relations, and the Third World*. Cambridge, UK: Cambridge University Press, 1993.

Jacobs, Didier. *Global Democracy: The Struggle for Political and Civil Rights in the 21st Century*. Nashville, Tenn.: Vanderbilt University Press, 2007.

Jervis, Robert. *System Effects: Complexity in Political and Social Life*. Princeton, N.J.: Princeton University Press, 1999.

Johnston, R. J., Peter J. Taylor, and Michael J. Watts. *Geographies of Global Change: Remapping the World in the Late Twentieth Century*. Oxford, UK: Blackwell, 1995.

Jones, Bruce, Carlos Pascual, and Stephen J. Stedman. *Power and Responsibility: Building International Order in an Age of Transnational Threat*. Washington, D.C.: Brookings Institution Press, 2009.

Jones, Ian, and Michael G. Pollitt. *Understanding How Issues in Business Ethics Develop*. New York: Palgrave Macmillan, 2002.

Jones, Seth G. *In the Graveyard of Empires: America's War in Afghanistan*. New York: W. W. Norton and Co., 2009.

Jones, Seth G., and Martin C. Libicki. *How Terrorist Groups End: Lessons for Countering al Qa'ida*. Santa Monica, Calif.: RAND, 2008.

Jones, Van. *The Green Collar Economy: How One Solution Can Fix Our Two Biggest Problems*. New York: HarperOne, 2008.

Jordan, Lisa, and Peter van Tuijl, eds. *NGO Accountability: Politics, Principles and Innovations*. London: Earthscan, 2006.

Kahler, Miles, and David Lake, eds. *Governance in a Global Economy: Political Authority in Transition*. Princeton, N.J.: Princeton University Press, 2003.

Kalathil, Shanti, and Taylor C. Boas. *Open Networks, Closed Regimes: The Impact of the Internet on Authoritarian Rule*. Washington, D.C.: Carnegie Endowment for International Peace, 2003.

Kapstein, Ethan. *Economic Justice in an Unfair World: Toward a Level Playing Field*. Princeton, N.J.: Princeton University Press, 2006.

Karns, Margaret P., and Karen A. Mingst. *International Organizations: The Politics and Process of Global Governance*. Boulder, Colo.: Lynne Rienner, 2004.

Kaul, Inge, and Pedro Conceição, eds. *The New Public Finance: Responding to Global Challenges*. New York: Oxford University Press, 2006.

Kaul, Inge, Pedro Conceição, Katell Le Goulven, and Ronald U. Mendoza, eds. *Providing Global Public Goods: Managing Globalization*. New York: Oxford University Press, 2003.

Keane, John. *Global Civil Society?* Cambridge: Cambridge University Press, 2003.

Keck, Margaret E., and Kathryn Sikkink. *Activists Beyond Borders: Advocacy Networks in International Politics.* Ithaca, N.Y.: Cornell University Press, 1998.

Kennedy, Paul. *The Parliament of Man: The Past, Present, and Future of the United Nations.* New York: Random House, 2008.

Khagram, Sanjeev, James V. Riker, and Kathryn Sikkink, eds. *Restructuring World Politics: Transnational Social Movements, Networks, and Norms.* Minneapolis: University of Minnesota Press, 2002.

Kidder, Tracy. *Mountains Beyond Mountains.* New York: Random House, 2003.

Klein, Michael, and Tim Harford. *The Market for Aid.* Washington, D.C.: International Finance Corporation, 2005.

Krasner, Stephen D. *Sovereignty: Organized Hypocrisy.* Princeton, N.J.: Princeton University Press, 1999.

Kumar, Krishna, ed. *Postconflict Elections, Democratization, and International Assistance.* Boulder, Colo.: Lynne Rienner, 1998.

Leguey-Feilleux, Jean-Robert. *The Dynamics of Diplomacy.* Boulder, Colo.: Lynne Rienner, 2008.

Linklater, Andrew. *The Transformation of Political Community: Ethical Foundations of the Post-Westphalian Era.* Columbia: University of South Carolina Press, 1998.

Lodge, George, and Craig Wilson. *A Corporate Solution to Global Poverty: How Multinations Can Help the Poor and Invigorate Their Own Legitimacy.* Princeton, N.J.: Princeton University Press, 2006.

Lomborg, Bjorn. *How to Spend $50 Billion to Make the World a Better Place.* Cambridge, UK: Cambridge University Press, 2006.

Lowe, Vaughan, Adam Roberts, Jennifer Welsh, and Dominik Zaum, eds. *The United Nations Security Council and War: The Evolution of Thought and Practice Since 1945.* Oxford, UK: Oxford University Press, 2008.

Lowenthal, Abraham F. *Global California: Rising to the Cosmopolitan Challenge.* Stanford, Calif.: Stanford University Press, 2009.

Marber, Peter. *Seeing the Elephant: Understanding Globalization from Trunk to Tail.* Hoboken, N.J.: John Wiley and Sons, 2009.

Margonelli, Lisa. *Oil on the Brain: Adventures from the Pump to the Pipeline.* New York: Doubleday, 2007.

McMillan, John. *Reinventing the Bazaar: A Natural History of Markets.* New York: W. W. Norton and Co., 2002.

Mertus, Julie A. *Human Rights Matters: Local Politics and National Human Rights Institutions.* Stanford, Calif.: Stanford University Press, 2009.

Migdal, Joel. *Strong States and Weak Societies.* Princeton, N.J.: Princeton University Press, 1998.

Mills, Greg. *From Africa to Afghanistan: With Richards and NATO to Kabul.* Johannesburg, South Africa: Witts University Press, 2007.

Moran, Theodore H. *Harnessing Foreign Direct Investment for Development: Policies for Developed and Developing Countries.* Washington, D.C.: Center for Global Development, 2006.

Moser, Caroline, ed. *Reducing Global Poverty: The Case for Asset Accumulation.* Washington, D.C.: Brookings Institution Press, 2007.

Moss, Todd J. *African Development: Making Sense of the Issues and Actors.* Boulder, Colo.: Lynne Rienner, 2007.

Mueller, John. *The Remnants of War.* Ithaca, N.Y.: Cornell University Press, 2004.

Munzele Maimbo, Samuel, and Dilip Ratha, eds. *Remittances: Development Impact and Future Prospects.* Washington, D.C.: World Bank, 2005.

Neuwirth, Robert. *Shadow Cities: A Billion Squatters, a New Urban World.* New York: Routledge, 2006.

Newman, Edward, Ramesh Thakur, and John Tirman. *Multilateralism Under Challenge? Power, International Order, and Structural Change.* Tokyo: United Nations University Press, 2006.

Nicolson, Harold. *Diplomacy.* Oxford, UK: Oxford University Press, 1939.

———. *The Evolution of Diplomatic Method.* London: Cassell, 1954.

Nilekani, Nandan. *Imagining India: The Idea of a Renewed Nation.* New York: Penguin Press, 2009.

Nolan, Janne. *Diplomacy and Security in the Twenty-First Century.* Washington, D.C.: Institute for the Study of Diplomacy, 2009.

Novogratz, Jacqueline. *The Blue Sweater: Bridging the Gap Between Rich and Poor in an Interconnected World.* New York: Rodale Books, 2009.

Ohmae, Kenichi. *The End of the Nation State: The Rise of Regional Economies*. New York: Free Press, 1995.

Palenberg, Markus, Wolfgang Reinicke, and Jan Martin Witte. *Trends in Non-Financial Reporting*. Berlin: Global Public Policy Institute, 2006.

Paris, Roland. *At War's End: Building Peace After Civil Conflict*. Cambridge, UK: Cambridge University Press, 2004.

Perkins, Dwight H., Steven Radelet, and David L. Lindauer. *Economics of Development*. 6th ed. New York: W. W. Norton and Co., 2006.

Pogge, Thomas W. *World Poverty and Human Rights: Cosmopolitan Responsibilities and Reforms*. Cambridge, UK: Polity, 2002.

Prahalad, C. K. *The Fortune at the Bottom of the Pyramid: Eradicating Poverty Through Profits*. Philadelphia: Wharton School Publishing, 2006.

Pritchett, Lant. *Let Their People Come: Breaking the Gridlock on International Labor Mobility*. Washington, D.C.: Center for Global Development, 2006.

Rangan, V. Kasturai, ed. *Business Solutions for the Global Poor: Creating Social and Economic Value*. San Francisco: Jossey-Bass, 2007.

Rashid, Ahmed. *Descent into Chaos: The U.S. and the Failure of Nation Building in Pakistan, Afghanistan, and Central Asia*. New York: Viking, 2008.

Ratha, Dilip, and Zhimei Xu. *Migration and Remittances Factbook 2008*. Washington, D.C.: World Bank, 2008.

Rawls, John. *Justice as Fairness: A Restatement*. Cambridge, Mass.: Harvard University Press, 2001.

Reinicke, Wolfgang. *Global Public Policy: Governing Without Government?* Washington, D.C.: Brookings Institution Press, 1999.

Reinicke, Wolfgang, and Francis Deng. *Critical Choices: The United Nations, Networks, and the Future of Global Governance*. Ottawa: International Development Research Centre, 2000.

Rice, Susan E., and Stewart Patrick. *Index of Weak States in the Developing World*. Washington, D.C.: Brookings Institution Press, 2008.

Ridley, Matt. *Nature via Nurture: Genes, Experience, and What Makes Us Human*. London: Fourth Estate, 2003.

———. *The Origins of Virtue*. London: Viking, 1996.

Rischard, Jean-François. *High Noon: Twenty Global Problems, Twenty Years to Solve Them*. New York: Basic Books, 2002.

Roberts, Adam. *The Wonga Coup: Guns, Thugs, and a Ruthless Determination to Create Mayhem in an Oil-Rich Corner of Africa*. New York: PublicAffairs, 2006.

Roberts, Paul. *The End of Food*. Boston: Houghton Mifflin Company, 2008.

Robertson, Robbie. *The Three Waves of Globalization: A History of a Developing Global Consciousness*. New York: Zed Books, 2003.

Rodrik, Dani. *In Search of Prosperity: Analytic Narratives on Economic Growth*. Princeton, N.J.: Princeton University Press, 2003.

———. *One Economics, Many Recipes: Globalization, Institutions, and Economic Growth*. Princeton, N.J.: Princeton University Press, 2008.

Ronfeldt, David. *Tribes, Institutions, Markets, Networks: A Framework About Societal Evolution*. Santa Monica, Calif.: RAND Corporation, 1996.

Root, Hilton L. *Alliance Curse: How America Lost the Third World*. Washington, D.C.: Brookings Institution Press, 2008.

Rosenau, James N. *Distant Proximities: The Dynamics and Dialectics of Globalization*. Princeton, N.J.: Princeton University Press, 2003.

———. *Turbulence in World Politics: A Theory of Change and Continuity*. Princeton, N.J.: Princeton University Press, 1990.

Rosenau, James N., and Ernst-Otto Czempiel, eds. *Governance Without Government: Order and Change in World Politics*. New York: Cambridge University Press, 1992.

Ross, Carne. *Independent Diplomat: Dispatches from an Unaccountable Elite*. Ithaca, N.Y.: Cornell University Press, 2007.

Ross, Dennis. *Statecraft: And How to Restore America's Standing in the World*. New York: Farrar, Straus and Giroux, 2007.

Rothkopf, David. *Superclass: The Global Power Elite and the World They Are Making*. New York: Farrar, Straus and Giroux, 2008.

Sachs, Jeffrey. *Common Wealth: Economics for a Crowded Planet*. New York: Penguin Press, 2008.

Sampson, Anthony. *Who Runs This Place?: The Anatomy of Britain in the 21st Century*. London: John Murray, 2004.

Santoro, Michael A. *China 2020: How Western Business Can—and Should—Influence Social and Political Change in the Coming Decade.* Ithaca, N.Y.: Cornell University Press, 2009.

Sassen, Saskia. *Territory, Authority, Rights: From Medieval to Global Assemblages.* Princeton, N.J.: Princeton University Press, 2006.

Satow, Ernest Mason. *Satow's Guide to Diplomatic Practice.* 5th ed. Edited by Lord Gore-Booth. New York: Longman, 1979.

Scholte, Jan Aart. *Globalization: A Critical Introduction.* New York: Palgrave Macmillan, 2000.

Sen, Amartya Kumar. *Development as Freedom.* New York: Alfred A. Knopf, 1999.

Sharp, Paul. *Diplomatic Theory of International Relations.* Cambridge, UK: Cambridge University Press, 2009.

Shaw, Martin. *Theory of the Global State: Globality as Unfinished Revolution.* Cambridge, UK: Cambridge University Press, 2000.

Signer, Michael. *Demagogue: The Fight to Save Democracy from Its Worst Enemies.* New York: Palgrave Macmillan, 2008.

Simmons, P. J., and Chantal de Jonge Oudraat, eds. *Managing Global Issues: Lessons Learned.* Washington, D.C.: Carnegie Endowment for International Peace, 2001.

Singer, Peter. *One World.* New Haven, Conn.: Yale University Press, 2002.

Singh, J. P. *Negotiation and the Global Information Economy.* Cambridge, UK: Cambridge University Press, 2008.

Slaughter, Anne-Marie. *A New World Order.* Princeton, N.J.: Princeton University Press, 2004.

Smith, David Livingstone. *The Most Dangerous Animal: Human Nature and the Origins of War.* New York: St. Martin's Press, 2007.

Smith, Rupert. *The Utility of Force: The Art of War in the Modern World.* New York: Allen Lane, 2005.

Snow, Nancy, and Philip M. Taylor, eds. *Handbook of Public Diplomacy.* New York: Routledge, 2009.

Sober, Elliot, and David Sloan Wilson. *Unto Others: The Evolution of the Psychology of Unselfish Behavior.* Cambridge, Mass.: Harvard University Press, 1998.

Soto, Hernando de. *The Mystery of Capital: Why Capitalism Triumphs in the West and Fails Everywhere Else.* New York: Basic Books, 2000.

Stern, Nicholas. *The Economics of Climate Change: Stern Review on the Economics of Climate Change.* London: HM Treasury, 2006.

Stopford, John, and Susan Strange. *Rival States, Rival Firms: Competition for World Market Shares.* Cambridge, UK: Cambridge University Press, 1991.

Stromseth, Jane, David Wippman, and Rosa Brooks, eds. *Can Might Make Rights? Building the Rule of Law After Military Interventions.* New York: Cambridge University Press, 2006.

Sullivan, Nicholas P. *You Can Hear Me Now: How Microloans and Cell Phones Are Connecting the World's Poor to the Global Economy.* San Francisco: Jossey-Bass, 2007.

Surowiecki, James. *The Wisdom of Crowds: Why the Many Are Smarter Than the Few and How Collective Wisdom Shapes Business, Economies, Societies, and Nations.* New York: Doubleday, 2004.

SustainAbility. *The 21st Century NGO in the Market for Change.* London: SustainAbility, 2005.

SustainAbility and the Global Compact. *Gearing Up: From Corporate Responsibility to Good Governance and Scalable Solutions.* London: SustainAbility, 2004.

Talbott, Strobe. *The Great Experiment: The Story of Ancient Empires, Modern States, and the Quest for a Global Nation.* New York: Simon and Schuster, 2008.

Thier, J. Alexander, ed. *The Future of Afghanistan.* Washington, D.C.: United States Institute of Peace, 2009.

Thompson, William R., ed. *Evolutionary Interpretations of World Politics.* New York: Routledge, 2001.

Toynbee, Arnold. *Civilization on Trial.* New York: Oxford University Press, 1948.

Trubek, David M., and Alvaro Santos. *The New Law and Economic Development: A Critical Appraisal.* Cambridge, UK: Cambridge University Press, 2006.

Tuchman, Barbara W. *A Distant Mirror: The Calamitous 14th Century.* New York: Alfred A. Knopf, 1978.

Vogel, David. *The Market for Virtue: The Potential and Limits of Corporate Social Responsibility.* Washington, D.C.: Brookings Institution Press, 2005.

Waddell, Steve. *Societal Learning and Change: How Governments, Business, and Civil Society Are Creating Solutions to Multi-Stakeholder Problems.* Sheffield, UK: Greenleaf Publishers, 2005.

Wallerstein, Immanuel. *The Modern World-System.* New York: Academic Press, 1974.

Webb, Adam K. *Beyond the Global Culture War.* New York: Routledge, 2006.

Wedel, Janine. *Shadow Elite: How the World's New Power Brokers Undermine Democracy, Government, and the Free Market.* New York: Basic Books, 2008.

Weiss, Thomas G. *What's Wrong with the United Nations and How to Fix It.* Cambridge, UK: Polity, 2008.

Wendt, Alexander. *Social Theory of International Politics.* New York: Cambridge University Press, 1999.

Wilson, Edward O. *Consilience: The Unity of Knowledge.* New York: Alfred A. Knopf, 1998.

Witte, Jan Martin, and Wolfgang Reinicke. *Business UNusual: Facilitating United Nations Reform Through Partnerships.* New York: United Nations Global Compact Office, 2005.

Wolf, Martin. *Why Globalization Works.* New Haven, Conn.: Yale University Press, 2004.

Wright, Robert. *NonZero: The Logic of Human Destiny.* New York: Pantheon Books, 2000.

Yunus, Muhammad. *Banker to the Poor: Micro-lending and the Battle Against World Poverty.* New York: PublicAffairs, 1999.

———. *Creating a World Without Poverty: Social Business and the Future of Capitalism.* New York: PublicAffairs, 2007.

Zielonka, Jan. *Europe as Empire: The Nature of the Enlarged European Union.* Oxford, UK: Oxford University Press, 2007.

Index

About the Author

PARAG KHANNA directs the Global Governance Initiative at the New America Foundation. Author of the previous international bestseller *The Second World*, he was picked as one of *Esquire*'s Most Influential People of the Twenty-first Century and featured on *Wired*'s Smart List. He has been a fellow at the Brookings Institution and researched at the Council on Foreign Relations. During 2007, he was a senior geopolitical adviser to U.S. Special Operations Command. He has written for major global publications such as *The New York Times* and *Financial Times* and appears regularly on CNN, the BBC, and other television media around the world. Khanna holds undergraduate and graduate degrees from Georgetown University and a PhD from the London School of Economics. He has traveled in nearly one hundred countries and has been named a Young Global Leader of the World Economic Forum.

www.paragkhanna.com

About the Type

This book was set in Sabon, a typeface designed by the well-known German typographer Jan Tschichold (1902–74). Sabon's design is based upon the original letter forms of Claude Garamond and was created specifically to be used for three sources: foundry type for hand composition, Linotype, and Monotype. Tschichold named his typeface for the famous Frankfurt typefounder Jacques Sabon, who died in 1580.